Texts collected by
J.-L. Chappelet and
M.-H. Roukhadzé

Sport Management
An International Approach

Texts collected by
J.-L. Chappelet and
M.-H. Roukhadzé

«Documents of the Museum»
Olympic Museum collection published by the International Olympic Committee
Commissioning Editor for the collection Marie-Hélène Roukhadzé

In the same collection:

Ferrán Brunet
Economy of the 1992 Barcelona Olympic Games, 1994
(In English, French and Spanish)

Nikolay Gueorguiev
Analyse du programme olympique 1896-1996, 1994

Elias Mbengalack
La gouvernementalité du sport en Afrique -
Le sport et le politique au Cameroun, 1994

Nikolay Gueorguiev
Analyse du programme des Jeux Olympiques d'hiver 1924-1998, 1995

Cover design:
Anne Egli-Decombaz
Photography
Allsport - Darrell Ingham

Cataloguing information:
Sport Management: An International Approach / under the dir. of Jean-Loup Chappelet.-
Lausanne: International Olympic Committee, 1996.- 188 p.; 30 cm.- (Documents of the
Museum)
ISBN 92-9149-010-5
Subjects: sport - management - various studies

Contents

The articles published in this publication do not necessarily reflect the opinion of the International Olympic Committee.

Preface

We are currently living in a golden age of sport. Never, since ancient times, has sport occupied as important a place in society as it does today. This status has been won throughout the 20th century by athletes themselves inspired by sporting excellence, particularly that of the Olympic Games.

A pyramid of association-style organizations has gradually formed, from the local club to the National Olympic Committee, passing through regional leagues and national federations. The leaders of these associations are essentially volunteers, who perform their functions by drawing on their professional expertise, which is often wide-ranging.

But the general administration and daily running of sport require increasingly specific knowledge. To preserve and maintain this golden age of sport, the leaders of the volunteer sports movement must become more professional. They must familiarize themselves with management techniques and adapt them to the sporting phenomenon which they know so well.

For the last twenty years or so, high-level athletes have no longer been amateurs in the sense of dabblers. They have become professionals, that is to say experts who like and fully master their sports technique. The same must be true of sports administrators and policy-makers who manage considerable human, financial and material resources, and have great responsibilities such as educating young people and public health.

Sport needs managers from within its ranks. For this reason, I welcome the publication of this book, hoping that it will contribute to a better understanding of sports management and better management of sports organizations throughout the world.

Juan Antonio Samaranch
President of the International Olympic Committee

The Authors

Tim Berrett is a doctoral student at the Faculty of Physical Education and Recreation of the University of Alberta in Edmonton, Canada.

Dr. **Thomas Bezold** is a research fellow in sports economy at the University of Bayreuth, Germany

Gonzalo Bravo is Sport Director at the Catholic University of Santiago, Chile.

Dr. **Jean-Loup Chappelet** is professor of public management at the Swiss Graduate School of Public Administration associated with the University of Lausanne, Switzerland.

Dr. **John Cheffers** is professor at the School of Education of Boston University, Massachusetts, USA. He was the Chief Executive Officer of the Australian Institute of Sport.

Dr. **Packianathan Chelladurai** is professor of sport management at Ohio State University in Columbus, Ohio, USA.

Dr. **Jean Camy** is professor of sociology at the Claude Bernard University in Lyons, France. He supervises the European Master in Management of Sport Organizations.

Dr. **Pierre Chifflet** is professor at the Joseph Fourier University in Grenoble, France, and is director of the Department of Sport and Physical Activity Sciences.

Dr. **Gabriel Colomé** is professor of political science at the Autonomous University of Barcelona, Spain.

John Deane is a lecturer at the Bowater School of Management and Marketing of Dearkin University, Burwood Campus, Victoria, Australia.

Dr. **Joy T. DeSensi** is professor at the University of Tennessee at Knoxville, Tennessee, USA. She is the editor of the Journal of Sport Management.

Dr. **Johan Gouws** is professor in sport management at the Rand Afrikaans University in Johannesburg, South Africa. He is vice-president of the Transvaal Rugby Union.

Dr. **Klaus Heinemann** is professor of sociology at the University of Hamburg, Germany.

Dr. **Heinz-Dieter Horch** is professor of sports economy at the German Graduate School of Sport in Cologne, Germany.

Dr. **Ian Jobling** is associate professor and director of the Centre for Physical Activity and Sport Education at the University of Queensland in Brisbane, Australia.

Dr. **M. L. Kamlesh** is professor and principal of the Lakshmibai National College of Physical Education in Trivandrum, Kerala, India.

Jean-Claude Killy is a member of the International Olympic Committee in France. He was a co-president of the Organizing Committee of the Olympic Winter Games in Albertville, France.

Dr. **Alain Loret** is professor of management at the University of Caen, France, and director of the Centre for the Study and Management of Sport Innovation.

Dr. **Marc Maes** is director of the Belgian Olympic Committee.

Dr. **Usha Sujit Nair** is a professor at the Lakshmibai National College of Physical Education in Trivandrum, Kerala, India.

Dr. **Mihály Nyerges** is a professor at the University of Physical Education in Budapest, Hungary.

Dr. **Jun Oga** is a professor at the University of Electro-Communications in Tokyo, Japan.

Dr. **Núria Puig** is professor of sport sociology at the National Institute of Physical Education of Catalonia in Barcelona, Spain.

Dr. **Berend Rubingh** is a lecturer in sport management at several European universities. He is director of the "Manage to Manage" consultancy and president of the European Association of Sport Management, the Netherlands.

Dr. **David Shilbury** is a senior lecturer in sport management at Deakin University in Melbourne, Australia.

H.E. Mr. **Pál Schmitt** is a member of the International Olympic Committee and president of the Hungarian Olympic Committee. He is currently Hungarian Ambassador to Spain.

Dr. **Trevor Slack** is a professor at the Faculty of Physical Education and Recreation of the University of Alberta in Edmonton, Canada.

Dr. **Daniel Soucie** is professor of sport management at the School of Human Kinetics of the University of Ottawa, Canada.

Dr. **Klaus Zieschang** is professor of sport science at the University of Bayreuth, Germany.

Introduction

The double singular of the title of this book is not satisfactory. Would it not be preferable to speak, if it were less offensive to the ear, of managements and sports?[2] Indeed, management and sport do not refer to single and homogeneous but multitudinous and varied entities.

That sport is not a homogeneous phenomenon, everyone will readily agree. There are, first of all, the various sports which some have tried to classify into almost as many categories as there are sports disciplines, categories that often intersect: team and individual sports, ball sports, water sports, combat sports, nature sports, motor sports, etc. But, even if we address sports as a whole, we tend to form other categories, consciously or otherwise. One of the oldest divisions and the one on which the revival of the Olympic Games was based is the distinction between amateur and professional (remunerated) sport. Despite developments in Olympic doctrine, this distinction remains relevant in the major team sports such as football, basketball and ice-hockey, and a number of individual sports, such as golf and boxing. Today, an implicit division has come about between those sports that are on the Olympic programme (35) and those that are not (some sixty other sports whose supreme governing bodies are members of the General Association of International Sports Federations).

Public authorities have developed the habit of classifying sports according to type of practice: school sport, extramural sport for the young and adult sport. In France, we speak of recreational sport, mass sport and high-level sport. The European "Sport for All" Charter distinguishes between competition sport, outdoor activities, aesthetic disciplines and keep-fit. In North America, sport is segmented in classic fashion into three particular markets: consumer sport (which concerns sports goods companies), spectator sport (represented by professional teams and the sports media) and participative sport (which encompasses everything from private body-building centres and university sport to Sunday jogging).

Among the participants, we may distinguish between those who are not organized and are independent of any structure, but who nevertheless express a new and ever stronger demand for sporting activities, and those who are organized in clubs, leagues and federations. The latter constitute what is known as associative sport. This kind of sport, the matrix of which is the non-profit association, is confederated within the Olympic Movement, which is coordinated by the International Olympic Committee.

All these different sports need to be managed. But with what management? That is the question.

That management is not homogeneous is not obvious to laypersons. For many years, management did indeed define itself as a science of action for the purpose of defining the one best way of resolving the problems facing companies. This classic school of management from the early part of the century was succeeded by the human relations school, then, after the second

---

[1] This question was posed by Heinz Keller, Director of the Federal Sports School in Macolin (Switzerland), at the conclusion of a sports management seminar organized by this school, 8th June 1995.

[2] In English, the expression "Sport Management" has tended to take the place of "Sports Management".

World War, by the contingency school and, finally, the systems school, which is dominant today.

Each of these schools gave rise to various management branches: scientific management, human resources management, management by objective, total quality management, strategic management, management by participation, which exist alongside specific fields of competence such as financial management and information systems management. Alongside these major branches, all kinds of managerial fashions have come into being, which have contributed not a little to the confusion of the last twenty years, and whose American names are generally not easily translated: reengineering, benchmarking, empowerment, learning organization, etc.; not to mention utterly ephemeral slogans such as "management by wandering around", "management by smiling around" and "chaos management".

For some twenty years now, public management has taken its place alongside the general management which is taught in business schools in view of the specific context of public administrations. By analogy, a form of intermediate sector management, half-way between public and private, has also developed, namely the non-profit association sector. This is of particular importance for associative sport.

Finally, it should be borne in mind that the act of managing always takes place within a cultural context. Latin-American management is not the same as that practised in North America, Asia or Africa. Indeed, in the light of national particularities, it could be contended that there are almost as many ways of managing as there are countries. The discipline of intercultural management has been developed precisely in order to remedy the problems encountered in this connection by multinational companies whose staff and operations belong to a variety of cultures.[3] Sports managers could doubtless learn something from this approach.

It is striking to note that most publications on sports management do not take into account the diverse nature either of sport or of management and adopt, without explicitly informing their readers, a given national context (that of their country or region), and particular forms of the sporting phenomenon, for example "sports business".

The present work is mainly devoted to associative sport. However, it has set itself the objective of presenting a global panorama of the way in which this type of sport is managed, hence the title "an international approach". The entire first part is devoted to the different visions of sports management in some ten countries on the five continents, including those on which the Olympic Games have been organized recently or will shortly be so: South Africa, Australia, Canada, Chile, Spain, France, Hungary (and the countries of Eastern Europe), India, Japan, the Netherlands. The articles have been written by the best national academic specialists. Several of them present the training programmes which are being set up in universities to teach and research this new discipline of sports management. This first part concludes with an article comparing the way German and Spanish sports clubs are managed.

The second part of the work sets out to identify a number of concepts towards a generic management of associative sport. It opens with contributions from two Olympic champions and IOC members who have become sports managers. The great skiing champion Jean-Claude Killy suggests that the ultimate aim of a sports organization is to generate emotion. The fencer

---

[3] See among many other books on this subject: Gauthey, F. & Yardel, D. (1990). *Le management interculturel*, QSJ - PUF, Paris. Ghoshal, S. (1989). *Managing Across Borders*. Harvard Business School Press, Boston.

and Olympic medallist Pál Schmitt sketches with broad brushstrokes the many managerial tasks of a National Olympic Committee, taking Hungary's as an example.

The remaining authors of this second part, well known in academic circles, address questions of importance for sports management such as the non-market economic context, operational management strategies based on sports values, strategic planning of national federations, the competences and knowledge necessary to the sports manager, ethics in sports management and sponsoring of national sports bodies, negotiation of sponsorships, quality management and multiculturalism. This second part concludes with the fascinating prospects offered by the sporting phenomenon as a new management model based on the three concepts of excellence, teamwork and coaching.

May this work help to reinforce the position of a specific form of management which, in the face of tremendous economic and political challenges, will enable associative sport to preserve its cultural and social goals for the good of the community.

Jean-Loup Chappelet
Swiss Graduate School of Public Administration,
Lausanne, Switzerland

Sport management in various parts of the world

Countries in French alphabetical order

Sport management in South Africa

Johan Gouws
Rand Afrikaans University,
Johannesburg, South Africa

According to writers such as Howell (1969), Loy (1975), Riordan (1981), Mandell (1984), Mergen (1986), Rizak (1986) and Van der Merwe (1990) the fact that sport as activity has existed since the times of the ancient Greeks indicates the importance of sport in our lives. This sport culture was transferred to students after the establishment of universities in 500 A.D. In England the first organized sport event was held in 1866. The Mokabi Union was established in 1912 and under the leadership of Pierre de Coubertin the Olympic Games were again held in 1896. Sport therefore is not only part of our everyday lives, but it has in fact developed into a business.

Lineberry (1960:16) pointed out that "... the first professional baseball team was owned by the players themselves, and embodied a kind of players' control over when, where and how they should play as well as how the profit should be shared". This control was however taken over by money magnates and the only basis for their decisions was, first and foremost, personal profit.

Takeshi (1986:4) refers to the Winter Olympic Games in Japan and states that "without the Olympics, it would have taken Sapporo at least 15 years longer to acquire these facilities and some of them, such as the subway, we might never have gotten".

The projected economic impact for Cape Town if the bid for the Olympic Games of 2004 is successful, is enormous. An increase in tourism of as much as 80% is envisaged whilst the cost of upgrading the transport system is estimated at R400 million. The chairman of the bidding committee estimates income for the Games at R4 billion without taking in consideration the improvement in housing and infrastructure.

In South Africa sport has become a major business. Laubscher (1989:12) has reported examples of sport persons who earn as much as R300 000 per annum and who have received R1000 for giving a talk. Retief (1990:64) refers to golf players' earnings in South Africa and Levine (1990:3) highlights the earnings of South African tennis players. The 1995 World Cup rugby competition had an income of more than R100 million and top South African rugby players earn a fortune. With this as background, another perspective must be put on the management of sport.

Sport management in perspective

Although the term Sport Management is a relatively new concept, writers such as Ulrich (1979), Parkhouse (1984), Van der Smissen (1984) and Parks and Quain (1986) plead that it be accepted as a field of study. Zeigler (1987:4) highlights the importance of the establishment of the North American Society for Sport Management in 1985 "... to promote, stimulate and encourage study, research, scholarly writing and professional development in the area of sport management." Pitts (1993:3) points out that sport in the USA had a turnover of 83 billion dollars in 1992 which makes the management of sport more complex than that of most businesses. Parkhouse (1991:381) warns that "... the future directions of sport management are determined by the impact of society itself, ... and the nature of professional leadership." Van der Zwaag (1984), Zanger (1984), Koehler (1988), Olafson (1988) Stotlar (1989) and Gouws (1994) confirm this point of view and recommend that aspects such as marketing management, information management, facility management and risk management be included in any curriculum of Sport Management training.

In the era of change in South Africa, the management of sport as a business but also as a vehicle for change has become essential.

Sport in South Africa

Although organized sport has been part of South African society since the 19th century, it was the influence of apartheid politics on sport which was noted by writers such as Lapchick (1979), Jarvie (1985), Guelke (1986) and Dunning (1990). Dr. Dönges of the National Party government made a policy statement on sport in 1956 when he declared that Whites and the different Black groups would administer their sport separately and under separate controlling bodies. No mixed sport would be allowed at any level. This was the beginning of sport isolation for South Africa. The South African government's view was that no international interference should be allowed in the South African management of sport.

On 11 April 1967 the then prime minister, John Vorster, made a statement in parliament emphasizing the importance of international sport links for South Africa. At this stage the MCC cricket tour to S.A. was in the planning stage. On 12 September 1968, Tom Cartwright withdrew from this team owing to an injury and he was replaced by Basil D'Oliviera, a South African born Black man. The South African government saw this as political interference and a week later the tour was cancelled. This was a moral victory for everybody involved in bringing about change in South African sport.

In 1972 Dr. Piet Koornhof was appointed as South Africa's first minister of sport. He managed to change government policy as far as granting of national colours was concerned. This allowed Blacks to obtain Springbok colours. On 18 May 1977 he made a policy statement in parliament and emphasized the importance of international sport participation as well as the important role sport must play in political and economic development.

Based on this apartheid in sport policy, different sport structures were established. The traditional sport structures were the South African National Olympic Committee (SANOC) which endeavoured to break the isolation by initiating discussions with different international sport bodies. Their efforts eventually led to the establishment of the Committee of Ten under the chairmanship of Sam Ramsamy. This committee reported back to the Association of National Olympic Committees of Africa (ANOCA) in March 1991 and the Interim National Olympic Committee of S.A. (INOCSA) was formed. The only other traditional structure was The Confederation of South African Sport (COSAS) which was established in 1988 representing most of the non-Olympic sport codes, with the exception of rugby, cricket and soccer which were not members of any national structure. The National Party government was instrumental in establishing COSAS and also supplied funds.

The non-traditional structures consisted of SANROC (S.A. Non Racial Olympic Committee) which was formed by Sam Ramsamy during the 1950's in protest against apartheid in sport. With John Harris he established an office in London in 1962 where they were instrumental in isolating S.A. from international sport participation. SACOS (S.A. Congress of Sport) was formed in 1972 with financial assistance from the Pan African Congress. At this stage it was the accepted structure representing Black sport in S.A. During 1990 the National Olympic Sport Congress (NOSC) was established with support from the ANC. When they had obtained the support from rugby, cricket and soccer, the NOSC positioned themselves strategically to become the most influential sport controlling body in S.A. Tshwete (1990:3) pointed out that in his future view of sport in S.A. the NOSC will play an important role, especially in the so-called townships. The president of the NOSC, Mluleki George (1990:6) also declared that "Sport is the vehicle of the mass democratic, non-racial and united South Africa in which sport persons could give full expression to their needs, aspirations and beliefs." Rees (1992:2) also pointed out that "... leaders of the NOSC feel that they are using sport to change society." In this new political climate with new role players in sport, a new perspective was imminent.

At a workshop in Port Elizabeth in June 1992, the NOSC, NOCSA and COSAS decided to establish structure and development programmes for sport in South Africa. This led to the establishment of the National Sports Council (NSC) with Mluleki George as chairperson, which controls all non-Olympic sport in South Africa. The main aim of the NSC is to ensure that members manage their sport effectively on national and regional level and that development at all levels takes place. The National Olympic Committee of S.A. (NOCSA) under the leadership of Sam Ramsamy, manages the S.A. Olympic team with emphasis on the development of athletes, coaches and managers. Ramsamy is also a member of the Executive Committee of the NSC.

In the draft White Paper on sport and recreation in South Africa which was published in April 1995, a national policy framework is proposed by the Department of Sport and Recreation. A foundation is laid for a culture of sport and a programme is proposed to mobilize the nation to play. Priorities outlined include to coordinate efforts of all the stakeholders in sport to take advantage of economics of scale. The Department of Sport and Culture will aim:
- to provide funds for the creation and upgrading of basic multi-purpose sports facilities in disadvantaged areas.
- to maintain the focus on the management of sport and recreation with emphasis on mass participation.
- to enhance health-consciousness by means of targeted programmes aimed at specific interest groups in society. These will include young people, street children, disabled persons, women, masters sport and corporate sport.
- to identify latent talent as an integral component of the process of upliftment and progress. Focus should be on both grassroot and elite level with the main thrust of activities being towards the grassroot level.
- to invest meaningfully in the preparation of participants who are called upon to represent the country in major competitions.
- to cement the sports unification process by instituting necessary affirmative action controls which will ensure that representative teams reflect all parties involved.
With these in mind against the background of a new political dispensation and streamlined sport structures, sport management in South Africa is also viewed from a different perspective.

Sport management in South Africa

Sport Management is defined as the utilization of resources to achieve the objectives of a sport organization. Leadership plays a very important role because these objectives can only be achieved through the efforts of people.

Although it is common knowledge that our athletes were disadvantaged because of isolation from international participation, few of us realize how much our sport managers lagged behind the rest of the world. We had almost no contact with international leaders in this field and because of isolation very little development and training were done. Sport was unprofessionally structured and most sport codes were managed by amateurs in an amateurish way. Notable exceptions were found in rugby and cricket because of the efforts of professional individuals.

The NSC embarked on an intensive national and regional development programme. With the assistance of several international experts, courses are presented for managers, administrators, coaches, officials and scientific support personnel. The NSC's Protea Sport Programme has three age-based components aimed at introducing sport to young people. The Super Kids Programme is a modified programme directed at crèche level kids and the focus is on encouraging children to play. The Sports Pioneer Programme focuses on children of 6-15 years and teachers involved in the programme will be trained in selected sports. The Isizwe Stars Programme is an advanced coaching programme aimed at children of 12-21 years, involving seven sports. The emphasis will be on the development of skills, including management skills. Sport academies will play an important role in developing skills especially for the talented athlete.

A delegation of sport managers, academics and sport scientists under the auspices of the NSC, went to Australia in 1995 to investigate the possibilities of establishing academies of sport in S.A. A report of this delegation was accepted by the NSC in November 1995 and a committee was established to manage the establishment of such academies. The main purpose of these will be to identify and develop athletes with potential and also to make facilities and expertise available to develop coaches. National Sport teams will also make use of these facilities and expertise in their preparation for international participation.

NOCSA has embarked on an intensive programme in preparing the Olympic team for the Olympic Games in Atlanta. A holistic approach is followed to prepare the team in all aspects which include testing, coaching, career guidance, financial assistance and management.

The Rand Afrikaans University established a chair in Sport Management in 1988 providing a B. Commerce degree for students in Sport Management. The syllabus includes subjects such as Business Economics, Business Psychology, Human Movement Sciences, Economics, Accountancy, Sport Management, Exercise Science, Sport Psychology, Sport Sociology and Sport Communication. This was followed up by an Advanced Diploma in Sport Management aimed at practitioners in the field of Sport Management. This diploma as well as a Diploma in Coaching were made available through distance learning in 1994. A further Advanced Diploma was developed to train teachers in the management and coaching of sport. An international conference on Sport Management has been held at the RAU each year for the past six years. Prominent speakers such as Sam Ramsamy, Richard Lapchick, David Stotlar, Beverley Zanger, Packianathan Chelladurai, Brenda Pitts and Frank Ashley have debated different aspects of sport management. The first Doctorate in Sport Management in S.A. was awarded at the RAU in 1994.

Conclusion

International isolation in sport has put South African managers, coaches, scientific support staff and athletes at a major disadvantage which cannot be rectified in one year. With the human resources available, the willingness to learn, and assistance from the international sporting community however, South Africa will be a force to be reckoned with in the near future. Every effort is made to develop our sport managers which will enable them to manage our sport strategically and ensure that we concentrate on the right priorities which will ensure success not only in the sport arenas of the world, but also within our country where sport will be the vehicle used in building our rainbow nation.

References

Dunning, E.- Sociological reflections on sport, violence and civilization. *International Review for Sociology of Sport*, 1990, 25(1), pp. 65-80.

George, M.- The NSC vision. *NSC News*, 1990, 2(1), pp. 2-4.

Gouws, J.S.- *Sportbestuur: 'n historiese, teoretiese en bestuursmatige fundering.* Dissertation for a D. Com., Rand Afrikaans University, Johannesburg, 1994.

Guelke, A.- The politicisation of South African Sport. In Allison, L. (Ed). *The politics of sport.* Manchester: Manchester University Press, 1986.

Howell, M.L.- *A historical survey of the role of sport in society, with particular reference to Canada since 1700.* Dissertation for a D.Phil., University of Stellenbosch, Stellenbosch, 1969.

Jarvie, G.- *Class, race and sport in South Africa's political economy.* London: Routledge, 1985.

Koehler, L.S.- Job satisfaction and corporate fitness managers. *Journal of Sport Management*, 1988, 2(2), pp. 100-117.

Lapchick, R.- *The politics of race and international sport, the case of South Africa.* Westport: Greenwood, 1979.

Laubscher, L.- Sportborgskappe: Die beker loop oor. *Finansies en Tegniek*, March, 1989, pp. 34-35.

Levine, B.- World champions. *Sports Illustrated,* December, 1990, pp. 6-8.

Lineberry, W.P.- *The Business of sport.* New York: H.W. Wilson, 1960.

Loy, J.W., McPherson, B.D. & Kenyon, G.- *Sport and social systems.* Reading: Addison-Wesley, 1975.

Mandell, R.D.- *Sport, a cultural history.* New York: Columbia University, 1984.

Mergen, B.- *Cultural dimensions of play, games and sport.* Illinois: Human Kinetics, 1986.

Olafson, G.A.- Personal style and administrative behaviour in amateur sport organizations. *Journal of Sport Management,* 1988, 2(1), pp. 25-28.

Parkhouse, B.- Shaping up to climb a new corporate ladder ...sport management. *Journal of Physical Education, Recreation and Dance,* 1984, 55, pp. 12-14.
Parkhouse, B.L.- *The management of sport.* St. Louis: Mosby, 1991.

Parks, J.B. & Quain, R.J.- Sport management survey: Employment perspectives. *Journal of Physical Education, Recreation and Dance,* 1986, 57(4), pp. 22-26.

Pitts, B.- Marketing in Sport and Recreation. *Conference at RAU,* Johannesburg, 1993.

Rees, C.R.- The NOSC and the non-racial sports movement: Towards post apartheid sport in S.A. *International symposium for Olympic Research*. Western Ontario: University of London, 1992.

Retief, D.- Tony wraps it up. *The allied M.-net Book of S.A. Sport*, 1990, pp. 10-12.

Riordan, J.- *Sport under communism*. London: C. Hurst & Co, 1981.

Rizak, G.- *Sport within the Chinese educational system*. Proceedings of the VIII Commonwealth and international conference on Sport, Physical Education, Dance, Recreation & Health, Glasgow, 1986.

Stotlar, D.K.- *Successful sport marketing and sponsorship plans*. Iowa: W.C. Brown, 1989.

Takeshi, I.- *Report on the Olympic Games in Japan*. Tokyo: IOC document, 1986.

Tshwete, S.- Planning the new S.A.'s role in sport. *NSC News*, 1990, 2(1), pp. 6-8.

Ulrich, D. & Parkhouse, B.- The application of motivation theory in management to the sport arena, *Quest*, 31, 1979, pp. 302-311.

Van der Merwe, F.J.G.- *Sportgeskiedenis*. Stellenbosch: Words Unlimited, 1990.

Van der Smissen, B.- A process for success: Sport Management curricula - An idea whose time has come! In B.K. Zanger & J.B. Parks (Eds). *Sport Management curricula: The business and education nexus*. Bowling Green: Bowling Green University, 1984.

Van der Zwaag, H.J.- *Sport management in schools and colleges*. New York: Wiley & Sons, 1984.

Zanger, B.R.K. & Parks, J.B.- *Sport management curricula*. Ohio: Bowling Green University Press, 1984.

Zeigler, E.F.- Sport Management: Past present & future. *Journal of Sport Management*, 1987, 1(1), pp. 4-24.

Sport management in Australia: a socio-historical overview and tertiary education perspective

Ian Jobling
Centre for Physical Activity and Sport Education,
University of Queensland,
Brisbane, Australia

John Deane
Bowater School of Management and Marketing,
Deakin University,
Burwood, Victoria, Australia

In anticipation of the 1908 Olympic Games in London the following exchange took place in the House of Representatives of the Australian parliament:

Mr Maloney: Subscriptions are being raised to enable representative Australians to compete in the marathon race in connexion (sic) with the revival of the Olympian (sic) Games. Since the representation of Australia at the carnival would do as much to advertise the Commonwealth as the visits of Australian cricket teams to the Old Country (Britain), does the Prime Minister think it would be possible for the Commonwealth government to subscribe, say, half the amount raised by the public for this purpose?

Mr Deakin (Prime Minister): Commencing with an avowal of innocence as to what a "marathon" race may be, but full of confidence in the capacity of Australians to hold their own in that or any other form of competition, I doubt whether it comes within the power of the Commonwealth, strictly interpreting the constitution, to interfere with the rights of the states in that matter. We shall consider the question.[1]

Two features of this extract - that sport is significant in promoting a national image, and the passing of the financial responsibility from the Federal to State governments - have continued to be issues in Australian sports policy and management to the present day. The purpose of this article is to firstly, and briefly, provide a socio-historical overview of the Australian sport system and the manner in which it is managed and, secondly, to outline sport management in Australia from a tertiary education perspective. A brief history of sport as a cultural phenomenon in Australia will allow readers to appreciate the evolution of a sport management system.

Socio-historical background of sport in Australia

The Commonwealth of Australia, comprising six states (New South Wales, Queensland, South Australia, Tasmania, Victoria, and Western Australia) and two territories (Australian Capital Territory and Northern Territory), is a large island-continent with a relatively small population. Of the population of 18 million people, 61% live in the state capital cities and another 10% live in another 6 bigger (over 100,000 citizens) cities[2]; it is one of the most urbanized countries in the world. Approximately 7 million persons are registered participants in sport and there are more than 10,000 sport organizations in which 66,500 people have paid employment. Of all of these people, more than 6,300 are in administrative or managerial positions.[3] The Australian sports system evolved from a community-based club structure, which predominantly catered for mass participation in sport; in this way individuals could participate at the level most appropriate to their capabilities.

Throughout our history many people have considered sport to be a particularly important institution in Australian society. Some observers have gone so far as to call it a national "religion" or "obsession". Certainly, over the last one hundred years, many visitors and observers from overseas have commented that sport has had a predominant effect on the culture, value systems and forms of expressions of Australians. As early as 1883, Richard Twopeny wrote *in Town Life in Australia* that "the principal amusements of Australians are outdoor sports of one kind or another".[4] The wife of a former United States ambassador to Australia in the 1960s wrote "living in Australia is like living in a gymnasium - there's always somebody practising something".[5] American journalist Herbert Warren Wind, wrote in *Sports Illustrated* in 1960 that "Australia is a sports-playing, sports-watching, sports-talking, altogether sports-minded country such as the world has never known before"[6]. Australian social commentator, Donald Horne, commented in 1964:

"Sport to many Australians is life and the rest a shadow. ... To play sport, or watch others and to read and talk about it is to uphold the national spirit and build its character. Australia's success at competitive sport is considered an important part of its foreign policy."[7]

Following the announcement in September 1993 that Sydney would host the Olympic Games in the year 2000, the Premier of New South Wales and President of the Sydney 2000 Games bid, John Fahey, stated:

"Holding the Olympic Games will inspire a generation ...when the Olympics are on - it is cartwheels around the back garden and across the lounge room floor. The Olympics in Sydney will inspire children to compete. They will be healthier, they will learn the pleasure of victory, the consolation of defeat, and in the end, we can perhaps teach our youth to take on the world and do their best."[8]

It is realized today that the "golden era" of Australian sport was the double-decade from 1950-1970. Ever since the Melbourne Olympic Games in 1956, the success of naturally talented Australian athletes was overcome by the European block countries' scientific preparation of athletes and by the sports organization of western nations. The glorious international reputation which Australians had enjoyed in sport seemed to be waning by the mid-1970s. Using Olympic gold medals only as a guide to the country's sporting excellence (a spurious measure but of particular importance to many Australians), one may ascertain the concern from the following results: Melbourne 1956 - 13; Rome 1960 - 8; Mexico City 1968 - 5; Munich 1972 - 8 (3 won by Shane Gould in swimming). At the Montreal Olympics Games in 1976, Australia won only one silver medal and four bronze medals. The print and electronic media reacted strongly to this "failure". John Daly, track and field coach at those Olympic Games, echoed the sentiments of many Australians who were shocked by the "poor showing" of their athletes, and demanded to know what had "gone wrong". Daly wrote:

"A public inquiry was initiated which ultimately resulted in greater government funding of Australian sport to bolster the system. For it was not the system [which was] at fault. Indeed, the club system of Australian sport still exists whereas most sports operated on a self-funded, ad hoc basis with volunteer "kitchen-table" administration and untrained coaches and "chook raffles" to boost their efforts before the 1970s and 1980s."[9]

It was not until 1939 that the Federal Government established a National Fitness movement by providing funds to set up councils in each State. However, financial support was meagre and even in 1968-69 the amount allocated for National Fitness Council purposes was only (Austn) $416,000 for the six States and Australian Capital Territory, an allocation of 3.4 cents per head of population. But in the *Australian Labour Party Policy Speech* delivered in November 1972, Gough Whitlam made a statement about the quality of life:
"There is no greater social problem facing Australia than the good use of leisure. ...It is, above all, the problem of urban societies and thus, Australian is the most urbanized nation on earth, a problem more pressing for us than any other nation on earth."[10]

Elected to office the next month, the Labour government established a Department of Tourism and Recreation. Frank Stewart effectively became Australia's first Minister for sport and he sought the advice of individuals and bodies associated with recreation, sport and physical education and a detailed report, *The Role, Scope and Development of Recreation in Australia* was tabled in parliament in May 1973. Based on the content, the term "sport" might well have been used instead of recreation. In his statement to Parliament, the Minister indicated:
"... most of [the] Cabinet submissions and budget requests would be based on recommendations contained within that report ... It is our responsibility to recognize for the first time in the history of Australia, that recreation and sport should constitute an integral part of our life and, as such, must receive serious attention and much more than token support from our governments."[11]

The government allocated $1 million in its first budget to assist Australian amateur athletes to participate in national and international teams, giving support to the Minister's statement that "our dedicated amateurs have been ignored long enough and we intend to remedy the situation".[12] The total allocation to recreation and sport in 1973-74 was approximately 5.2 cents per head. In 1974 a task force headed by Dr Allan Coles considered the extent of support for elite athletes.[13] The Australian Sports Institute report was tabled in parliament in November 1975 but its recommendations were not implemented because, in a unique turn of political events, the Labour government was dismissed by the Governor-General and replaced in a subsequent election by a Liberal-Country Party coalition government. In this new administration, sport was allocated to the Ministry of Home Affairs. However, following Australia's dismal performance at the 1976 Olympic Games in Montreal and a general decline in athletic achievement at the international level, an Australian Institute of Sport (AIS) was established in Canberra on January 26 (Australia Day), 1981. Athletes at the AIS receive scholarships, which may include accommodation, educational allowances, clothing and equipment for training and competition, coaching, domestic and international travel and competition, and the support services provided by sport science and medicine. Specialist training and competition facilities were developed in Canberra for the "institute" sports, as well as residential accommodation, a sports science and medicine centre, and an administration and information resource centre.

When the Labour Party was returned to government in 1983 the Minister for Sport, Recreation and Tourism, John Brown, while expanding and decentralizing the AIS, proposed that an Australian Sports Commission (ASC) function as a statutory authority. The ASC, established in September 1984, had three main objectives: to sustain and improve Australia's level of achievement in international sport competition; to increase the level of sport participation in sport by all Australians; and to increase the level of assistance from the private sector.

In late 1987 the ASC, AIS and elements of the Department of the Arts, Sport, the Environment, Transportation and Tourism (DASETT) were amalgamated to form a new commission under a second Australian Sports Commission Act. The then Chairman, Ted Harris, described the ASC's function as "promoting sport for the community and increasing the level of sports participation by Australians .. Equally it is seeking to improve the level of performance of Australian athletes nationally and internationally".[14]

It is clear that the ASC has assumed responsibility for sport in Australia and seeks to redress the situation that the first Federal Sports Minister, Frank Stewart, described in 1974: "Australian sport is among the most unorganized and un-coordinated in the world ... in the past our champions succeeded in spite of our organization, not because of it".[15] This comment not only changed significantly the extent of involvement in elite sports by federal and state governments, it rallied a call for specialized management education for those responsible for the administration of sport. It was envisaged that the skills derived from that education would include policy and planning formulation, promotion and marketing, accounting and finance, computer literacy, personnel, and resource and time management. The former playing career of an aspirant to a sport management position would no longer be the paramount factor which determined the success of an applicant in securing a position. Tim Wendel wrote in 1988 that, in America:

"There was a time when the path from the playing field to the front office of a professional team was a direct line. But now a new route has emerged: through the halls of academia".[16]

Why sport management education?

In its 1990 report on sports funding and administration, the House of Representatives Standing Committee, under the chairmanship of the Honourable Steve Martin, MHR, observed:

"... there is a need for a core of full-time experts to provided specialized administrative skills ... High calibre administrators must be trained ... not all skills can be learned on the job."[17]

Later, the Director-General of the Victorian Department of Sport and Recreation, Tom Hogg, reiterated this concern, stating that: "... there is an urgent need to upgrade the quality of sport administration ... [and] ... a need for more management-trained administrators".[18] There was a recognition of the growing complexity of Australian sport as it became interdependent with commercial interests and, in many respects was required to interface with a more sophisticated government sports bureaucracy. Clearly, the management of sport required the input of specialized personnel.

As far back as 1973, sports academic John Bloomfield, who had been commissioned by the Australian Government's fledgling Department of Tourism and Recreation, advocated that "the Australian Government retain the voluntary leadership system but that it attempt to introduce more professional and semi-professional leadership in the near future."[19]

Bloomfield further advocated that the Australian Government should financially support sport through national sporting associations of Australia.[20]

Clearly, Australia was endowed with a wealth of experience and expertise in sport administration, if the successful hosting of the Olympic Games in Melbourne in 1956, and the British Empire and Commonwealth Games in Perth in 1962 were anything to go by. Yet the harnessing of that expertise in formal education programmes was limited to being conducted by agencies such as the State National Fitness Councils.

The 1975 *Report of the Australian Sports Institute Study Group*, chaired by Allan Coles, acknowledged the contribution made to Australian sport by volunteers, declaring that "while interest and enthusiasm are essential pre-requisites for any administrator, they are hardly sufficient in themselves to equip individuals with the background needed."[21]

While reiterating that any recommendations made by the Study Group should not be perceived by volunteers or part-time administrators to be threatening or discouraging,[22] it implied the need for greater professionalization. The Report clearly observed that, not only did Australian sport lack direction and coordination[23], but that "effective administration is one of the more outstanding deficiencies in Australian sports organizations."[24]

Recommendations on the professional education of sport administrators fell short of tertiary level study; instead the Report recommended that the Australian Sports Institute "establish courses for sports administrators and officials in conjunction with national and international federations".[25] These were to take the form of part-time residential or short correspondence courses.

By 1981, however, an undergraduate degree in Sports Studies, incorporating a major study in administration was operational at the then Canberra College of Advanced Education (now known as the University of Canberra), partially funded by the federal Department of Sport, Recreation and Tourism.[26] It was recommended that this Department should organize a series of workshops and produce a handbook aimed at those organizations without full-time administrative staff with a view to promoting better programme understanding and administration.[27] Pyke and Woodman observed in 1983 that, apart from a variety of short course packages aimed at improving expertise in select subject areas such as sports marketing and sports law, there were few tertiary-level courses in Australia which permitted some specialization in administration.[28]

Experience and expertise appears to have been sport-specific, passed inter-generationally as by baptism-of-fire, endowment and oral tradition. Insularity was characteristic. Jack Carroll recently gave an insight into the two major classes of sport administrator prevalent in those years. The traditional part-timer or "kitchen table administrator"[29] typically worked in a voluntary capacity, had "competed at high level" and had a long history in the sport being administered. The traditional full-time sports administrator was "more likely to have tertiary qualifications and less likely to have competed at a high level".[30]

Even in the early 1990s, tertiary qualified sport managers were by no means the great majority. In 1990 Dianne Whitelaw surveyed 249 senior managers in the Australian Football League, the National Basketball League, State and National Cricket Associations, State and National Tennis Associations and found about 52 per cent had tertiary qualifications ranging from Associate Diploma to Masters degree level.[31] Whitelaw stated further that almost half of all graduates (46.75%) had a business qualification; the second most common area of training was teaching/education with 37.67% of all graduates.[32] An insignificant proportion of personnel held specific Sport Management or Sport Administration qualifications.[33]

In 1989 Brown and Spinks, commenting on the professional development of sport administrators, believed that the more traditional settings for such development in Australia have been in tertiary programmes in Sports Studies, Human Movement Studies, and Physical Education.[34] Their major concern was that such programmes offered "only a fleeting view of issues that receive considerable critical analysis in well established business and management programmes".[35]

Earle Zeigler, writing about North America, has suggested that "an organizational, administrative or managerial revolution has occurred and will continue to occur because of the ever-increasing complexity of society".[36] One is tempted to consider that conditions in Australia are symptomatic of that complexity also. Sport managers in Australia need to respond effectively to the impact made on sport and technological developments, socio-cultural diversity and expectation and the changing nature of our surroundings.

Tertiary education and sport management

It is commonly agreed that the impetus for tertiary level sport management education had its origins in 1957. Envisaging a massive growth in sport at all competitive levels, Walter O'Malley, the owner of the Los Angeles Dodgers, encouraged James G. Mason of the University of Miami in Coral Gables, Florida, to prepare a sport administration curriculum.[37] It was nearly ten years later that Mason, then at Ohio University, commenced a graduate programme in sport administration. By 1973, the university of Massachusetts at Amherst programmes at the undergraduate and postgraduate levels were in operation and, according to Mullin[38], by 1977 six institutions throughout the USA offered tertiary level programmes. Originally, the Ohio course required students to take physical education units but, according to Mason, "those requirements were dropped and a more interdisciplinary approach was adopted".[39]

In some quarters this adoption foreshadowed a drift of responsibility for sport management education away from the physical education and athletic departments. Some have argued that the sport manager must have an empathy with and a sensitivity to the sort and athletic experience. Hager, from the Sport Management Division of the School of Health, Physical Education and Recreation of Bowling Green State University believed that:

"Excluding a strong foundation in sports activities would be tantamount to sending a sailor out to sea without sails for the boat. The Sport Manager with a basic understanding of motor learning and biomechanics must develop the physical skills needed to incorporate this knowledge... If the Sport Manager is going to be a director of sport, an administrator of sport, or a promoter of sport, then self-actualizing experiences in a variety of sports are critical to professional education."[40]

Given the sport background of the overwhelming majority of applicants for places in sport management programmes, compulsory or required physical activity units may do little more than complement an already established empathy for the sport experience. This leads to another concern expressed about the modern sport manager. Jack Carroll described a third class of manager - the "office-desk administrator - as someone who is "less likely to have competed at a higher level and most significantly, has no competitive background in the sport being administered".[41] This has been a concern for Jim McKay who, when reviewing an advertised position for an executive director of the Australian Women's Hockey Association, said:

"*For the position it was essential to have excellent managerial and coordination skills, desirable to be experienced in sports administration and preferable to have a knowledge of hockey. These requirements indicate the extent to which grassroots volunteers have been displaced by managerial experts. Presumably the successful applicant ... [may] ... never have seen a hockey game.*"[42]

This concern may be intuitively driven and that perhaps active or vicarious participation in a sport is less important pre-requisite for an efficient and effective manager. Indeed, as will be suggested later, there are some sport studies which may have greater priority.

In 1988, 109 institutions in the USA were identified as offering sport management degrees: 51 at undergraduate level only, 33 at graduate level only, and 25 at both levels[43] with about 3,000 students enrolled. There appears to be a diversity of bases to such courses, much the same as it has been in Australia where, in 1989, Mahoney and others identified 9 courses which met sport management criteria of:

(a) a clear orientation to management as a principal feature of the course rationale.
(b) sport management was clearly identifiable within the published course structure.
(c) clear use was made of terminology and content as outlined by the Sport Management Task Force of the National Association of Sport and Physical Education.
(d) sufficient time appeared to be devoted to the area of study within the course unit described.[44]

Courses generally emanated from faculties of Physical Education in the United States and from Applied Science or Arts in Australia, with fewer from Business faculties in either country. Such was the diversity of background or content of sport management programmes in the USA that the National Association for Sport and Physical Education (NASPE) gave a Sport Management Task Force responsibility for formulating *Guidelines for Programmes Preparing Undergraduate Students for Careers in Sports Management*.[45] The 1987 Task Force suggested at both the undergraduate and graduate levels:

The curricula in Sport Management may typically be divided into three major components: (1) the foundational areas of study, (2) the applied areas of study, and (3) the field experiences.

The foundational areas consist of courses typically offered through the business department ... the Applied areas of study build upon the Foundational areas and deal specifically with the sport enterprise ... The field experiences component includes part-time experiences called "internships" for which academic credit is received.[46]

Ulrich and Parkhouse, in their consideration of curriculum design in 1982, attempted to determine whether coursework met job-related needs as a step to improving the quality of sport management courses. Their survey of 145 graduates showed that the most applicable or relevant courses include the internship, public relations, communications, management principles, and athletic administration.[47] These areas were closely followed by accounting, finance and applied economics.

In 1986, Parks and Quain found in their survey of 365 sport management practitioners in the United States that the most desirable competencies arising from studies in management, promotion, marketing and sport were human relations, personnel and time management and writing, closely followed by public speaking and money management.[48]

The problem of national course accreditation has more recently been addressed by the North American Society for Sport Management (NASSM) and National Association for Sport and Physical Education (NASPE) Joint Committees. It was recommended that to establish parameters of the minimum Sport Management coursework required a full degree in Sport Management.[49] The guidelines, according to the joint committees, would be adopted for use in the NASSM-NASPE Curriculum and Accreditation Guidelines for Sport Management Programmes.

Perusal of the draft proposal suggests nine content areas, each with an array of possible theoretical courses. If anything, the joint committees appear to have re-jigged the 1987 Task Force Guidelines and broadened the scope of studies for accreditation purposes. Notably absent from the suggested curricula content are physical activity units, although it is noted that such units are often mandatory for undergraduate students regardless of course specialization in the United States.

In their examination of accreditation for sport management programmes in 1991, Fielding et al. reported that the NASPE-NASSM chairpersons took the joint committee's "recommended curriculum content guidelines"[50] to their parent organizations, which endorsed them. Continued study and development of the competency-based curriculum and of an accreditation model were recommended and future reports were desired.

In their survey of over 200 academics teaching sport management programmes in over 100 North American institutions, Fielding et al. found that 43% of respondents opposed programme accreditation, 32% were in favour and 25% uncommitted.[51] These researchers found that among the academics there is little agreement on what constitutes educational quality, what competencies are necessary for success, and what coursework is necessary to prepare students for successful careers in the sport industry.[52]

So what should be the curriculum of Australian sport management students? At present there are neither guidelines nor accreditation standards at State or National level, but it appears that institutions are following something like the model suggested by the 1987 Task Force and are cognizant of the work of the Australian Society of Sport Administrators (ASSA), but who will ultimately accredit programmes of tertiary education? It seems that among the challenges facing tertiary sport management courses in Australia into the third millennium, the more important will be the issues of development of a nationally recognized curriculum model, a national accreditation process, and the problem of supply outstripping demand for graduates if the exponential growth of courses as experienced in the United States is experienced in this country. It has been suggested that the ultimate accrediting authority, and perhaps the final arbiter of curriculum worthiness, will be the marketplace. It nevertheless behoves all academics and institutions conducting or seeking to conduct sport management programmes to consider carefully what constitutes a professional education. According to Fielding and others, "many sport management students"[53] in North America would not achieve or possess qualities of a professional education on graduation such as:
"... a minimum body of knowledge commonly possessed by members of the profession; skill in handling source materials and adding to the acquired body of knowledge; the ability to think, analyse, and act in the presence of new or unprecedented situations; and an ethical attitude toward the uses to which a member of the profession my put knowledge or skill."[54]

It would indeed be unfortunate if Australian academics and institutions neither foreshadowed nor recognized the challenges facing the discipline in their own country nor gleaned some of important insights from the experiences of their overseas counterparts.

Conclusion

In November 1995, a sport management conference hosted by Deakin University in Melbourne, envisaged the formation of the Sport Management Association of Australia and New Zealand (SMAANZ). Leading academics and sport industry representatives addressed the issues of linking academia to the industry, facilitating a dialogue between academics responsible for curriculum design in sport management in Australia and New Zealand and linking the new association with the International Alliance for Sport Management. It was felt that the formation of the association was a critical part of the growing professionaliztion of sport management.

Since the early 1990s several Australian universities have established undergraduate and post-graduate programmes in sport management. At the undergraduate level in 1995 the following universities offered degree programmes: Deakin University, University of Ballarat, and the

Victoria University of Technology (all in Victoria); Southern Cross University, the University of Western Sydney, and the University of Technology - Sydney (all in New South Wales); and the University of Canberra (in the Australian Capital Territory). At the post -graduate level programmes were offered at Deakin University, the University of Ballarat and the Victoria University of Technology, Southern Cross University, the University of Canberra, Griffith University (in Queensland), and the University of Technology - Sydney[55]. They emanate from a variety of faculties, including Arts, Applied Science and Commerce, and typically draw upon the services of others for curriculum delivery. Each programme would, by university requirement, be subject to the scrutiny of an industry-based advisory panel, which would meet the programme staff on a regular and formal basis.

The undergraduate programmes have attracted many thousands of school-leaver applicants and, as the universities have placed quite rigid quotas on intake, the level of pre-university academic performance has predominated in the selection procedures. As a consequence, the academic quality of successful applicants has been high and has been complemented by programmes of high academic rigour. Typically, students of sport management programmes have been encouraged, through fieldwork placements and research work, to establish strong network relationships with the sports industry.

The profile of staff expertise has seen the emergence of specific sport management qualifications, as personnel are drawn from Europe and North America and as Australian staff are encouraged to engage in the new research culture abounding in the universities. Newly emerging Australian graduates have been encouraged to consider academic paths after a period of industrial experience.

The Australian experience in sport management and sport management education has been one of quite dramatic and justified change over recent years and it is clear that there has been considerable response to the concerns of the 1970s. It is our belief that Frank Stewart, the nation's first Minister for sport, would be well pleased with the developments which have taken place.

[1] Hansard.- House of Representatives, March 20, 1908, p. 1330.

[2] Australian Bureau of Statistics.- *Year Book Australia*, 1993, Canberra, Australian Bureau of Statistics, 1994.

[3] Commonwealth of Australia.- *Going for Gold. The First Report of an Inquiry into Sports Funding and Administration*, Canberra, Australian Government Publishing Service, 1989.

[4] R.E.N.- Twopeny, *Town Life in Australia*, London, Elliot Stock, 1883, p. 204.

[5] Dunstan, Keith.- *Sports*, Melbourne, Cassell, 1973, p. 3.

[6] Warren Wind, Herbert.- "Over the rainbow", *Sports Illustrated*, May 16, 1960, p. 84.

[7] Horne, Donald.- *The Lucky Country*, Penguin, London, 1966, p. 40.

[8] *Australian Olympian*.- Spring, 1993.

[9] Daly, John.- "Australia's national sport - winning", *Australian Journal of Physical Education*, Vol 57, pp. 5-14.

[10] Whitlam, E.G.- Australian Labour Party Policy Speech, Blacktown Civic Centre, 1972, p. 35.

[11] Stewart, Frank.- Speech at the inaugural dinner of Australian Sports Council, August 28, 1974.

[12] Stewart, Frank.- Press Release, August 22, 1978, p. 1.

[13] Coles, Allan.- *Report of the Australian Sports Institute Study Group*, Canberra, Australian Government Printing Service, 1975.

[14] Australian Sports Commission.- *Sport to the Year 2000*, Canberra, Australian Government Publishing Service, 1987, p. 1.

[15] Stewart, Frank.- quoted in Ian Jobling, "A ministry of recreation and sport at the national level of government", *Report of the British Commonwealth and International Conference on Health, Physical Education and Recreation*, University of Otago, Dunedin, 1974, pp. 71-81.

[16] Wendel, Tim.- The academic approach to sport, *Sports Inc.*, April 25, 1988, p. 18.

[17] Commonwealth of Australia.- *The Second Report on an Inquiry into Sports Funding and Administration*, Canberra, Australian Government Publishing Service, 1990, p. 12.

[18] Hogg, Tom.- "The future of sport in Australia", *Sport Report*, Confederation of Australian Sport, Canberra, Summer, 1990-91, Vol. 10, No. 4, p. 22.

[19] Bloomfield, John.- *The Role, Scope and Development of Recreation in Australia*, Canberra, 1973, p. 74.

[20] Ibid.- 1973, p. 78.

[21] Department of Tourism and Recreation.- *Report of the Australian Sports Institute Study Group*, Canberra, 1975, p. 74

[22] Ibid.- 1975, p. 75

[23] Ibid.- 1975, p. 29.

[24] Ibid.- 1975, p. 63

[25] Ibid.- 1975, p. xix.

[26] Parliament of the Commonwealth of Australia.- *The Way we P(L)ay: Commonwealth Assistance for Sport and Recreation*, Canberra, 1983, p. 72.

[27] Ibid.- 1983, p. 43.

[28] Pyke, Frank and Woodman, Laurie.- "The education of sports coaches and sports administrators in Australia", *Proceedings of the VIII Commonwealth and International Conference on Sport, Physical Education, Dance, Recreation and Health - Conference '86*, Glasgow, E. & F.N. Spon, London, 1986, p. 29.

[29] Carroll, J.- "From the kitchen table to the office desk: the hanging faces of sports administrators in Australia", *Conference Proceedings Management in Sport*, Vol. 1, University of Canberra, 1989, p. 64.

[30] Ibid.

[31] Whitelaw, Dianne.- *Careers in Sport Management*, Graduate Diploma in Careers submission, Victoria College, November 1990, p. 2.

[32] Ibid.- p. 22.

[33] Ibid.- p. 72.

[34] Brown, P. and Spinks, W.- "The professional preparation of sports managers: a leisure-based perspective", *Conference Proceedings: Management and Sport*, Vol. 1, University of Canberra, 1989, p. 21.

[35] Ibid.

[36] Zeigler, Earle.- "Sport Management: past, present, future", *Journal of Sport Management*, Vol. 1, No. 1, 1987, p. 8.

[37] Mason, J. G., Higgins, C.R. and Wilkinson, O.J.- "Sports administration education 15 years later", *Athletic Purchasing and Facilities*, January 1981, p. 44.

[38] Mullin.- 1980, p. 1.

[39] Mason et. al.- 1981, p. 45.

[40] Hager, S.A.- "Curricular questions confronting Sport Management", in B.K. Zanger and J.B. Parks, (eds) *Sport Management Curricula: The Business and Education Nexus*, Bowling Green, 1984, p. 119.

[41] Carroll.- 1989, p. 64.

[42] McKay, Jim.- *No Pain, No Gain? Sport and Australian Culture*, Prentice Hall, New Sydney, 1991, p. 43.

[43] Sports Inc.- May 23, 1988, pp. 42-44.

[44] Mahoney, D., Deane, John, Holden, A. and Smart, J.P.- "Sports management: a business faculty perspective", *Management and Sport Conference Proceedings*, Vol. 1, Canberra, 1989, p. 8.

[45] Sport Management Task Force of the National Association for Sport and Physical Education.- *Guidelines for Programs Preparing Undergraduate and Graduate Students for Careers in Sports Management*, September 1987, p. 1.

[46] Sport Management Task Force.- 1987, p. 3.

[47] Ulrich, D. and Parkhouse, Bonnie.- "An alumni oriented approach to Sport management design using performance ratios and a regression model", *Research Quarterly for Exercise and Sport*, Vol. 53, No. 1, 1982, p. 68.

[48] Quain, R. J. and Parks, J. P.- Sport Management survey: employment perspective", *Journal of Physical Education, Recreation and Dance*, Vol. 57, No. 4, 1986, p. 20.

[49] North American Society for Sport Management (NASSM) and National Association for Sport and Physical Education Joint Committees.- *Professional Preparation Curriculum Content Guidelines for Programs in Sport Management - First Draft and Proposal*, October 1989, p. 1.

[50] Fielding, L. W., Pitts, B. G. and Miller, L.K.- "Defining quality: should educators in Sport Management programs be concerned about accreditation?", *Journal of Sport Management*, Vol. 5, No. 1, 1991, p. 2.

[51] Ibid.- 1991, p. 12.

[52] Ibid.- 1991, p. 13.

[53] Ibid.- p. 91.

[54] Ibid.

[55] Shilbury, D. and Deane, J.W.- "Opportunities in Sport Management" in *1996 Preliminary Universities Guide*, Graduate Connection, Balgowlah, 1995, pp. 11-12.

The development of competence in sport management: a Canadian perspective

Daniel Soucie
University of Ottawa,
Canada

In Canada, as well as in many countries around the world, sports management has recently made giant strides both as a professional occupation (Soucie, 1994a), and as an academic discipline (Parks, 1992). Indeed, in the past twenty years or so this field has been witness to an increasing demand for competent people to manage sport organizations. Universities around the world have responded with numerous academic programmes to meet the needs of this emerging profession (Thoma, 1993).

Canada is respected worldwide as a true sporting nation. It has frequently hosted the world through major sport events. "Sport is integral to Canada and Canada is committed to sport... Cradle-to-grave, we value lifelong physical activity and sport as a cultural trademark of our society" (Minister of Fitness and Amateur Sport, 1992, p .7). Furthermore, as evidenced by the recent hosting in 1995 of the first World Forum on Physical Activity and Sport, Canada is a world leader in the debate and resolution of the major issues facing the sport movement.

Canada, along with the United States, has led the way in promoting the development of academic professional preparation programmes in sport management (Soucie, 1988). Furthermore, Canadian academics exercise strong leadership within the North American Society for Sport Management which is responsible for the promotion of research and professional development in this area (Zeigler, 1992). The purpose of this short article is to examine the field of sport management as an occupation and as a career in Canada, and to briefly discuss the need for management competency development in sport.

The need for efficient sport management

There are indeed vast resources in the world of sport which require efficient management: financial, material and human resources. Whether it is at the professional or the amateur and recreational level, there exist literally thousands of sport-related organizations, associations or clubs which necessitate sound management. As is the case for any business-related or service-related enterprise, such sport organizations have missions and goals, structures, policies, procedures and rules, and tasks and functions which are all designed to rationally and systematically guide human interaction. Sport organizations therefore possess the same basic bureaucratic characteristics which are common to all organizations. Their resources need to be properly channelled and coordinated in an effort to achieve the stated purposes in the most efficient manner. In bureaucratic structures, specialization is also required so that responsibilities can be delegated to persons holding competence (specialists, professionals) in specialized areas.

The efficient use of resources is particularly important at the present time in Canada as the country struggles with the slow economy and must subserve to international money markets. As a consequence recent government cutbacks are placing higher demands on the delivery of sport and forcing sport managers to deliver quality and relevant services in times of tenacious restraint and increased public scrutiny. More than ever our society needs competent, politically astute and change-conscious professional sport managers.

What do sport managers do?

DeSensi et al. (1990) have suggested that sport management includes "any combination of skills related to planning, organizing, directing, controlling, budgeting, leading, and evaluating within the context of an organization or department whose primary product or service is related to sport and/or physical activity". According to Chelladurai (1994), sport management can be defined as "the coordination of resources, technologies, processes, personnel, and situational contingencies for the efficient production and exchange of sport services" (p. 15). Sport managers are therefore persons who act in managerial leadership roles in the production and marketing of sport services.

In Canada sport managers are typically involved in various and quite diversified managerial responsibilities depending on the specific type of sport organization, whether it is operating at the national, provincial or municipal level, its size, and the sport manager's relative position within the organization's hierarchy. Tasks of sport managers (or administrators as they are most often referred to in Canada) mainly consist of planning and supervising various activities and services that aim for satisfaction of various needs and expectations of different sport "clients", whose personal objectives range from simply watching sports, to participating in recreational sport programmes, to excelling in high performance sport. The role of the sport manager is "to enhance sport performance and/or participation and/or to enhance efficient supervision and governance of sport" (Harris, 1993, p. 392).

Titles of managers and administrators in Canadian sport vary considerably. They may be called directors, department heads, presidents, supervisors, coordinators, general managers, chief executive officers, etc. They may be paid professionals or simply volunteers. They are often formally appointed by the organization, but they can also be elected by their peers. The formal authority that they hold varies considerably from one situation to another. Hence, some sport managers are accountable for larger amounts of resources (human, material or financial) than others. However, regardless of their official title and their level of authority and responsibility, all sport managers, in varying degrees, do the same fundamental thing - that is, they must plan and organize different aspects of sports programmes, and then direct and guide the resources towards their execution.

Sport management as a career

Sport management is the main source of income, and a full-time job for many. Individual careers therefore do exist in sport management. In Canada, career opportunities in sport management have been classified (Soucie, cited in Haggerty & Chelladurai, 1991) as follows :
(1) Amateur sport: as executive or general director, technical director, programme supervisor or coordinator within sport governing bodies at the federal and/or provincial level;
(2) Educational institutions: as director of intramural or inter-scholastic sports programmes at the high school, college or university level;

(3) Municipal recreation and parks departments: as manager or supervisor of sports/recreational programmes for children, youth, the elderly, etc.;

(4) Government agencies: as manager of sports, recreation and fitness policy programme units within government;

(5) Private sports clubs: as manager in fitness, tennis, squash and racketball clubs or centres, as well as programme manager in outdoor education centres, summer camps, camping and youth centres in the private sector;

(6) Private agencies: as manager of various sports and recreation programmes in agencies such as Red Cross, Royal Life Saving, YMCA/YWCA, National Lifeguard Service, etc.;

(7) Facility management: as director of operations in arenas, sports centres and facilities at the municipal level;

(8) Merchandise and equipment enterprises: as production or marketing manager of sports equipment and merchandise;

(9) Professional sport: as programme manager, publicity director, marketing and promotion agent, negotiating agent for professional athletes, etc.;

(10) Professional associations and multi-sport organizations and agencies: as manager of various programmes in national, provincial or international associations in sport, coaching, recreation or fitness.

Sport management is therefore unique, and clearly points to a definite and unique "field of competence" which requires specific knowledges and skills (Soucie, 1994b). In Canada our "best qualified" sport managers have often been, and in many cases still are, the ones who have "come up through the ranks", the ones with experience and seniority. While these variables have great importance in the recruitment of competent sport managers, as we shall now discuss, specific professional and academic training in sport management is highly desirable.

What is a competent sport manager?

We often hear people criticize and say of some managers that they are "incompetent". Whereas it may be true that some people acting as administrators or managers are less than perfect, most managers have some competence in some aspects of the requirements of the position. There is a difference between ideal and actual competence. Competence is a relative term and it is multifaceted. In other words there are many dimensions of one's competence as a sport manager. What then exactly is competence in sport management?

As stated by McCleary (cited by Zeigler, 1987, p. 17), "to be competent is to possess sufficient knowledge and ability to meet specified requirements in the sense of being able, adequate, suitable, capable". Competence derives from several interrelated dimensions: knowledge, experience, traits, and skills.

Knowledge relates to factual information which the manager possesses. Knowledge acquired through general education and specific and specialized training is essential in the development of expertise as a sport manager. Guidelines prepared by the North American Society for Sport Management list the following core knowledge content in sport management: human behaviour, ethics, marketing, communication, finance, economics, legal aspects, leadership and organizational theory.

But management is not just a science; it is also an art. This is why experience is also important. The acquisition of knowledge is not strictly done through formal education. Sport managers also learn on the job and develop their knowledge base through trial and error, and through exposure to the field. That is why, for example, experience either as a coach or an athlete, or as an administrator or manager in other fields can also be an important contributor to competence.

Traits correspond to innate attributes as well as personality characteristics which can be either inherited or acquired. Personal traits which may be relevant to management are numerous, and include such characteristics as self-confidence, emotional stability, congruence, integrity, energy level, initiative, stress tolerance, empathy, tact, charm, etc. Such individual characteristics are particularly relevant in the development and maintenance of good interpersonal relations and effective communication in organizations. They are therefore very much a part of what management competence is all about.

Skills are also numerous and important in leading people towards organizational goals. Skills refer to personal abilities that an individual is adept at or has some propensity for. Skills correspond to know-how that managers have the potential to work at, develop and improve, and are acquired through training, experience and education. Skills pertinent to sport management have been classified differently by different researchers. Taxonomies usually include technical, interpersonal and conceptual skills.

Technical skills, which mainly have to do with "things", relate to know-how about such things as methods, processes, procedures, and techniques to resolve organizational details and problems. Interpersonal skills, which mainly deal with "people", relate to know-how about such things as human behaviour, ability to understand the feelings, attitudes and motives of others, ability in oral and written communication, ability to foster cooperative relationships, etc. Conceptual skills, which relate mostly to "ideas and concepts", are concerned with general analytical ability, logical thinking, deductive and inductive reasoning, problem-solving ability, creativity, anticipating, visioning and strategic-thinking ability. In addition to these skills, Zeigler and Bowie (1995) refer to "conjoined" skills or "developing the various managerial skills in combination or proportion to achieve both immediate and long-range objectives and goals" (p. iii).

As stated earlier, competence is an elusive concept and people have very different and subjective perceptions of what it is to be an effective and competent manager. Furthermore, the managerial effectiveness of any sport leader is affected by many other contextual factors like for example the formal power bases of the incumbent (Babiak & Soucie, 1994). People in organizations typically expect administrators to make firm decisions, but one can only act in as much as he or she has the formal authority to do so.

Sport management academic programmes in Canada

Universities in Canada have taken on the responsibility for the development of competence in the field of sport management. Programmes are designed in such a way as to develop the desirable traits, skills and knowledge base of future sport managers. Practicums and internships are also important components of these programmes and provide students with an opportunity to gain valuable experience in working directly in the field. These are often the cornerstone of the students' academic experience and they help them to develop professional attitudes, behaviours, and values. They help students to understand and grasp early the hard realities of organizations. Finally, these experiences help students to develop knowledge as to how to implement some of their own ideas and effect change in sport organizations.

Many of the 38 Canadian universities with undergraduate degrees in physical education and kinesiology offer courses in sport management. Some universities have focused undergraduate programmes in this area, e.g. Laurentian University (Sudbury) and York University (Toronto). At the graduate level, of the 26 universities with graduate degrees, 10 institutions offer a specialization in sport management: U. of Alberta, Memorial U., U. de Montréal, U. of Ottawa, U. of Saskatchewan, U. of British Columbia, U. of New Brunswick, U. of Victoria, U. of Western Ontario, and U. of Windsor (Soucie, 1995).

Academic programmes are also designed so as to develop critical and reflective skills to allow sport managers to look at problems from new and innovative perspectives. That is why courses in philosophy and ethics of sport, and in history and sociology of sport, are essential so that future sport managers gain an understanding of the broader social context of sport.

Universities are also involved in the development of a body of knowledge which is useful and meaningful to practising professional sport managers. In the field of sport management "research seeks to understand the world of sport organizations and to systematically investigate the many variables that may have an impact on the efficient management of sport (Soucie & Doherty, 1995, p. 620)". That is why another important component of professional preparation in sport management, particularly at the graduate level, is the development of research skills. As stated by Di Brezzo (1993), "being a professional is more than associating with a specific activity, career, or group. Professionals must understand their craft - the attributes, techniques and ethics of that career" (p. 48).

Most academic programmes prepare "generalists" in sport management and prepare future managers for a variety of managerial and administrative positions. This approach is pertinent since, as stated earlier, most sport managers and administrators in Canada are called upon to exercise different roles and perform diversified tasks in sport settings.

Conclusion

The existence of a vast number of organizations and associations that relate to sport and physical activity in our society cannot be denied. Because quality of life is now considered by many as their prime objective, it can be speculated that the end of the present century will witness further emergence of sport organizations, particularly in the area of recreation and participative sports. These organizations need to be governed by the best qualified individuals that the profession can offer. Therefore, advanced education and specialized training at university level in sport management is highly desirable.

Specialized university programmes constitute an important phase in the recognition of a professional occupation. Social recognition of an occupation such as sport management will take time, but this process is being accelerated when professional sport managers with university education secure important management positions at the highest levels of competence within the public and private sectors. Professionals with academic credentials assume more demanding positions, thereby contributing to the autonomy of the occupation.

References

Babiak, K. & Soucie, D.- *Managerial leadership effectiveness in national sport organizations.* Paper presented at the 1st ICHPER-SD Asia congress, Kuala Lumpur, Malaysia, November 1994.

Chelladurai, P.- Sport management: Defining the field. *European Journal for Sport Management*, 1994, 1 (1): pp. 7-21.

DeSensi, J. et al.- Sport management curricular evaluation and needs assessment: A multifaceted approach. *Journal of Sport Management*, 1990, 4, pp. 31-58.

Di Brezzo, D.- Being professional - How does research fit? *Journal of Physical Education, Recreation & Dance*, 64, 1993, (7): pp. 48-49.

Haggerty, T. & Chelladurai, P.- Physical activity programme management. In C. Bouchard, B.D. McPherson, & A.W. Taylor (Eds.). *Physical Activity Sciences*, 1991, pp. 207-212. Champaign, II: Human Kinetics.

Harris, J.D.- Using kinesiology: A comparison of applied veins in the subdisciplines. *Quest, 45*, 1993, pp. 389-412.

Minister of Fitness and Amateur Sport.- *Sport: The Way Ahead* - Minister's task force on federal sport policy. Ottawa: Minister of Supply and Services Canada, 1992.

Parks, J.B..- Scholarship: The other "bottom line" in sport management. *Journal of Sport Management*, 1992, 6, pp. 220-229.

Soucie, D.- *Promotion of sport management programmes in Canada.* Paper presented at 3rd annual conference of the North American Society for Sport Management, Urbana-Champaign, Illinois, 1988, June.

Soucie, D.- The emergence of sport management as a professional occupation: A North American perspective. *European Journal for Sport Management*, 1994a, 1 (2): 13-30.

Soucie, D.- Management theory and practice. In E.F. Zeigler (Ed.). *Physical education and kinesiology in North America: Professional and scholarly foundations.* Champaign, Illinois: Stipes, 1994b.

Soucie, D.- *Les sciences du sport au Canada: Un aperçu de la recherche institutionnelle.* Communication présentée au 6e Congrès de l'Association des Chercheurs en Activité Physique et Sport. Pointe-à-Pitre, Guadeloupe, 1995, November.

Soucie, D. & Doherty, A.- An overview of past, present, and future sport management research in North America. *Proceedings of the 2nd European Congress on Sport Management*, 1994, pp. 619-634. Florence, Italy: Istituto Superiore di Educazione Fisica.

Thoma, J.E.- *Sport management education:* A world view. Paper presented at the 8th annual conference of the North American Society for Sport Management, Edmonton, Alberta, 1993.

Zeigler, E.F.- Sport management: Past, present, future. *Journal of Sport Management*, 1987, 1, pp. 4-24.

Zeigler, E.F.- Using the rays from history's shining lantern as we face an uncertain future. *Journal of Sport Management*, 1992, 6, pp. 206-214.

Zeigler, E.F. & Bowie, G.W.- *Management competency development in sport and physical education.* Champaign, Il.: Stipes, 1995.

Sports administration in Chile through its sports structures

Gonzalo Bravo
Club Deportivo Universidad Católica,
Santiago de Chile, Chile

*The present article is based on the study presented in the report **Diagnóstico sobre el sistema deportivo en Chile** (1995), produced in 1994 by the Advisory Council (Consejo Asesor) of the President of the Republic for Sport and Recreation, of which the author was a member of the executive team. The principal aim of the study and subsequent report was to prepare a first draft of a sports law for Chile.*

The organization of sport in Chile, as in many countries, is dictated by the participation and interaction of a considerable number of governmental and private organizations, including the General Directorate of Sport and Recreation (DIGEDER), which is the largest governmental organization concerned with sports administration. On the level of governmental organizations there are also organizations depending from or connected with DIGEDER, which administrate and develop sport at the various territorial levels, such as regions, provinces and communes, throughout the country (Consejo Asesor, 1994a).

Among the private bodies involved in sports administration in Chile there are the Chilean Olympic Committee, the Sports Federations, the Sports Associations and other related organizations.

The governmental structure of sport

The General Directorate for Sports and Recreation or DIGEDER is a centralized public service organization reporting to the sub-secretariat for War in the Ministry of National Defence. DIGEDER is the successor of the former State Sports Directorate that was created in 1948. Under current legislation (Law 17.276 of 1970), DIGEDER is in charge of sports and recreation policy in the country, and serves as coordinator of the sports organizations and recreation institutions connected with the government (Consejo Asesor, 1994a).

By law, DIGEDER is authorized to perform its activities in three areas: (1) institutional development and coordination; (2) promotion of sports and recreational activities; (3) development of sports and recreational infrastructure.

DIGEDER, as a public service organization, and according to the provisions of the sports law, No. 17.276 of 1970, has bodies that represent it throughout the country. These bodies correspond to Local Sports Councils and Provincial Sports Councils. The former act at communal level, and are private companies that take instructions from DIGEDER. There are 325

Local Sports Councils nationwide, which have relations with the Provincial Sports Councils and various associations and clubs existing at communal level (Consejo Asesor, 1994a).

The Provincial Sports Councils act at provincial level, and also at regional level, but under the name of Regional Sports Coordinators, which are only nominal organizations since they are part of the function of the Provincial Sports Councils[1].

Funding for DIGEDER's activities comes through the fiscal budget, which is made good through the public budget law, and from revenue from betting on sports (Law 1.298, 1975; Law 19.135, 1992), which in practice has become the main source of funds for the institution (DIGEDER, 1993). Nevertheless, in the 1987-1993 period there was a considerable fluctuation in this revenue, which went from 80% in 1989 to 39% in 1993. In 1980 the betting system raised revenue equivalent to 87 million dollars, as compared with 1990 when it raised only 8 million dollars (DIGEDER, 1994a).

The substantial decrease in revenue from the sports betting system has provoked a serious crisis in the Chilean sports system. In fact, the dependence on a single source of financing has meant that short-term projects have been favoured over long-term initiatives aimed at more important ends, which has produced a limitation in the capacity, both of users and leaders, to generate new sources of financing. Thus, it is currently becoming essential to diversify sources of financing, creating revenue-generating instruments through various legal bodies to allow the involvement and participation of the private sector.

Private sports structures

Private sports organizations and structures are defined as all those not in the organizational structure of the governmental department represented by DIGEDER, even though many sports organizations in Chile receive some kind of subsidy from DIGEDER.

The sports structures in the private sector include the so-called "organizaciones funcionales de deportes" or functional sports organizations, which encompass the Chilean Olympic Committee, the sports federations and various channels, areas or sectors of participation including various organizations such as the school sports sector, the university sports sector, the labour sports sector, the professional sports sector, and the community sports sector (Consejo Asesor, 1994a).

Administration of federation sport

The organization of federation sport in Chile, as in many countries, is handled by the sports federations themselves, which in turn are represented by the Chilean Olympic Committee (COCH), which is the governing body of competitive federation sport in the country. The

---

[1] These were created to comply with the legal administrative structure of the public services of the country as a result of the process of regionalization completed in 1976, whereby public monies had to be handed over and administrated at regional level through the regional ministerial secretariats. The Defence Ministry has no regional ministerial secretariats, but the Regional Sports Coordination was created in order to administer, control and finally to transfer public funds to sport. In Chile there are 14 Regional Sports Coordinations, one for each region, plus two in the Santiago metropolitan area.

COCH is a company under private law, which means it can receive monies from both the public and the private sectors. The COCH consists of 43 federations, which are subdivided into those governing Olympic sports and those governing non-Olympic sports. As a member of the Olympic movement, it collaborates with the sports federations, authorizes the Chilean team members to represent Chile in international competitions such as the Pan-American Games and the Olympic Games, and supervises the technical standards of national athletes.

The Chilean sports federations encompass 1.17 million athletes, 88% of whom are footballers, which leaves 140,000 in other sports (Consejo Asesor, 1994b).

The administration of federation sport is carried out by the federations themselves, who possess autonomy as far as their organization and internal regulations are concerned, and have legal status and links with their international counterparts. The majority have paid staff for general administrative work. Of the federation leaders in managerial posts, 37% are active athletes, 21% former athletes and around 19% parents of athletes (Consejo Asesor, 1994b). Nevertheless, a significant percentage of federation presidents have held leading positions in clubs and associations, which indicates that the tendency towards having amateur leaders, who start at the bottom and gradually take on posts with greater responsibility, continues.

As far as specialized training of leaders is concerned, 23% have taken part in courses abroad and around 29% have some training at national level. As far as professional and administrative staff were concerned, in the 34 federations consulted there were 60 administrators working full-time and 47 part-time, on tasks ranging from management and accounting to administrative secretaries. As far as the appointment of national coaches was concerned, around 27% of federations made appointments from year to year, 6% every two years, 5% every four years, 24% subject to competence, 21% in another way and 9% did not have national coaches (Consejo Asesor, 1994b).

Funding for federation sport is provided mainly through laws 1.298 (1975) and 19.135 (1992) which grant elite sport 15% of the total budget allocated to sport. Of this, 13% is distributed among the 43 sports federations and the remaining 2% goes to the Chilean Olympic Committee. The National Association of Professional Football (ANFP), which is part of the Chilean Football Federation, is not included in this, since it receives a direct percentage from DIGEDER.

The budget given to the 43 federations for 1994 came to just under 3 million dollars, which highlights the scarcity of resources for federation sport and suggests that the federations should seek new sources of revenue for their activities. In this regard around 35% of them seek funds in the private sector through advertising and marketing, and 29% claim to have no other funding apart from that provided through DIGEDER (Consejo Asesor, 1994b).

The budget allocated by DIGEDER to each of the federations cannot be used freely; spending has to comply with certain standards. The almost 3 million dollars that were allocated to federation sport in 1994 could only be used to cover costs in the following areas: training of elite athletes (39%), federation administration (25%), international competitions (23%), national competitions (10%) and organizational development and distribution (3%) (DIGEDER, 1994b; Fuentes, 1994).

Nevertheless, and in view of the scarcity of resources available for federation sport, particularly at the elite end, as from 1992 an aid programme for exceptional athletes, called TOP, was instigated, granting a monthly stipend to those athletes with a genuine hope of excelling on an international level, whether in South America, the American continent as a whole, internationally or at the

Olympics (DIGEDER, 1994a). The total revenue for 1994 came to 700,000 dollars, which went to help 119 athletes (DIGEDER, 1994c).

Among the main problems caused by the scarcity of resources for federation sport is the lack of coverage for amateur sport, both in the written press and on television, which makes it difficult to sell as a product. Also important is the lack of professional marketing experts within the different federations: only one federation replied that it had a marketing manager (Consejo Asesor, 1994b).

Administration of school sport

Sport in schools takes place mainly as part of extra-curricular education, which in the case of Chile has a take-up rate of only 16% of the school-age population, i.e. around 480,000 students.

The administration of the school sport system is handled mainly by the Education Ministry's office for extra-curricular education, which coordinates with the offices of the regional ministerial secretariats for education, and with the different municipalities. Funding for the National School Games is provided by DIGEDER. Preparation of the prior stages, i.e. communal and regional stages, and also the development of sports activity within colleges, is financed by municipal contributions intended for the various colleges and high schools.

Private high schools are responsible for their own jurisdiction and have overall funding. In this sector of education, the extra-curricular education department does not have the influence and control that it can exert in most of the country's other colleges and high schools. Sports organization, administration and policy are the autonomous preserve of the education ministry. Nevertheless, although the level of organization, administration and funding of sports programmes in private schools is excellent, sports participation from this sector represents a minimal percentage of the total participation of Chilean school children.

Administration of university sport

University sport is structured through four organizations that encompass almost all the universities and other centres for higher education in the country. The four organizations divide their spheres of activity in accordance with the institutions they represent: state universities, which are those that receive a subsidy from the state; private universities; professional institutions; and finally, technical training centres. In total they encompass around 300,000 students, of which it is estimated that no more than 15% take part in any sports programme, whether within the university or at a level of inter-university competition (CONAUDE, 1994).

State universities, which represent 50% of the students in Chile's universities, are organized through the Comisión Nacional Universitaria de Deportes (CONAUDE), the National University Sports Commission. Within this organization, internal sports activities are administered by the universities themselves. Inter-university competition is handled through CONAUDE itself, which dictates guidelines, establishes policies, creates regulations and coordinates the participation of universities in the national university championships (Cornejo, 1994). Funding for university sport is provided by the universities themselves and by DIGEDER.

CONAUDE is the Chilean organization that interacts with the International University Sport Federation (FISU). It is run by professionals from state universities, acting in a voluntary capacity.

Administration of labour sport

As far as labour sport is concerned, a group of organizations in Chile administer programmes concerning sport and recreation in this sector. These include the Canal Deportivo Laboral (CANADELA), created in 1976 as a result of the reorganization of national sport into "canales" or "areas". CANADELA is a non-profit organization with the mission of involving the labour sector in sporting activities. Its activities extend to almost all labour institutions in industry, agriculture, mining, commerce and construction sectors.

In recent years various bodies have arisen alongside CANADELA, largely upon the initiative of the private sector, to administer and promote sport. These include the sports corporation for metalworking industries, the sports corporation for companies in the construction sector, and the sports banking group, for banking and finance employees, to name a few. However, despite the rise in the number of such organizations, participation in sport in Chile by the labour sector is still low, particularly in view of the fact that in the four organizations mentioned above, which represent around 96,000 workers, only a little over than 20,000 claim to participate in any of the sports activities organized in their place of work (Flores, 1994; Mejías, 1994).

Another aspect is the low level of participation from companies making up the various organizations for labour sport. In the case of companies in the metalworking sector, only 9% of the total of 800 companies in the sector take part in the sports programmes, representing around 3,000 workers (Flores, 1994). In view of the significant efforts that have been made to try to bring sport into the work place, particularly by the private sector, the scarcity of available resources and the lack of sport promotion campaigns appear to be the main obstacles in the way of the development of sports activity in this sector. In addition, most organizations have no premises of their own, and no insurance to cover sports accidents, which is why a considerable proportion of their resources is spent on hiring sports facilities and paying for accidents occurring during sports competitions.

Funding for labour sports comes mainly through the payment of social contributions by the workers themselves; in some cases it is the union itself that negotiates a subsidy for these enterprises with the company. DIGEDER's contribution to these purposes is minimal and is limited mainly to financing sports competitions between the companies belonging to the Canal Deportivo Laboral. Other programmes are administered by the sports offices of each organization, with a minimum of hired personnel who are responsible for general administration.

Administration of professional sport

When speaking of professional sport in Chile it is possible to concentrate exclusively on football, since it is the oldest and only sports activity that has remained in the professional category in our country; moreover, it is possible to say that it is perhaps the only sports activity that has a real impact on Chilean culture.

At different times professional cyclists, professional boxers, professional tennis players and, in latter years, professional basketballers have existed, but these cases essentially concern athletes who receive honorariums for participating in some competition or other, which does not necessarily imply that the structure of the sport is professional, as is the case with football.

The Chilean football federation is the governing body of Chilean football, and is made up of two associations: the national amateur football association (ANFA) and the national professional football association (ANFP). The latter encompasses the country's 32 professional clubs, sixteen in the first division and sixteen in the second. The ANFP is affiliated to two international organizations: the International Football Federation (FIFA) and the South-American Football Confederation. The highest organ of the ANFP is the council of club presidents, comprising 32 representatives, which elect the board of directors every four years, the advisory committee and the discipline commission (Nuñez, 1994).

Although on the one hand football is the sports activity with the greatest impact and coverage at national level, it is also true that there is a clear disparity between conditions in the clubs, both in the first and the second division, that take part in professional competitions, with some clubs making a profit and others running at a deficit for years.

The problems of professional football have been dragging on for years: as early as 1987 DIGEDER carried out a serious study to diagnose the situation of Chilean football. Officials from both the first and second divisions pointed out that the main reason for the crisis and problems of football had its roots in leadership aspects, particularly the lack of planning and organization. The other major problem was financial: at the time it was pointed out that financing had to come from the state through DIGEDER and the national professional football association itself (DIGEDER, 1987).

In addition, it was recognized that one of the main sources of financing was gate money in the stadiums. There are not many clubs, however, that can live off gate money. The average audience between 1984 and 1988 was 5,939 spectators per match (Vergara, 1994), while in 1993 audiences fluctuated between 2,500 and 21,000 spectators per match, and the total audience for first division matches was approximately 1.8 million, yielding gate receipts of 6.5 million dollars, 65% of which was earned by 5 of the 16 first division teams (Alonso, 1994).

Among the main forms of financing for professional clubs are gate receipts, the sale of players, advertising and television rights and the contributions generated by DIGEDER for national competitions. Another new form of funding for professional football is the recent addition of cable television, which during 1994 signed an important exclusivity contract with the national professional football association, for three years, and for the sum of 18 million dollars, whereby the clubs receive a percentage of the deal. The effects and repercussions that this deal will have on the development of professional football in Chile are still unknown, since with the increasing importance of cable television, attendance at football matches could drop further.

The governing body of professional football finances its operations through selling the rights to broadcast matches, gate money for international matches, contributions from clubs, stadium fees and contributions from DIGEDER. In 1993 it received around 3.3 million dollars (Becerra, 1994). The ANFP's administration is professional and has full-time administrative and technical personnel.

Administration of communal sport

Sport in Chile's communes is developed through various organizations which, in many cases, have overlapping fields of activity. The law (18.695, Art. 3 and 4) allocates responsibility for developing sport to the municipalities. In this way most municipalities have their own sports department, along with an extra-curricular education department, which acts as coordinator of extra-curricular sporting activities along with the colleges and high schools of the commune. There also exist local sports councils at communal level.

Although Chile has a variety of organizations for developing sport at commune level, there is a lack of coordination and clarity of objectives among them. These organizations evidence a great redundancy of functions and in many cases bad management of the meagre resources available. Sport at commune level is administered by paid professionals.

Both sports departments and local sports councils have full-time or part-time personnel. They hire the physical education teachers that are in charge of the activities. The infrastructure available varies from municipality to municipality, as do the sports activities practised, the budget available and the level of participation and interest of the inhabitants. Funding for commune sport comes from two sources: the allocation of resources by DIGEDER to the sports department and the local sports councils, and the resources generated by the municipality itself through taxes and contributions, and earmarked for sport. At national level DIGEDER contributes to communal plans for developing training programmes for young people, popular sport and popular recreation. Contributions to these programmes for 1993 came to around 5.5 million dollars (DIGEDER, 1994d).

Conclusions

Administration of sport in Chile involves the participation of a significant number of governmental and private organizations. Nevertheless, although there is a network of organizations covering a wide spectrum of the sports sector, there is a clear lack of policy at national level to coordinate efforts for better use of the scant funds available for sport in Chile, public funds which in 1994 came to almost 30 million dollars. Although there are no studies that quantify investment by the private sector, it is estimated that it brings considerably larger sums into sport. As far as the human resources in charge of sports administration are concerned, to date there is no research enabling us to establish the profile of the Chilean sports administrator. The available antecedents imply only that the personnel working in this sector are a combination of volunteer and professional workers, and that sometimes the professional or paid personnel lack formal training to carry out the responsibilities in this sector. This is due mainly to the virtual non-existence of training courses or programmes, particularly at university level, for professionals working in this sphere.

The report presented in January 1995 by the Sports Advisory Council to the President of the Republic (Consejo Asesor) offers a series of concrete proposals to develop sport in Chile. Indications are given as to the role of a new and modern structure for sport in Chile, the future of this growing country's sports culture, the development of physical education and sport in schools, the development of high-level sport and the involvement of the private sector in sports funding.

References

Alonso, Victor.- *La torta del fútbol es para Colo Colo*. Santiago de Chile. La Segunda, 1994, December 12, pp. 17-18.

Becerra, P.- *Financiamiento del fútbol profesional*. Gerente de finanzas de la asociación nacional de fútbol profesional ANFP. Santiago de Chile (personal interview), 1994, August 19.

CONAUDE.- *Evaluación diagnóstica CONAUDE 1993*. Comisión Nacional Universitaria de Deportes. Santiago de Chile, 1994.

Consejo Asesor.- *Diagnóstico sobre el sistema deportivo en Chile y antecedentes de los sistemas deportivos de otros países*. Consejo Asesor del Presidente de la Republica para el Deporte y Recreación. Santiago de Chile, 1994a.

Consejo Asesor.- *Cuestionario a federaciones deportivas*. Consejo Asesor del Presidente de la Republica para el Deporte y Recreación. Santiago de Chile, 1994b.

Cornejo, Miguel.- Antecedentes de la comisión nacional universitaria de deportes. Presidente de CONAUDE. Santiago de Chile (personal interview), 1994, September 20.

DIGEDER.- *Análisis diagnóstico y formulación de una estrategia de desarrollo para el fútbol chileno*. Dirección General de Deportes y Recreación. Santiago de Chile, 1987.

DIGEDER.- *Estructura jurídica, sistemas operativos y de control*. Dirección General de Deportes y Recreación. Santiago de Chile, 1993.

DIGEDER.- *El plan nacional de deportes y recreación y su proceso de aplicación*. Dirección General de Deportes y Recreación. Santiago de Chile, 1994a.

DIGEDER.- *Proyecto de planificación y presupuesto anual 1994 del programa de alto rendimiento*. Dirección General de Deportes y Recreación. Santiago de Chile, 1994b.

DIGEDER.- *Asignaciones a deportistas programa TOP*. Dirección General de Deportes y Recreación. Santiago de Chile, 1994c.

DIGEDER.- *Plan y presupuesto anual 1994*. Asignación de recursos a programas y sub-programas. Departamento de planificación de la Dirección General de Deportes y Recreación. Santiago de Chile, 1994d.

Flores, Maximiliano.- Deporte y recreación laboral. Coordinador de deportes de la corporación deportiva y cultural de la asociación industrial de metalurgía y metal mecánico CORDEMET. (Personal interview), 1994, August 4.

Fuentes, Juan.- Distribución de recursos a federaciones deportivas. Jefe del departamento técnico de DIGEDER. Dirección General de Deportes y Recreación. Santiago de Chile. (Personal interview), 1994, September 20.

Mejías, Gustavo.- *Deporte y recreación laboral*. Gerente del canal deportivo laboral CANADELA. Santiago de Chile (Personal interview), 1994, August 1.

MINEDUC.- *Archivos de matrícula año lectivo 1993*. Santiago de Chile. Ministerio de Educación Pública, 1994.

Nuñez, Sergio.- Antecedentes generales de la asociación nacional de fútbol profesional ANFP. Secretario ejecutivo. Santiago de Chile. (personal interview), 1994, August 2.

Vergara, H.- El público ¿un oxígeno que se extingue? Revista minuto 90, 1989, April 18, pp. 30-31.

Sport management in Spain

Gabriel Colomé
Centre d'Estudis Olímpics i de l'Esport,
Universitat Autónoma de Barcelona,
Barcelona, Spain

The structure of sport in Spain has developed from the new situation created when the country reverted to democracy after the death of General Franco in 1975. Whereas under Franco sport had been structured along the lines of the centralist and centralizing State, the new democratic State adapted its structure to the new structure of Spain itself, with its Autonomous Communities. The State of Autonomies, which was born in the 1978 Constitution, and evolved after the approval of the Autonomous Communities' Statutes, defines the extent of each administration's and institution's responsibility for sport. It is mid-way between a Federal State and a Regional State, and includes Autonomous Communities with both kinds of jurisdiction, i.e. either closer to the federal model or closer to the regional model, although the tendency, as laid down in the Constitution itself, is gradually moving towards a federative structure.

The law on sport, 10/1990 of 15th October, regulates the judicial framework in which the practice of sport should develop within the State. The preamble to the law explains:
"Although the allocation of competence with regard to sport and the promotion of sport is given in the various Statutes of Autonomy — for which reason this law does not attempt to perform re-allocations that are not its to perform — nevertheless, (1) such allocation must first be placed strictly within the context of the territorial scope of the respective Autonomous Communities, and (2), sport is a matter — to employ constitutional terms — over which various claims for competency and jurisdiction can be made. Thus there are coordinated activities and cooperation projects between the State Administration and the administrations of the Autonomous Communities to cover those concurrent claims for competency, which no doubt encourage a more dynamic sports policy with a positive knock-on effect.

"As far as the first point is concerned, it seems clear that the competitive aspect inherent in sport, both at national and international level, justifies the State's involvement. As the Constitutional Tribunal said in its day, Autonomous Communities' management of their own interests certainly does not imply the transferral of interests that belong to national Spanish sport as a whole, such that it is absolutely essential to connect public intervention with the environment in which sport takes place. This enables the boundaries of the jurisdiction and authority of the State and the Autonomous Communities to be better defined."

"As far as the second point is concerned, it is also clear that sports activity is a cultural event, in which the State should and must become involved under the terms of the Constitution, if only to facilitate the necessary communication between the various autonomous bodies. And, notwithstanding that the competence exercised over education, research, health or trade legislation supports State activities in the area, in their supra-autonomous aspects. This is in complete accordance with the authority assumed by the Autonomous Communities in their

Statutes of Autonomy, which has caused some territories to promulgate their own sports legislation."

The organization of sport

The Sports Law defines the various components of the sports-institutional framework: the Consejo Superior de Deportes, sports clubs, Spanish sports federations, professional leagues and the Spanish Olympic Committee. We shall examine the internal elements of each component and how they fit together.

The activities of the State Administration in the domain of sport corresponds to, and is governed directly by, the Consejo Superior de Deportes (CSD). This sports governing body is led by a President who is appointed directly by the Council of Ministers, with the rank of Secretary of State.

The CSD is the highest authority of sport in Spain. It has authority over regulations, control, sanctions, education, science and finance (article 8 of the law).

Sports clubs can be categorized as:
a) elementary sports clubs;
b) basic sports clubs;
c) Sociedades Anónimas Deportivas (sports associations in the form of limited companies).

All clubs, whatever their specific aim and the legal form they take, must be registered in the register of sports associations (Art. 15.1). In order to take part in official competitions clubs must first become members of the corresponding federation. This registration must be made through the federations of the autonomous communities when these are members of the corresponding Spanish federation (Art. 15.3).

The Spanish sports federations are private bodies with legal status, whose area of competence extends to all the territory of the State in those areas over which it has jurisdiction; they are made up of provincial federations, sports clubs, athletes, officials, judges and referees, professional leagues if these exist, and other interested bodies involved in promoting, performing or contributing in some other way to the development of sport (Art. 30).

In those Spanish sports federations where there exist official national professional competitions, professional leagues are created, exclusively and mandatorily composed of all the clubs that take part in such competitions. The professional leagues enjoy an autonomous status with respect to the Spanish sports federation. The professional leagues have the authority, among other things, to organize their own competitions in coordination with the respective Spanish sports federation (Art. 41).

The Spanish Olympic Committee (COE) is the sole representative in Spain of the International Olympic Committee. The COE organizes the entries and participation of Spanish athletes in the Olympic Games, collaborates in their preparation and promotes the practice of the activities represented at the Games. Article 48 of the Sports Law mentions the COE specifically, saying "the Spanish Olympic Committee is a non-profit-making association with a legal personality, whose aim is to promote the Olympic movement and propagate the Olympic ideals. To this end the Spanish Olympic Committee is declared an association of service to the public." This consideration is extremely significant since such bodies receive a series of fiscal benefits, priority when it comes to obtaining resources for sports promotion plans and programmes from State and local administrations, and preferential access to official State credit facilities.

New developments: Sociedades Anónimas Deportivas and Professional Leagues

This Sports Law introduces two important new concepts in sports management. First, professional sports clubs being categorized as Sociedades Anónimas Deportivas (SAD) and second, the creation of Professional Leagues to oversee competitions.

The SADs are based on the idea of transforming the professional clubs which, before the Sports Law was introduced, had little responsibility for their own management (this could lead to clubs going bankrupt and being dissolved without anyone bearing clear responsibility), and establishing a framework of legal and financial responsibility for clubs performing professional activities on a nationwide scale. The aim of the Law is to establish a new form, by converting professional clubs into SADs, based on the general provisions of any other Sociedad Anónima (roughly equivalent to a limited company), and including specific provisions for the world of sport. The directors of sports clubs that have become SADs are legally and financially liable.

In the case of football only four clubs did not have to become SADs: Athletic de Bilbao, Real Madrid, FC Barcelona and Osasuna de Pamplona, since when the law came into force they fulfilled the requirement of being financially sound. Apart from Osasuna, they are all historic clubs that have always played in the first division since their creation in 1929.

The reason these four clubs did not have to become SADs was that since the 1985-1986 season they have all had a positive capital balance, and were allowed to keep their legal status if their general assembly authorized it. Moreover, the board members of these clubs are jointly liable for any negative financial balance generated during their administration. Before the beginning of each financial year the board of directors has to submit on behalf of the club, to the professional league, a banker's reference guaranteeing to underwrite fifteen percent of the expense budget. This sum can be called in by the Professional League and the guarantee is renewed annually throughout the administration.

FC Barcelona is a case apart as far as financial management is concerned. The creation of the Fundación del Barcelona from financial contributions paid by supporters in return for a plaque bearing their name in the Stadium, pursues the aim of having a powerful vehicle for channelling their financial potential with the support of the new legislation on Foundations and Patronage. Barcelona is not a typical example, compared with most other professional sports clubs.

The second new concept in the Sports Law is the obligation to create Professional Leagues within the federation, made up exclusively and mandatorily of all the clubs participating in official professional competitions. The Professional Leagues organize their own competitions in coordination with their respective Spanish sports federation. This new structure and division of tasks, as in other European countries, allows the problems inherent in the management of the professional competitions to be managed by the professional clubs within this new autonomous body. It enables better rationalization of functions between federations and Professional Leagues without impairing the competence of each, since efforts towards the development of sport, whether professional or not, are clearly delimited.

The world of sport, as the last link in a chain that unites leisure elements such as the practice of sport with the entertainment aspect of elite sport, had to adapt its structure to a modern society that was moving towards democracy. Although Spain's political transition was an example for others to follow, sport and its institutions had to follow the same path to transformation and modernization. It could not remain the last bastion of outmoded times. The democratization of its institutions was a pending matter that Spanish sport finally approved. Furthermore, the new elements such as the conversion of professional sports clubs into Sociedades Anónimas Deportivas, the liability of their directors and the creation of the professional leagues to be responsible for organizing competitions, bring the Spanish model closer to the usual practice of the European Union countries.

Sport management in France

Jean Camy
Université Claude Bernard,
Lyon, France

Introduction

It might appear to be an impossible task to give a short presentation of how sport is organized and managed in France. Indeed, this is assuming that it has been possible both to identify the most significant components in this extraordinarily complex and continuously developing system and to detect the major trends in its development, having defined the relationship between the system and the players involved in it. It presupposes that it has been possible, throughout our analysis, to identify specific features of the French situation and what makes it unique as compared with other countries[1].

Such an ambitious project involves a number of risks, one of which might be to produce a caricature revealing, on the one hand, a set of structural characteristics which appear to pose an implacable logic and, on the other hand, as a counterpoint, an interplay of those involved amounting to poorly understood effects of position and status.

We cannot be certain that we have been able to avoid this danger even if we try to indicate that this system is also the product of seemingly minute adjustments and localized debates on the subject. The diversity of local practices and sports organizations leads us to consider that sports management is a search for guidelines capable of taking advantage of ideological, organizational and functional contradictions at every level in the system.

It is futile to give an account of how sport in France is managed without first defining the subject-matter. "Sport" can be said to correspond nowadays to very different situations compared with 40 or 50 years ago. We must therefore first give a brief account of this field of activity and the various practices which have grown up within it.

Such diversity goes some way to reveal new collective players in a field which is increasingly complex and the system we will endeavour to describe is based on the coordinated or sometimes competing activities of a large number of organizations. Interaction between organizations, the compulsory relationships between them, and the degree of autonomy or dependence which characterizes them, lead to a (provisional) overall equilibrium which lends some of its originality to the system.

This system would be no more than an empty mechanical structure were it not given life by those whose status and relative position partly underlie patterns of behaviour which are

---

[1] To this end, we will use mainly two publications, one of which was produced by the AENOC (Association of European National Olympic Committees), now the EOC (European Olympic Committees), the second being published by the Commission of the European Communities (DG X) Ed. Gen. J. Wegener.

increasingly subject to requirements for "rationality" and "efficiency" emanating both from a principle of internal evolution (the search for progress) and also from pressures exerted by partners (in the public sector or economic sector). From this standpoint, we are witnessing a sensitive transformation of the ways of mobilizing human resources. More than ever, sports organization management has to be able to control different if not contradictory forms of commitment: that of professionals who are sometimes organized into "corps", who base themselves on a contractual approach, and that of volunteers who are often motivated by the idea of community and sharing but who are also able to adopt a more idealistic exchange approach.

Sports organizations and practice in France

As in most other Western European countries, sport in France has experienced both massive growth and great diversification since the Second World War. In addition to the development of traditional sporting disciplines, this movement also benefits from the incorporation into the sporting movement and the transformation ("sportization") of physical disciplines, such as gymnastics and traditional popular games, as well as the progress made by sport as a support for physical education in schools. Mention should also be made of the effects of the shift in use of the word "sport" which nowadays tends to denote all forms of physical activity regardless of their aim (leisure, fitness training, competition). Sport's current success is a result of the convergence of a growth in sporting activities proper, the "colonization" or "conquest" of related fields, and its increased importance. Despite difficulties in defining the object and interpreting certain results, it is possible to state that, over 40 years, the number of qualified or non-qualified participants in sport has increased five-fold to reach 20% and 30%, respectively, of the French population today, i.e. one in every two French people[2].

Diversification in sporting disciplines is no stranger to this massive growth insofar as it has permitted the incorporation of further people who wish to take part. Sport is increasingly relevant for people who are younger or older than those who have traditionally taken part (middle- and upper-class young males). Women are much better represented than ever before and the most underprivileged social strata have seen numbers of those taking part in sport rise substantially.

With its new intake, the nature of sport is partially changing. Initially regarded as an activity affording "education through competition", a means of surpassing oneself and improving one's skills, it is becoming more an opportunity for mixing socially and relaxing, a way of maintaining one's health and a means of social integration. A contrasting landscape has replaced a relatively monolithic whole.

In basic terms, sport could be divided into 6 major categories with varying aims:
- *"High-performance sport"*, which is becoming more and more professional in nature, its development largely being based on its capacity for media coverage, and organized in an entrepreneurial manner in step with its development.
- *"Competitive sport"*, the heir of modern sport which was born in the United Kingdom in the 19th century and which has been transformed as it has become increasingly distant from its aristocratic origins, the principal vector still being the community-orientated sports movement.

---

[2] On this subject, reference is made to the statistics of the Ministry for Youth and Sports relating to qualifications (Sports Management databank, April 1995) and to the data presented by the INSEE (Surveys published in 1967 and 1990 on "How the French spend their leisure time").

- *"Sport for fitness"*, which corresponds to the contemporary interest in the human body and people's enthusiastic pursuit of health.
- *"Educational sport"*, actually a physical education which is compulsory in primary and secondary education, which has made sport its principal vector.
- *"Sport for integration"*, which is used for its socializing capabilities in populations regarded as marginal or in danger of becoming marginal (problem youngsters, the elderly).
- *"Sport as a form of play"*, as an accompaniment to holidays and leisure for a great many French people.

All the above forms have their own organizations where they are practised, without these organizations having a monopoly of one particular form.

We cannot expect to offer, here, a precise presentation of the interplay between the people principally involved, the producers of goods and services, who are active in the "sports field". All we can hope to give is a basic initial definition of the main categories they represent, with the principles of action that motivate them, and to give a brief description of the types of interrelationships that have been established between them (especially since these various categories are extremely heterogeneous). Those directly managing the sporting disciplines we have just listed may be grouped into four main types:

1) *Sports clubs* which are members of *federations* and which, in France, are represented by the CNOSF (French National Olympic and Sports Committee), the CROS and CDOS (Regional and Departmental Sports and Olympic Committees). Nearly 160,000 clubs, covering over 10 million qualified people, are members of approximately 120 sports federations. They are run by more than one million volunteers and employ, at an estimate, over 15,000 people.

2) The national, regional or local *public sports body* which is particularly strong in France (9,000 state employees, agents from the Ministry for Youth and Sports and its decentralized structures: over 15,000 representatives in the field for bodies which depend on local or regional authorities).

3) *Schools* (or, rather, secondary teaching establishments where 35,000 teachers are responsible for the Physical and Sports Education of twelve million youngsters attending school. One might question the inclusion of this group in the "sports system", but, owing to the large numbers of those involved and the resources it employs, and although it operates as a largely independent sub-group, it is important to take it into account.

4) The last group is more vague in terms of organized structure and hierarchy and consists of all *commercial businesses with a sports-related activity*. The geographical extent and the diversity of these structures, plus the absence of any unified organization makes it very difficult to evaluate its size. Nevertheless, it seems likely that over 40,000 people are employed in this sub-group.
Still further structural categories ought, in fact, to be distinguished:
- Professional organizations staging regular sports events (certain professional sports clubs) or more specialist events (Tour de France, etc.).
- Structures offering leisure activities and sports tourism (gyms, private tennis or golf clubs, etc.).
- All other providers of sports services.

What is the relative importance of these categories of players?
We will base our answer to this question on two principal points of reference, namely financial resources and the human resources employed.

As in all Western European countries, sport in France is financed principally by the household budget; however, if one attempts to measure the contribution from other categories, the exceptionally important role played by central government and, on a wider basis, by public bodies, is revealed[3].

Country	% Financing guaranteed by the State	% Financing guaranteed by local communities	Total public financing
Germany	0.55 %	26.45 %	27.00 %
Spain	3.30 %	10.70 %	14.00 %
France	9.00 %	27.00 %	36.00 %
Italy	6.00 %	08.00 %	14.00 %
United Kingdom	0.80 %	15.20 %	16.00 %

The financial contribution which may be attributed to the commercial sector is much more difficult to assess. If sponsorship is included (and this represents virtually half the sector's contribution), a sum comparable to that represented by State financing is obtained.

This initial assessment of the relative size of the various categories of those involved may be supplemented by an evaluation of the human resources employed.

State employees predominate and their numbers (nearly 40%) in relation to all staff whose professional activity is principally in sports management are even more spectacular than those for government financing.

Profession	Staff Numbers	Percentage
Primary/secondary teacher	35,000	29.10 %
Ministry for Youth and Sport officials	9,000	07.50 %
Officials in the field (Field education officials and advisers)	15,000	12.50 %
Others	61,000	50.90 %
Total	120,000	100.00 %

Those persons whose principal activity is sports management (estimate)

This economic information ought to be viewed in conjunction with remarks on the legal framework of each sporting discipline and the organizations which implement it. France is one of those Western European countries where the State is omnipresent[4]. A law defines the objectives and the respective roles of the various players. Sports federations are given the freedom to concentrate on general-interest assignments, thereby creating a quite explicit situation of dependence which is currently seen in a wide range of activities.

---

[3] According to W. Andreff (under the direction of) Les enjeux économiques du Sport en Europe, financement et impact économique, "CDDS" report, Council of Europe, 1993.

[4] M. Pescante, "Les différents modèles européens de législation sportive".

These federations may be classified into three categories[5]:

1 - Those which are completely dependent on the Ministry of Sports (at least two thirds of resources originate from the subsidy granted to them). The pentathlon, wrestling, field hockey, weight-lifting, rowing, kayaking and fencing are among the Olympic federations in this category.

2 - Those which are very largely dependent on the Ministry (the subsidy represents between one third and two thirds of resources). The Olympic federations in question are: ice sports, boxing, baseball, athletics, swimming, volleyball, cycling, gymnastics, archery, badminton, sailing, handball, table tennis, shooting, skiing, judo and basketball.

3 - Largely independent sports (less than 20% of resources coming from the Ministry for Youth and Sports). The Olympic federations in this category include those for equestrianism, football and tennis.

As may be seen, the vast majority of Olympic sports federations are highly dependent financially on the Ministry.

If the State subsidy is calculated as a percentage of the federations' (consolidated) budget, it is 32% for the Olympic federations, 16% for non-Olympic, single-sport federations and 20% for multiple discipline federations[6].

State aid to the sports movement also includes making state employees available to the sports federations. More than 1600 technical managers form the majority of the federations' permanent professional staff and the importance of their role in the life of these organizations is easy to imagine.

The situation of sports clubs reveals an average degree of dependence which is even higher in the case of communities since subsidies and indirect aid (provision of facilities and staff) represent more than 60% of their consolidated budgets[7].

To summarize the situation of sport in France and of its organization, we are certainly in possession of an original model which gives the public authorities, State and Communities an exceptionally important role.

The system's overall equilibrium has, however, developed since the 1960s. The position of central government and the latter's services was first strengthened to a singular degree up to the beginning of the 1980s, but making the Ministry for National Education responsible for physical education (previously supervised by the Ministry for Youth and Sports), was the first blow delivered to the latter. Although its effect was to weaken the latter, it did not thereby manage to form a new centre of decision-making dominating the entire system.

In fact, within the Ministry for National Education as a whole, Physical Education is not of central importance and this Ministry has no ambitions or special project to develop in the field of sport.

---

[5] Source: Ministry for Youth and Sports databank, December 1995. L. Boyer & D. Charrier. Consolidated subsidies and budget.

[6] Idem: An organization in a highly specific situation has a great effect on this entire category. The results given do not take this organization into account.

[7] W. Andreff, Op. cit.

Whilst strengthening the powers of local public authorities (communes, departments, regions), decentralizing legislation has also contributed to a reduction in the Ministry's direct influence. These local public authorities are nowadays much courted by the sports movement, particularly by clubs, having become their principal partner.

The commercial sector has also seen an increase in its importance since the beginning of the 1980s. This increasing importance, which we have been unable to measure globally, shows through in some of the segments studied, particularly as regards the sports event. In fact, in order to play a major role, as is the case, for example, in the United States, this sector undoubtedly lacks organized representation. The influence of the commercial sector has spread progressively within the sports movement by contributing to the development within it of the contradictory "amateur status" and "professional status". The sector covering tourism and commercial leisure sports is even less structured than that of the professional sports event and a large number of sports associations in some sensitive sports (tennis, golf, equestrianism, etc.) has grown up, frequently at the fringes of the sports movement itself, as institutional support for the professionals' activity.

To sum up: it is thus possible to see that the French "Sports System" is a much more widely spread entity than twenty or thirty years ago. The relative influence of the various players involved has changed and openness is now the order of the day. It calls into question firstly a globally weakened Ministry, but one which maintains its influence by closely supervising the majority of sports federations, while controlling both the training system and the regulations relating to the professional practice of sport. It also concerns communities which have become the inevitable partner of sports clubs and which greatly influence national political direction. It is giving more and more space to a lucrative private sector whose influence is particularly great in top-level sport, tourism and leisure sports. Finally, it mobilizes the organized sports movement itself which is experiencing greater and greater difficulty in controlling the three influences on it. This is not without effect on the way in which the sports movement is managed: entrepreneurial or bureaucratic models spreading through the French sports movement's managerial practices are no strangers to these eventualities. However, they also correspond to developments firmly rooted in the sports organizations themselves.

Management in sports organizations in France

We still do not have reliable and systematic data on profiles of managers and directors in French sport[8], but we do know that sports management and the way in which it develops relies very largely on the human resources available to it.

Management of the various structures in sporting disciplines exhibits characteristics which are peculiar to it, namely the presence of a high proportion of volunteers capable of carrying out all tasks, be these technical, administrative or management tasks. This form of employment of human resources is found on a massive scale at all levels of the sports movement, and also amongst those who are politically responsible in the community. Their involvement is much more marginal in the commercial and schools sector.

The situation develops very quickly and talk is now increasingly about the "professionalization" of sports organizations.

---

[8] Research on this subject at a European level will probably be undertaken in 1996.

This process, as studied in the literature[9], corresponds to three phenomena which are distinct but undoubtedly linked:

- Firstly, rationalization of operation of the structure concerned, i.e. more systematic matching up of the organization's objectives and its means for achieving these, which is usually reflected in a greater division of work and forms of bureaucratization[10].

- Secondly, via a requirement for and mobilization of increased skills on the part of persons forming part of the structure. When not already the case, this may be reflected in payment for the services rendered in this way.

- Finally, through the formation, by these highly qualified people, of "professional corps" with a definite identity and which exert a high degree of influence on the operation of the organizations they may be required to supervise.

There is no doubt that sports organizations, particularly those committed to a search for excellence, are faced with a growing requirement for resources to be mobilized. However, experience and the few analyses which have been carried out in the Lyons region demonstrate that this mobilization of resources affects more than just material matters. In a number of cases, structures are capable of replacing economic resources, equivalent services coming from an appeal for a high "capital stock". Overall, the ability to increase one's economic resources is a prerequisite of the professionalization of sports organizations and, in a reciprocal manner, an increase in the resources available encourages professionalization.

However, contrary to the arguments developed by the supporters of the contingency theory, the adaptation of an external demand to requirements will not transform organizations such as those to be found in the field of sport. Federations or clubs, in particular, are too steeped in their message to be receptive to the needs of potential participants. Yet, the desire to achieve the highest level may have given rise to habits and practices which have placed them in increasingly dependent situations, financially speaking, vis-à-vis the authorities. The movement towards rationalization developed by the latter for some time, now, in France, has led them, more and more often, to accompany their subsidies with a presentation of "plans" or "agreements of objectives". These new requirements assume, at least apparently, that sports organizations will adopt a new, more strategic approach.

Those responsible for the federations mostly have to manage on an ad-hoc basis. Very few have been able to develop long- or medium-term strategies and virtually none have a framework enabling them to evaluate and plan the organization's operation. In fact, very often, the response is still a formal one and little in their actual operation changes [11].

The demand for professionalization usually emanates from the structure itself and is accompanied by calls for rationalization and planning which are, of course, found in companies. "Economization" (marketing) of relationships (contractual approach) contributes to a great extent to facilitating the shift from routine and/or improvised operation to planned operation. Admittedly, other pressures may also be exerted on sports organizations to push them into planning their activities and development. National or local public authorities have, very widely, developed contracts with sports organizations (Contracts of Objectives with the Ministry of Sports in the case of the federations).

[9] For example, A. Etzioni, The semi-professions, 1973.

[10] I. Thibault, T. Slack & B. Hinings, "Professionalism, Structure and Systems: The Impact of Professional Staff on Voluntary Sport Organizations", International Review for Sociology of Sport 1991.

[11] B. Ramanantsoa & C. Thiery-Basle, Organisations et Fédérations sportives, PUF, 1989.

One of the most substantial effects of "rationalization" in the operation of sports organizations in France is the transformation in methods of recruiting managers, particularly at local level. As in all similar structures, access to managerial posts is via a very long process of initiation into the life of the club or federation: firstly (and usually) as a participant, then a low-ranking manager, with the highest-level posts being reached only very late in a career.

Nowadays, the trend is increasingly towards the recruitment of managers on the basis, firstly, of their assumed competence. Some clubs even "head-hunt" qualified volunteers. "Communion" in respect of common values may be a thing of the past.

The process of evolution of sports organizations has sometimes (too simplistically and, largely, incorrectly) been described as a progressive or step-by-step passage from voluntary association to business. This concept takes no account of the special conditions permitting the mobilization of human resources within an associative framework and ignores the diversity of ways of linking up to an organization, even if this is a business. In fact, all organizations play a part in forming physical and symbolic links between their members, in publicizing and legitimizing their inherent values, and in allowing a "sense of belonging" to develop, which forms the cultural basis of the organization.

When dealing with something as sensitive as amateur status and voluntary work, which have played a key role in the development of modern sport even if professionalism has been in evidence for a long time, major adaptation and reinterpretation work is essential.

The "professionalization" of an organization encourages a number of changes in terms of the "values" and "beliefs" which motivate members.

Such declared values, i.e. those celebrated in a number of communal rituals, are not necessarily those which actually motivate members as a whole. However, the persistence of a collectively shared fiction is essential to mobilize energies, particularly when no more than symbolic profit can be hoped for. An organization, a club or a federation is capable of justifying its existence because it constructs links between its members and with its social and cultural environment in specific ways.

The ambiguity necessary (because it has to associate contradictory objectives) to the operation of sports organizations is not, however, a source of inefficiency. The "strategies" adopted more or less conscientiously usually correspond to the prevailing compulsory relationships within the organization and it would be futile to wish to clarify, at any price, the aims pursued.

One of the indicators of the degree of professionalization of sports organizations is, naturally, the professionalization of its executives, more particularly of its "executive managers". The appearance of professionals is not a phenomenon generated from outside, although it may sometimes correspond to extreme environmental pressures.

Although this process is not completely remarkable, it is interesting to note that the first "professional corps" to develop in the sports sector are the trainers, and then the professional players. In the case of the former, distinct professional organizations bring together state technical executives and trainers who are not State employees. Players are grouped into different organizations on the basis of the sport they play.

It is estimated that there are approximately 120,000 people whose main professional activity consists of sports management. Virtually all are "technicians", i.e. specialists in the teaching or training of the sport. Virtually all the organized professional corps, be these physical-education teachers, ski instructors or educationalists in the field, belong to this same professional category.

The professionalization of sports management grew up essentially around technical posts, which is not unusual. However, the extent to which this phenomenon has occurred in France is quite exceptional. The majority of sports-management professionals are in the public sector (over 70,000 State or field employees out of the 120,000 polled).

That sport is managed principally by State employees and elected volunteers is a peculiarly French phenomenon and is not without consequence as regards the manner in which problems are understood and dealt with.

It is also interesting to note the virtual absence of professional managers. It seems that France is particularly behind in this field, and that elected managers have virtually no highly trained professionals to substitute for them. The few people of this type, in the federations, are usually State employees who have rarely been trained for this role. This situation is both a symptom of the resistance of elected managers to the arrival en masse of high-ranking professionals into these functions and the expression of their sensitive character within the context of the sports movement.

Conclusion

The highest State authorities require France to have an original "co-management" model[12].

This formula presupposes two things we would like to question:
- The first is the balance between the power of the State and that of the associative sports movement and its representative bodies. The question of balance is obviously a question of viewpoint and is extremely difficult to evaluate in absolute terms. However, the few points of comparison with other European countries which we have set forth here lead us to speak of a "French exception" in terms of sport. The authorities and, particularly, central government play an exceptionally important role in matters of regulation and human and financial resources.
- The "co-management" formula could also imply that there are two partners. As we have seen, bodies other than the State and the sports movement are playing an increasingly active role within this sports system. Although the most spectacular is undoubtedly the increasingly omnipresent media "partners" as a whole, the most important are most certainly the local communities who own and manage virtually all the sports facilities and finance essential to the sports clubs' activities.

Each of them has an individual driving force: in the case of public-sector organizations, this is "bureaucratic", where struggles for development (or at least maintenance) of the structure are weakly oriented towards a systematic analysis of economic or social requirements; it is "a mission" in the case of the associative sector which attempts to convince us of the benefits of sport as traditionally conceived by a population which is not always capable of withstanding constraints on time and space to such a degree; and it is "entrepreneurial" in the case of those who believe that sport, like a show or leisure activity, may be used for economic development (or the enrichment of a few).
Is it possible to expect to be able to coordinate the activity of these organizations, given that so many factors appear to oppose it?

---

[12] G. Drut, Ministry for Youth and Sports, "Modernisation dans la fidélité", Le Figaro, 25 October 1995.

We should note, firstly, that approaches are not free from internal contradiction. We have identified a few of them and they can be relied upon to enable the system to develop and respond to a greater degree to the expectations of participants (or of potential participants).

However, this evolution would undoubtedly be more rapid and less chaotic if the relative importance and the role of each of the players involved were redefined. We would be tempted to suggest that "cultural property" in sport should belong to those who take part in it, in its various forms, and to their legitimate representatives; that economic exploitation in sport should take place but should respect this "property" and recognize the rights attaching to it; and that the role of the authorities could be concentrated both on recognizing unsatisfied social needs (without doubt, more in the form of encouragement than as a direct operator) and on facilitating dialogue and coordination between largely autonomous partners as a whole. This would undoubtedly be a challenge for Sports Management in France in the next millennium!

Sport management in Eastern Europe, especially in Hungary

Mihály Nyerges
Hungarian University of Physical Education,
Budapest, Hungary

Sport management in the Eastern European countries before the change of regime

As indicated below, management was not adopted in the former socialist countries until a few years ago. Before the change of regime, western management theories could not find their way into the organizational systems of sport either. What were the reasons? We can simply say that they were not needed.

General statements

In all socialist countries, PE and sport played a significant role. Within them, competitive sport was of outstanding importance owing to its political representational function: outstanding sports achievements were identified with the success of the socialist system, and in some countries - including Hungary - sports success was used to restore the nation's self-respect lost in World War II. And the political representational function of sport has not lost its importance since the change of regime.

Sport was always considered a significant social issue and so was dealt with by the state. Popular sport was declared to be free but in practice that meant that the money to be spent on sport was not included in salaries (the same applied to medical treatment and education). Sport facilities were provided by the state and not by the enterprise sector. This caused serious problems after the change of regime when the state withdrew from the financing of sport. The state no longer wanted to support sport and the economic sector was not yet prepared to do so. The transition from state control and financing to operations in market economy is a hard process. Under the new circumstances it was imperative to adopt management and sports management systems.

In all socialist countries sport was managed under direct or indirect party control and the involvement of the state and other control organizations was regulated officially.

Particularities

In addition to the many similarities, there were also differences in the various sports structures. The regular restructuring of sports management in some countries such as in Bulgaria, Czechoslovakia, Poland and Hungary implied that the sports management organized according to the Soviet pattern did not fit into their particular conditions. So these countries tried to find their own form of operation.

In the Eastern European countries, there were three basic models of sports management:

State controlled sports management: the system of central control is set up along the same lines as the other state organizations. Central control is exercised by the national sports office and enforced through the local administrative sports organizations, the boards and managers of which are appointed and not elected.

Alongside them, social organizations also operate under central control.

The system is characterized by double control enforced through the regional/local state organ (e.g. district or country council) and through the sports organization of the state organ (sports department of the council).

This model was characteristic of the Soviet Union, Poland and Rumania. In all three countries the central sports management organ was under the direct control of the Council of Ministers. In the Soviet Union, the cooperation of the coorganization was not voluntary but governed by the state. In Poland and Rumania the national sports federations could operate fairly independently. In Rumania some sports clubs were given priority and enjoyed extra support from the state for champion training.

Social (mass organizational) sports management: physical education and sport are not directly controlled by the state but considered as a social task. The sports organization is an independent social organization and its board and managers are elected. It cooperates with the central or regional state organizations and other organizations under the terms of separate agreements.

This model was characteristic of the sports management of Czechoslovakia. The central sports management organ was not directly controlled either by the Council of Ministers or by the party. The sports clubs were also independent.

Mixed sports management: the state and social sports management organizations operate in parallel. The state organizations have the tasks of planning, financing, investing and co-ordinating, while the social organizations manage and control the actual sports activities.

This model was characteristic of the sports management structure of Bulgaria and the German Democratic Republic. In both countries the central sports management organ was under the control of the Council of Ministers; the president of the sports management organ in Bulgaria was a member of the Cabinet. In Bulgaria, the social sports management organization operated in the form of an association. Its sub-organizations were the national sports federations, the latter being subordinated to it. In the German Democratic Republic, the social organization involved in sports management was also an association but directly controlled by the party, and the national sports federations were subordinated to the social sports management organization. Here the sports clubs were controlled centrally and some of them were given preferential treatment (as in Hungary).

There are no clear models in practice; they can only be defined on the basis of their dominant features. Certain differences are also shown in the same model regarding the independence of the sports clubs, the structural levels and the role of coorganizations etc.

All the models show the central control of sport and the dominance of social activity at the level of execution (sports clubs).

The science called "management" in the western world was given the name "organizational and management theory" in Hungary, for historical reasons. As a consequence of the particular developments in Eastern Europe and Hungary, scholars starting from organizational activities took the organizational approach when adopting this science in Hungary. The explanation lies in the economic management system of that time: in economies controlled by plan directives, the managers had to only perform a part of the managing functions because it did not fall within their competence to set the targets and determine development tendencies. The targets were set and controlled centrally, so the managers' task was to realize them. In economies controlled by plan directive, resources were centralized and then allocated. Managers could therefore only dispose of resources allocated to their organization and it was not their duty to provide for them. Their activities were not evaluated by economic efficiency and profit but by the observance of regulations and fulfilment of the envisaged plans, irrespective of how the organizations' operation was affected.

Therefore, the early period which started nearly 25 years ago was dominated by the organizational approach for the above described reasons. Nevertheless, with the changes taking place, the economic reform in 1968 and the introduction of the western management concept into the Hungarian economy, management was gradually given priority and it was also acknowledged officially that organizing can only be a part of managerial functions.

This introduction aims at giving an explanation of why management is considered a novelty in Hungary and also in the other Eastern European countries.

Particular development of organizational and management theory

As for management and organizational concepts, if we compare western development with that of the Eastern European countries including Hungary, as set out below, there are marked conceptual differences.

Eastern Europe
The development of management and organizational thinking in the East-European countries can be divided into three stages:
1. The initial development
2. The plan directives system of the Stalin era
3. Adoption of progressive western management theories
The above stages of development show different characteristics in each country: in the last stage, for instance, strong efforts to adopt the western schools were evident in Poland, while in former East Germany organizational and management theory still bore the marks of the central plan directives system.

The initial development
In case of the Soviet Union the initial development stage covered the period up to the 1930s when the Stalin-type plan directives system was introduced. In the case of the European socialist countries, it covers the years between 1945 and 1948 before socialism was introduced. In the German Democratic Republic, the classical school was characteristic for the initial period, namely German Taylorism, rationalization and Weber's organizational concept.

In Poland, the foundations of organizational science were laid down in the years of the turn of the century. The teachings of Adamiecki agree with Taylor's conception in concentrating on the physical circumstances of labour. The Organizational Scientific Institute that started its operations in 1925 under the leadership of Mr. Adamiecki set the aim of developing organizational science.

In Czechoslovakia a new control and internal accounting system was introduced in the 1920s, and organizations were set up as independent units which were allotted weekly targets and funds to cover costs and also allowed to grant premiums to employees working with the unit.

The plan directives system of the Stalin era

This system was gradually introduced in the socialist countries after nationalization, earlier in the Soviet Union, and existed till the end of the 50s. Its main features were as follows:

The major element of economic management was the plan, which was approved at top level, and plan targets were allotted to the lower levels in the form of directives. The managers had the task of providing for the fulfilment of targets.

It is characteristic of the organizational system of economic management that the specialized ministries had double roles: as authorities, they had specialized administrative functions, but on the other hand, they controlled the companies pertaining to their sector. The medium-level control organs falling under the supreme authorities were also specialized, involving a strong specialization of the companies as well.

The industrial companies were only engaged in production; they did not deal with sales, as sales were under the control of another specialized ministry.

The same applies to research and development which did not fall within the companies' activities.

A characteristic feature was the large-sized organization, not for reasons of economic efficiency but rather for controllability.

The plan stipulated not only targets for the companies according to their activities but also functional duties as to the applicable raw materials, resources etc.

This economic management system is a paternalistic system. The paternalistic state plays the role of a father not only towards the employees and the citizens in general but towards the companies as well. In such a system there is no room for individual decisions made by the companies, and profitability makes no sense, nor is it a criterion since a company is deemed to be efficient if it hits the target and the only criterion is the observance of directives.

Management science ceased to exist in that era; only certain organizational issues might have cropped up to a limited extent.

Efforts to adopt progressive western management theories

The new period of progress brought about the revival of the management and organization science silenced in the Stalin era, and from the 1960s onwards the management of labour has regained importance.

The renascent formalistic schools (management of labour based on classical Taylorism and rationalization based on neo-Taylorism) were not inconsistent with the formalistic concept of the plan directives system.

This period can primarily be characterized by progressive tendencies in labour management, systems theories and management concepts.

Hungary

Hungary's development went through approximately the same phases as the Eastern European countries in general. The theories of the initial period were based on the Taylor-Fayol school and were influenced by the German organizational theory. The Stalin era meant practically suppression, and the progressive tendencies of the recent period have been formalistic thinking, socio-scientific approaches (mainly sociological approaches since the 1970s) and the latest concepts. A significant difference as compared to East-European progress is that in Hungary, western theories could be adopted almost freely as early as the 1960s.

The early period of the progress of management and organization science

With Taylorism finding its way to Hungarian management science relatively soon in the 1910s, the movement of rationalization spread in the economy. It is a characteristic feature that several studies in the field of management science were written by engineers.

The period of the Stalin-type economic management system based on plan directives

In the nearly 10-year period starting in the late 1940s, management and organization science had no chance in Hungary, just as in the other socialist countries. In 1950, the organizational departments of the companies were wound up pursuant to a government decree, and with this measure, professional organizing activities ceased to function in Hungary. (According to the official statement the tasks of organization fall within the competence of managers, so there is no need for separate organizational departments.) Management was not dealt with scientifically either, and managers' activity consisted merely of the execution of directives. In the training of managers priority was given to ideological training as against professional training.

The revival of management and organization science

After being silenced for ten years, management and organization science began to develop once more in 1957. To be more precise, the organizational part of the science made progress as shown by the relatively large number of publications on the subject.

At the end of the 1960s, the Organizational Science Committee was established at the Hungarian Academy of Sciences, implying official, academic acknowledgement of this field of science.

At the beginning, the main directions of research were progress management and organizational set-up, later including network planning, and, finally, cybernetics, information and systems theories were also accepted. Decision theory began to develop as well, and from the 1970s, human-concentrated thinking has also gained importance.

From the 1980s, efforts have been made towards integration and research into socio-technical systems.

In 1980, the Academy of Sciences set up the Management and Organization Sciences Committee (in place of the Organizational Science Committee) which reflects a change of conception.

Sport management in East Europe

How long has it been since we could talk about sport management in East-Europe? Well, management is pretty new in the field of sport; it was launched at the end of 1980s. The former economic system in East-European countries provides the reasons for this occurrence.

Under the socialist regime, sport had no financial resources of its own. It was financed by the government through various channels, such as the central budget, local council budgets, state-owned business organizations and tax preferences. As is well known, he who gives the money, lays down the rules. Sport was organized by the central sport office and controlled by the government.

If we claim that management is the process of 1) setting goals and aims, 2) arranging for financial, human and physical resources and 3) achieving desired results through efficient utilization of resources, there was no management in the true sense before the change of regime.

The system in which the expenditure of companies on sports played the role of the "extended hand" of state support practically ceased to operate by the end of the 1980s, i.e. the change of the system. Political and economic restructuring in recent years have brought about radical changes in sport as well. A new type of state administration structure has taken shape, and at the same time, the old sports organization model based on centralized government control ceased to function. The shift towards a market-oriented economy fundamentally affected the system of sport financing: this rapid change has put sport in an awkward position. Nowadays sport has to raise its own funds, so the people who are involved in sport are very aware of the need for management.

References

Nyerges, M.- Basic principles of the Organization and Leading Theory, *textbook, TK*, 1979.

Laki, Nyerges, Pethō.- Top Sport from outside perspective, *Magyarország*, 1984, pp. 24-28.

Laki, Nyerges.- Empirical study on the First Class Hungarian Handball Championships, *ILK*, 1984.

Laki, Nyerges, Pethō.- Challenge of the Top Sport in Hungary, *Sport*, 1985.

Nyerges, Petróczy.- Basic principles of the Sport Management, *textbook HUPE*, 1995.

Nyerges, M.- Organization of Physical Education and Sport, Kalokagathia, I.

Laki, Nyerges.- Way of living of the Hungarian Top Athletes, *Elet-és Tudomány*, 1985, no. 33.

Laki, Nyerges.- Top Sport, Professions, Incomes, *TFTK*, 1981, no. 3.

Laki, Nyerges.- Top Sport and Society, *TFTK*, 1980.

Kun, L.- International History of Physical Education and Sport, *Sport Bp.*, 1979.

Földes, E., Kun, L., Kutassi, L.- History of Hungarian Physical Education and Sport, *Sport Bp.*, 1979.

Sport management in India

Packianathan Chelladurai
The Ohio State University,
Columbus, Ohio, United States of America

M. L. Kamlesh & Usha Sujit Nair
Lakshmibai National College of Physical Education,
Trivandrum, Kerala, India

An understanding of sport and its development in a given country is greatly facilitated by a general description of the population and economic characteristics of that country. Accordingly, let us look at the main characteristics that influence sport development in India. India is the largest democracy in the world in terms of population. Its current population is 901 million (International Monetary Fund, 1995), and it is expected to pass the billion mark very soon. The population growth of India was 2.1% in 1991 compared to 0.7% in the U.S. (Kamlesh, Chelladurai, & Nair, in press). The enormity of this annual increase of 17.75 million people is highlighted when we compare it to the total populations of many other countries.

From the economic perspective, India is making enormous progress in the agricultural, industrial, business, transportation, technological, and educational fields. The average growth in the gross domestic product (GDP) of India over six years from 1986 to 1991 was 5.38% compared to 2.02% in the U.S. and 2.07% in Canada (United Nations, 1994). Despite the phenomenal growth in the economy of the country, India's standing in the international community has been restricted by the fact that advancing patterns of economic growth are offset by growth in the population. In other words, the wealth created on the economic scene is being shared by an ever-increasing population. According to the United Nations reports, the per capita gross domestic product for India was 310 U.S. dollars in 1992 as compared to $ 21,562 in Canada and $ 22,219 in the U.S. Even when the figure for India is converted to purchasing power parity, it comes to only $ 1,350 (United Nations, 1994).

India is composed of 25 states that have been largely drawn up on a linguistic basis. Incidentally, there are seventeen official languages in India. Therefore, it is not surprising that several of the state-level political parties have been formed in defence of the local language and its growth. That the state-level parties have a strong hold on the electorate sometimes leads to frictions within and among the state governments, and between the states and the central government. Apart from the diversity in languages, there are also religious and racial differences that create problems at times. It is remarkable that, despite all the internal turmoil, India has remained democratic in every sense of the term. Governments have been elected, toppled, and/or re-elected through democratic elections at both the central and state levels.

Governance of Indian sport

The performances of India's national teams in international competitions have been mediocre except in the case of cricket in which India is one of the top-ranked teams in the world. An obvious reason is the per capita income which ranks below that of many developed countries. That means that the vast majority of the population does not enjoy the same levels of disposable income as in many other countries. Thus, individuals and families do not have the wherewithal to engage in sporting activities, much less to pursue excellence in sport. Therefore, it is not surprising that, till this date, all efforts in promoting sport within the country have largely been left to various levels of government. The following brief outline of government involvement in sport is extracted from the more comprehensive work of Kamlesh (1988), Kamlesh, Chelladurai, and Nair (in press), and Nair (1993).

Union government
The first step the Indian government took after independence to foster sports was the creation of the All India Council of Sports (AICS) in 1954. It served as a link between the government and the sport sector, and as an advisory body to the government on (a) national sport policy; (b) the disbursement of government grants to the sport governing bodies; (c) designing the structure and processes of sport governing bodies; (d) coaching elite athletes; (e) selection of specific national teams to be financially supported by government in international competitions (it was not possible for any team or athlete to travel abroad without AICS' approval); (f) construction of sports facilities around the country; and (g) selection of sportspersons for the "Arjuna" award, the highest award in India for outstanding sports performance.

The year 1982 marked the creation of a separate Ministry of Sports within the broader Ministry of Human Resource Development. This was followed by the setting up of the Sports Authority of India (SAI) in 1984 as the apex body for all of sport in India. The approach to sports development taken by the Indian government has been focused on (a) development of coaches, (b) training of physical education teachers, (c) promotion of participation in sport and physical activity, and (d) creation of sport infrastructure for both training and hosting international fixtures and meets. From a management perspective, these thrusts make eminent sense as they are designed to achieve three sufficiently distinct purposes - pursuit of excellence, pursuit of knowledge in sport and physical activity, and pursuit of healthy life style.

At present, the programmes of the central government aimed at promoting sport include grants to (a) state governments and national sport organizations for the creation of sports infrastructures; (b) rural schools to build basic sport facilities; (c) universities and colleges to build sport structures, conduct interuniversity tournaments, and offer scholarships to outstanding athletes; (d) state sports councils for the development of mass-oriented playing fields, stadia, and sports complexes; (e) national sports federations for conducting national championships, preparing national teams, and participation in international competitions; (f) schools in the form of prize money for those schools which win district championships; (g) athletes as cash awards for winning medals in international competitions; (h) sport scholars for research, and for travel to conferences, technical training, and workshops; and (i) physical education training institutes to update their programmes and improve facilities as specified. In addition, the central government has created the "Arjuna" awards for outstanding sportspersons, and the "Dronacharya" awards for outstanding coaches. Recently, the government has set up the National Welfare Fund for Sports Persons to assist former athletes who need financial assistance.

Apart from providing monetary support to various sport-related projects, and controlling to some extent the internal and international affairs of sport, the Indian government maintains two separate projects of its own. Firstly, the government set up the Netaji Subhas National Institute of Sports in 1961 to train coaches in various sports including track and field. At present, there are three more branches of the NIS at Bangalore, Calcutta, and Gandhinagar. Secondly, the Government established the Lakshmibai National College of Physical Education, Gwalior in 1957 as a model for physical education institutions in India. (It is now known as the

Lakshmibai National Institute of Physical Education and considered as a university). A branch of the college has been created at Trivandrum. While these two institutions serve as prototypes for state level institutions, the Indian government also sets guidelines for state governments to follow in specifying requirements for physical education teachers.

As for promotion of mass sport, the government began with the National Physical Efficiency Drive in 1959, and the creation of the National Fitness Corps in 1966. At present, the Department of Youth Affairs has set up several programmes aimed at growth and development of youth (e.g., Nehru Yuvak Kendra Sanghthan, National Service Scheme, and National Youth Federation). Some of these programmes include training in sport and physical activity, and are organized under the purview of the subordinate units in various states.

In a similar fashion to most nations in the world, India has also used sport as a diplomatic tool to achieve its foreign policy goals. The first notable instance was when Jawaharlal Nehru, the first Prime Minister of India, used the first Asiad (organized by India in 1951) to bring together the Asian nations as a prelude to the formation of what is presently known as the Non-aligned Movement (NAM) which is the third block of nations contrasted with the western and former communist block countries. India was the first nation to take action on the sporting scene against the South African policy of apartheid. India did not allow its Davis Cup team to play against the South African team in 1974 despite the fact that it was the first time the Indian team had advanced to the finals (Haylett & Evans, 1989). Another notable instance was when the government stopped the Indian contingent from participation in the Moscow Friendship Games in 1957 as a protest against the Soviet invasion of Hungary.

State governments
The state governments have set up state sport councils whose function, structure, and processes are similar to those of the Sports Authority of India but restricted to their respective jurisdictions. In addition, most states in India have created the district sports council to promote and support sport within each district. In general, the state sports councils have followed the guidelines and directives of the Union Government in promoting sports in their respective states.

Typically, state sports councils have instituted specific programmes in support of (a) facilities and equipment, (b) state level sport governing bodies, (c) district level sports councils, and (d) the development of coaches and athletes (Nair, 1993). Some more progressive states such as Kerala and Punjab have set up sports hostels and sports schools wherein outstanding young athletes are housed and trained in various disciplines (Nair, 1993). The government pays for the board, lodging and training of these athletes. Normally, these hostels and schools are affiliated with the local educational institutions for academic purposes.

Most state governments also (a) offer cash awards for high-level performances in national competitions (usually placing in the top three positions); (b) reserve seats in academic institutions for promising athletes, (c) employ athletes in their own departments on a quota basis, (d) offer pension and insurance schemes for athletes, and (e) require educational institutions to offer academic credit for athletic performances (Nair, 1993). The idea of offering academic credit for athletic endeavour is, however, seen as contaminating the academic process (Kamlesh et al., in press; Nair, 1993).

It must be pointed out that although the Sports Authority of India and its state level counterparts are designed to be arms-length organizations, they continue to be dominated by government representatives. Typically, these organizations are headed by a minister of the government and tightly controlled by senior bureaucrats of the respective governments. The other members of the organization may be nominated by the government and/or elected by lower level bodies such as state or district sports councils, and sport governing bodies. In so far as the government(s) provide the funds, the golden rule is operative. That is, "one who has the gold makes the rules." From this perspective, these organizations tend to be virtually government agencies.

As can be seen from the above, the policies of both the national and state governments do focus on elite sport as well as mass sport. Unfortunately, the public and the media pay attention only to the elite-oriented sport programmes, and inevitably offer their criticisms and suggestions for those programmes.

Educational sector

Most of the states stipulate that every school must have at least one physical education teacher while some states insist on one physical education teacher for every 250 students in the school. Unfortunately, however, this progressive legislation does not carry much weight because most of the schools in the country do not have the playing fields or other sport structures to facilitate sport teaching and/or sport participation. It is also ironic that most schools in general do not schedule physical education classes in the regular timetable.

Every district has a government official to supervise physical education in schools, who in turn is supervised by a state-level inspector of physical education. These government officers are also in charge of selecting and training district- and state-level teams, and organizing competitions in a variety of sports in their respective jurisdictions. There is also the School Games Federation of India which is solely concerned with organizing national scholastic competitions.

A similar pattern exists among universities and colleges. Every university/college will have one or more directors of physical education (equivalent to athletic directors in the North American context) whose responsibilities include facilitating sport and physical activity participation among students and faculty, selecting and training college/university teams, and organizing competitions. The University Sports Control Board, a unit of the Association of Indian Universities, supervises and partially finances the organization and conduct of interuniversity competitions at the regional and national levels.

Amateur sport organizations

The promotion and governance of amateur sport in India rests largely with the Indian Olympic Association and the national sports federations/associations. The Indian Olympic Association is the apex voluntary organization and is comprised of the representatives of the state Olympic associations and the national sports associations. Each national sport association is a voluntary body made up of representatives of the state associations which, in turn, consist of representatives of district associations. The clubs form the foundation of the organization of amateur sport. Except for a few national sports associations such as the Board of Cricket Control in India, all of the 53 national sports associations are compulsorily affiliated to the Indian Olympic Association. Within the framework of the national policy and without violating the Olympic Charter, the national sports associations (NSAs) are free to formulate and implement their developmental policies and action plans. While a few NSAs are financially sound, most of them receive regular, substantial financial support from the Government of India for (a) conducting coaching camps for their elite athletes, (b) organizing national championships for various age groups - senior, junior, sub-junior, and (c) maintaining their administrative offices. These NSAs sponsor national teams for international competitions subject to the concurrence of the Indian Olympic Association, and clearance from the Union Government. The NSAs resent the fact that the Union Government exerts considerable control in the affairs of the NSAs, and feel that their autonomy is violated. The continuing conflict between the NSAs and the government has adversely affected the development of elite sport.

The state and district sport associations manage amateur sports within their respective geographical jurisdictions. Their effectiveness, however, has been curtailed for several reasons. First, a lack of popularity of some sports makes it hard for grass roots organization of the sport. Second, because, most officials are either businessmen, bureaucrats, or politicians they do not possess the insights to develop the sports under their charge. Thus, they turn out to be simple patrons rather than competent sport leaders. Third, lack of financial resources does not permit them to provide facilities and equipment to support their units, and/or organize an adequate number of competitions. Finally, as they are autonomous units, they are not accountable to anyone. Thus their sloppy management is neither noticed nor questioned.

The club system in India does not approach the organizational scope and sophistication found in many European countries. Typically, a few individuals interested in playing a particular sport will form a club in their locality and continue to participate in the sport as a recreational and leisure pursuit. As they gain some proficiency in the sport, they may seek affiliation with the district sport association and enter a few competitions. If and when they are successful in tournaments, the local public may show greater interest in the club and support it through donations. But their success is largely dependent on the initiative and tenacity of the playing members, and, to some extent, that of the local patrons. Further, these clubs operate mostly in the urban areas. The rural areas where 85% of India's population resides are devoid of sports clubs, and thus the vast reservoir of sporting talent is untapped.

Factors inhibiting sport development

There are several factors that limit the efforts toward promotion of sport in India. The most significant factor is the economic one. As noted earlier, the per capita income is rather low leaving very little disposable income to enable the masses to engage in leisure pursuits including sport.

Second, despite government's emphasis on sport and sport development, sport does not rank high in government's priorities. Therefore, the budget allocation is very small. The central government has allocated 500 million rupees for sport for five years beginning in 1991-1992. Under current exchange rates, the figure is equivalent to about 15 million U.S. dollars. That figure pales in comparison to the annual budget of about 30 million dollars for individual athletic departments in large universities in the US (e.g., the Ohio State University athletic department). Although the policies of the Indian government are well thought out and rank among the best national sport policies around the world, these policies cannot be effectively implemented with such minimal financial allotments to the sport sector.

Among the social factors that impinge on sport development is the greater concern with academic pursuits rather than an emphasis on sport and sport development. It is very typical for a family to encourage its children to spend their free time on academic studies. Participation in sports is seen as a diversion from studies and thus it is strongly discouraged.

Another limitation stems from differing orientations of the state governments. Apart from linguistic barriers, divisions based on religion and caste also create divergent opinions on many matters including the affairs of sport. These divisive forces inhibit a unified thrust toward sport development.

It was noted that the poor economic condition of the masses is the major reason for the low level of sport development in India. Recent reports, however, suggest that the picture is changing. It is reported that the middle class in India is growing fast. Estimates of the size of the middle class in India range from 30% to 50% of the population. Based on the most conservative estimate of 30%, the size of the middle class will be about 300 million members. This figure is larger than the total population of most countries including the United States. The implication is that the growing middle class will also have the income to participate in more leisure activities including sport. It can be expected that, with such increasing participation in sport, the cream of the crop will rise to the top and be more competitive on the international scene.

The advent of sports coverage on radio and television also augurs well for the development of sport and increased participation in physical activity. First, these broadcasts help to create public awareness of healthy and active lifestyles. People are constantly encouraged to engage in some form of vigorous physical activity. As the media begin to cover more and more of the sporting events, the public becomes aware of the nuances of the various sports and show greater interest in them. This process is expected to result in greater community support for sport. An example is the status of cricket in which India has attained international excellence. Cricket has found a place in the national psyche. The astounding following for the game can be attributed perhaps to the fact that the game was introduced in India by the British, and that the Indians may take delight in beating the former "masters" at their own game. The public is well informed of the game and its outstanding players from around the world. Even the governments declare holidays during test matches. The point is that if India can do so well in one sport, it can also do well in other sport forms which do not enjoy much mass and spectator support at the moment. With increasing support for these sport forms, India has the potential to become a super power in sports.

As the extent of sport coverage increases, many business houses and industrial corporations have also taken to sponsoring individual athletes, teams, and events. The various levels of government have also allowed the business and industrial enterprises to claim tax exemptions for their expenditures toward sport promotion (Kamlesh et al., in press). It is hoped that this upward spiral of sports coverage, community interest, commercial involvement, and government encouragement will further the progress of sport in India. A final point relates to the process of liberalization undertaken by the Union and state governments. It holds two promises for sport in India. First, the governments may loosen their grip on governance of sport which would permit each sport governing body to devise its operational procedures to suit its specific circumstances. Second, such liberalization would encourage the business and industrial world to get more involved in promotion of sport particularly at the educational level. In the final analysis, India can be expected to compete effectively in international competitions in many disciplines.

References

Haylett, J. & Evans, R.- *The illustrated encyclopedia of world tennis.* New York: Marshall Cavendish Limited, 1989.

International Monetary Fund.- *International Financial Statistics Yearbook.* Washington, DC: International Monetary Fund, 1995.

Kamlesh, M.L., Chelladurai, P., & Nair, U.S. (in press).- *National sport policy in India.* In A.T. Johnson, L. Chalip, & L. Stachura (Eds.). National sport policies: An international handbook. Westport, CT: Greenwood

Nair, U.S.- *Government and sport in Kerala, India.* Journal of Sport Management, 1993, 7, 256-262.

United Nations.- *United Nations statistical yearbook,* 1992. New York: United Nations, 1994.

The management of sport for all programmes in Japan

Jun Oga
The University of Electro-Communications,
Tokyo, Japan

Development of the Japanese economy and changes in Japanese lifestyles

The Japanese economy developed remarkably after the Second World War. Especially in recent years, it experienced huge growth. According to the Annual Report on National Accounts 1995, the Nominal Gross Domestic Product in 1993 was 4,667.6 billion US dollars (with one US dollar per 100 Japanese yen). It has quadrupled during the last two decades. The development of the Japanese economy has caused many changes in the social conditions of the Japanese people. Three significant changes can be seen. They are an increase in family income, a reduction in working hours and the development of infrastructure, including sports facilities. According to the Annual Report on Family Income and Expenditure Survey 1994, the average family income of all workers' households rose to 5,705.5 dollars per month in 1993. The White Paper on Labour 1994 showed that the average number of working hours per month decreased to 159.4 hours as the five-day working week gained acceptance. According to the Investigation on the Current States of Sports Facilities in Japan, in 1990, the number of public sport facilities was 62,786. During the last 15 years, it increased 3.2 times.

These changes have had an impact on the lifestyles of the Japanese people. The Japanese are becoming increasingly interested in leisure activities and sport in particular.

The present situation of sport and exercise participation

The Cabinet Public Relations Office of the Prime Minister's Office has conducted the Public Opinion Survey concerning Physical Fitness and Sports almost every three years since 1957. These surveys, each involving 3,000 subjects over 20 years of age from all over the country, show the percentages of people who do some form of sports and exercise in a year. In 1957, the average percentage for men and women was 14%. Then it rose rapidly, reaching 60% in 1972, about a fourfold increase. In 1976, the percentage had reached 65%, and it grew to 67% in 1994. As the Japanese population was about 120 million people, the number of sports participants was estimated at 80.4 million on the basis of these figures. This shows that the habit of enjoying sports has taken a firm hold on Japanese lifestyles.

However we have three considerable problems concerning sports participation. Firstly, it is necessary to increase women's participation, because women's participation was seen to be less than men's. The difference between women's and men's participation was 10%. Secondly, the percentage of those showing regular participation, at least one activity a week, was 42% of all sports participants. Regular sports participants are estimated at 28% of all Japanese. This percentage must be increased. Finally, the rate of club participation was shown to be only 16% of the population as a whole. To promote sports for all throughout Japan, it is necessary to increase sports club participation.

In types of sports in which people participated in a year, the rates of sports participation were as follows : light exercise and sports 23.4%; outdoor activities 6.5%; competitive sports 2.5%; light sports and outdoor activities 19.4%; light sports and competitive sports 2.4%; outdoor activities and competitive sports 1.8%; and the three types together 10.0%.

As for kinds of sports, the participation rates for the top ten sports were as follows: walking 24.3%, callisthenics 21.1%, bowling 18.5%, light ball games 18.3%, sea swimming 13.3%, light swimming 13.0%, golf 12.8%, skiing 10.9%, fishing 10.6% and running 7.6%. These figures indicate that most Japanese people participate in sports and exercise with the idea of sports for all instead of elite sports.

Organizations for promoting sport for all programmes

The reason for increased sports participation is that national and local governments have endeavoured to improve conditions so that people can enjoy sports and exercises at any time or place. Also, various sports organizations and private commercial (for-profit) sports facilities have played a significant role in promoting "sports for all" through various activities.

A. The system of administrative organizations for sports promotion

The Japanese administrative system consists of the national government, 47 prefectural governments and 3,400 municipal governments. The function of national government is fundamentally to give guidance, advice and financial aid to local governments. The function of prefectural governments is to do the same for their municipal governments. The administrative organization in charge of sports is the Physical Education and Sports Bureau of the Ministry of Education, Science, Sports and Culture at the national level, and the physical education or sports division of the board of education of the local government at the prefectural and municipal levels. Sports promotion, including the development of sports facilities, improvements in sports for all activities, the promotion of competitive sports and the enrichment of school physical education activities, are carried out with the co-operation of these specialized administrative organizations. In undertaking sports promotion, it is vital that a wide range of expert opinion be appropriately reflected in actual policy. For this reason, the Health and Physical Education Council serves as an advisory body to the Minister for investigating and deliberating on important issues regarding sports promotion. Furthermore, the Sports Promotion Law prescribes that a council on sports promotion should be established at the prefectural level, and a similar council may be established at the municipal level.

B. Sport Promotion Policy

Since 1985, urbanization, increased leisure time and the rising proportion of the aged in the population have led to increased participation frequency and participant diversification and elevation of the promotion of sports for all activities to a major national issue. In 1989, the Health and Physical Education Council reported its findings in "Strategies for the Promotion of Sports Towards the 21st Century". This report emphasized the significance of broad promotion of both competitive sports and sports for all, and also set down the following fundamental guidelines for sports promotion policy for the 21st century: (a) to provide guidelines for the improvement of sports facilities for local governments as one means of enriching sports facilities; (b) enrichment of sports for all by promoting the spread of a wide range of sports events and activities, training sports leaders, etc.; (c) promoting competitive sports through raising the quality of sports leaders, establishing leadership systems and encouraging research in sports science; (d) promoting international exchange in sports, (e) encouraging the healthy development of professional sports; (f) securing funds for sports promotion activities.

In 1988, to meet the growing and diversifying public demand for sports and to improve the competitive level of the nation's athletes, the Ministry restructured one of its administrative divisions dealing with sports to form two separate divisions: the Sports for All (Lifelong) Division and the Competitive Sports Division. Presently various policy measures are being implemented to accomplish the goal set out in the 1989 Report.

C. Activities of the Sports for All Division

A high-priority policy task of the Division is to achieve a society in which sports can be enjoyed by everyone, regardless of age or level of physical ability, throughout all periods of their lives at convenient times and locations. Three conditions must be met to develop sports for all: providing sports facilities, training and securing personnel with excellent leadership abilities and hosting events to meet public needs. For promoting sports for all programmes, the total budget, excluding the budget for building sports-related facilities, is 31.4 million US dollars in 1995.

1. Improving Sports Facilities

According to an Investigation on the Current States of Sports Facilities in Japan, the total number of sports facilities has doubled during the last two decades and currently is estimated at about 300,000. An institutional breakdown of facilities shows that school physical education facilities comprise approximately half of all sports facilities. Recently, marked growth can be seen in both public sports facilities and private facilities including both for-profit and non-profit facilities managed by enterprises. Public facilities now represent around 20% and private facilities around 25% of total sports facilities. Looking at types of facilities, there are approximately 50,000 sports grounds, 50,000 gymnasiums, 40,000 swimming pools and 30,000 tennis courts.

According to the "Survey on Exercise and Sports 1991" commissioned by the Ministry, when asked about improving sports facilities, 61.7% of the respondents said they would like to have nearer and more convenient sports facilities available. This shows that it is necessary to improve public sports facilities and school physical education facilities for use in sport for all programmes, taking into account the role of commercial (for-profit) sports facilities. The Ministry is providing financial assistance through local government for the development of sports facilities. In the 1995 Annual Budget, 123.6 million dollars in subsidies has been allocated for building facilities and also 8.8 million for development of school physical education facilities by providing facilities with lighting and upgrading sports clubhouses, etc., for the community. Consequently the percentage of public elementary and secondary school physical education facilities open to local people has increased to 68% of all school facilities in 1990.

At present, the Ministry is urging local governments to carry out planned developments of sports facilities using the guidelines in the Strategies for the Promotion of Sports Towards the 21st Century.

2. Training and Securing Sports Leaders

As the majority of people enjoy sports activities and as their goals and needs for sports become diversified and more sophisticated, it is important to train and secure high quality sports leaders. At the municipal level, the social education director in charge of sports, physical education advisors and other staff at the municipal board of education engage in planning and designing policy for promoting sports for all. In order to enhance the quality of these sports leaders, various training activities are being carried out at the national and prefectural level. In 1987, the Ministry established the "Regulations for Accreditation of Qualification Examination Programmes for Social Physical Education Leaders". Through these regulations a system was created whereby the Ministry accredits those training and qualification programmes conducted by sports associations which came up to a certain standard and which should be encouraged in order to raise the quality of sports leaders. As of 1995, the following training and qualification programmes are being accredited : (a) programmes for community sports leaders and coaches (29 different sports), (b) programmes for leaders and coaches in competitive sports (30 sports), (c) programmes for training staff at commercial sports facilities (5 sports), (d) programmes for "Sports Programmers" (a sports leader who produces programmes and provides advice and practical sports guidance for a range of persons of differing ages and degrees of physical strength), (e) programmes for recreation leaders and (f) programmes for youth sports leaders (who provide children with the proper sports guidance). Sports associations conduct these programmes, organize examinations, and award qualifications to those candidates who score above a certain level. The contents of these courses and examinations are wide-ranging and include, among other subjects, an introduction to social physical education, sports management, sports medicine, sports physiology, sports psychology, leadership theory, etc. Also included are basic theory and training skills for related sports as well as practical training and coaching. As of 1994 the number of leaders trained under this system had reached approximately 69,600. It is hoped that through this system, future sports leaders and coaches will be appropriately placed in sports facilities related to their training and also that these kinds of qualification activities will be a basic requirement for organizations of sports events and sports meets.

3. Development in Sports for All Promotion Activities

As the government body which is closest to the people, municipalities play an important part by directly providing local residents with the actual places and opportunities for sports for all activities by carrying out a variety of activities and events such as sports and recreational meets, physical strength and abilities testing, sports classes, etc. In order to encourage municipalities in their projects, the Ministry is conducting "Sports for All Promotion Projects" as a type of support activity. The actual activities include (a) promotion and development of a range of sports activities according to age and other special characteristics of the population, (b) exchange activities such as international programmes for sports for all and sports programmes in depopulated communities, (c) activities for assisting the development of sports clubs at the community level and (d) activities for the promotion of sports-related consultation. Also, the Ministry is conducting "Sports Activity Promotion Community Projects" which are carrying out pilot studies on the prospects of school-community co-operation in sports activities.

With a view to promoting sports activities prefecture-wide, prefectures are carrying out basic and wide-ranging activities such as prefectural sports events, meets and the training and securing of sports leaders. The Ministry is conducting financial support programmes for prefectures such as the "Sports Programmer Training Programmes" and "Sports Leaders Bank Programme" through which it underwrites a part of the cost for training, distributing lists of them to various sports facilities in the prefectures. In addition the Ministry also supports the dispatching of social physical education leaders in order to strengthen the social physical education system.

4. Holding Nation-wide Sports-for-All events

The Ministry has been holding two significant nation-wide sports-for-all events. They are the "National Festival of Sports and Recreation" and the "Annual Conventions on Sports for All". The former is a national event where a broad range of sports-lovers, young and old, can deepen exchanges and enjoy sports and recreation in a fun and relaxed atmosphere. Since the first Festival was held in 1988 the event has become a familiar one. The festival offers a wide range of separate sports events in which people can freely participate, the focus of most of these events being new and unique types of sports. Festival-goers are also given the opportunity to try out a variety of new kinds of sports and to attend a symposium. The festival boasts an attendance of about 300,000 persons ranging from children to the elderly.

For the successful promotion of sports for all, co-operation among a broad range of related organizations including sports associations, local governments, the industrial sector and others is essential. In order to foster such a co-operation, the Ministry has annually held a "Sports for All Convention" since 1989, at which representatives of various levels of the public and private sectors can come together to exchange opinions and discuss various issues for the promotion of sports for all.

5. Development of a Sports Promotion Fund
The establishment of a sports promotion fund which would provide a secure, continuous and flexibly applicable flow of funds to help to raise the nation's competitive level and promote various activities which popularize sports had long been hoped for by people in the sports world. In 1990, the Sports Promotion Fund was set up with government funds. The Fund is composed of a government grant of 250 million US dollars and contributions from the private sector. The following activities are supported through the working profits from the Fund: (a) training activities conducted by sports associations; (b) organization of athletic meets at the national and international levels as well as study meetings and intensive courses; (c) support for trainers and athletes so that they can devote themselves to their activities without undue financial worries; and (d) projects to support large-scale international athletic events. Through the establishment of this Fund, the Japanese support structure for sports promotion has been strengthened. Although, originally, the Fund was applied only to athletic training projects and activities related to competitive sports, butsince 1991 support has also been provided for projects and activities related to sports for all. In regard to actual awards granted, a total of 473 were approved in 1994 and the total amount of funding awarded amounted to 8.6 million dollars.

6. Fostering Development of Sports Associations and Sports Clubs
In Japan, sports associations also play a major role in the promotion of sports for all. As in the past, the Japan Amateur Sports Association, central athletic associations for respective sports and others sports-promotion associations have furthered activities such as: establishing rules for competition, holding national events, leadership training, club development, research surveys, etc. In recent years, along with the diversification in sports, both the type and character of organizations have broadened. In addition to associations for a new type of sports such as India Ka and others, there are now associations for sports instructors, youth sports promotion associations, sponsoring agencies, the Sports Safety Association which provides insurance or compensation in case of sports related accidents, and others. The Ministry intends to further promote the development of various kinds of sports associations which are dealing with the diversified public demands through financial support from the Sports Promotion Fund and other measures.

By definition, sports clubs are gatherings of sports aficionados. They are managed autonomously and voluntarily and they help to cope with meeting the public demand for sports. It is important for furthering the promotion of sport for all to encourage the development of sports clubs. According to the Public Opinion Survey concerning Physical Fitness and Sports, the percentage of people who joined sports clubs was 16% in 1994, remaining virtually unchanged since 1983. In response to this the Ministry has begun a "Programme to Develop Associations of Local Sports Clubs", i.e. aid to municipalities for sending sports leaders to sports clubs, and a "Programme for Developing Children's Sports Clubs" through which children can enjoy continuous sports activities. With the expectation that sports clubs will be a force in helping to develop regular participation in sports and become a base for promoting sports for all, the Ministry is working towards their promotion and development by fostering inter-club co-operation.

Sports organizations for promoting sports for all programmes

A. The Japan Amateur Sports Association

The Japan Amateur Sports Association (JASA) was established in 1911, as an organization uniting the amateur sports world of Japan and a public service organization to popularize sports, to develop physical strength and sportsmanship among the Japanese people. The role of JASA assigned at the outset has succeeded in two major tasks: "Promotion of National Sport" and "Improvement of the Competing Standard of International Level Athletics".

However, in 1989 the Japanese Olympic Committee (JOC) was re-established as an organization with the status of a juridical person, in order to cope with the progressing international sports scene. Thus JOC has come to take charge of the task while the JASA has entered a new phase devoting all its energies to the "Promotion of National Sports". The main tasks are as follows: (a) developing sports leaders in accordance with the Regulations on Authorization of the Enterprise for Judging Knowledge and Skills of Sports Leaders; (b) the National Sports Festival, the National Meeting of Junior Sports Clubs and other events which are held under the auspices of JASA, the Ministry of Education, the host prefecture and other associations; (c) fostering junior sports clubs; (d) propagation of sports for all; (e) international exchange through exchanging competition and simultaneous exchange; (f) participation of sports for all movement through co-operation with the International Assembly of National Organizations of Sports and the Trim and Fitness International Sports for All Association; and (g) research on sports science by the Research Institute of Sports Science. Today 51 national sports federations and 47 prefectural sports associations are affiliated with the JASA. The yearly budget for promoting sports is 27 million US dollars. The number of authorized sports leaders is over 66,000 and the number of children and leaders participating in junior sports clubs is 1.2 million.

B. The National Recreation Association of Japan

The National Recreation Association of Japan (NRAJ) was founded in 1938 and in 1948 it resumed its activities to help improve the quality of life for the Japanese people. The goals of NRAJ are to improve people's health, promote international relations, increase people's quality of life through participation in leisure time activities and act as the main administrative body for the recreation movement in Japan. The NRAJ performs a variety of functions in administrating and delivering recreation services to member associations, other recreation related organizations and people at large. The Association provides (a) in-service courses for training of recreation leaders, (b) research on leisure, (c) a monthly magazine and books publication, (d) hosting for numerous industry conferences and seminars, (e) recreation events for community participation (National Recreation Congress, Nation-wide Walk Rally Meets, etc.), and (f) international relations with the World Leisure and Recreation Association, etc. The NRAJ has as its affiliates 47 Prefectural Recreation Associations and 32 associations. The yearly budget is 13.3 million dollars and it has approximately 37,000 qualified leaders.

C. The Sasakawa Sports Foundation

The Sasakawa Sports Foundation (SSF) was established by the The Sasakawa Foundation in 1991. The Foundation's operational plan incorporates the following programmes: (a) subsidization of various activities and events held by sports organizations, (b) international exchange projects adopting a policy of sports for all, (c) collecting and disseminating information on sports for all, (d) promoting public awareness of the importance of sports and (e) research on current sports in order to contribute to the propagation of sports for all. The main task of the Foundation is to subsidize activities and events so as to offer opportunities for everyone to participate in sports whenever and wherever they desire. The activities covered by these subsidies are athletic meets and events open to the general public and sports lessons and classes aimed at popularizing specific sports in Japan. In 1995, the foundation gave grants to 662 activities of 560 sports associations totalling 4 million US dollars.

Contribution of Private Commercial Sports Facilities

The increase and diversity of the sports demands of people and the extra margin of family finance have brought prosperity to the sports services industry. According to the Investigation on the Current States of Sports Facilities (1985), the total number of private commercial sports facilities such as profit sports clubs and centres was approximately 30,000 and the market value of the sports service industry was estimated at 30.5 billion US dollars, as shown in the White Paper on Leisure 1995. Concerning the sports demands of people, callisthenics, bowling, light swimming, golf and skiing featured in the top ten sports which people played (from the Public Opinion Survey concerning physical Fitness and Sports). Their sports use both commercial and public sports facilities in neighbourhoods; the percentage using commercial facilities was 35.5% and the percentage using public facilities was 30.8% according to the Survey on Exercise and Sports 1991. It shows that nowadays private commercial sports facilities have been contributing to promote sports for all activities in Japan.

References

Cabinet Public Relations Office of Prime Minister's Office.- *Report of Public Opinion Survey Concerning Physical Fitness and Sport 1994*. Author, 1994, Tokyo.

Economic Planning Agency.- *Annual Report on National Accounts 1995*. Economic Research Institute of the Economic Planning Agency, 1995, Tokyo.

Foundation of Leisure Development Centre.- *White Paper on Leisure 1995*. Author, 1995, Tokyo.

Health and Physical Education Council.- *Strategies for Promotion of Sports Towards the 21st Century*. Edited by Ministry of Education, 1989, Tokyo.

Japan Amateur Sports Association.- *Annual Report 1994*. Author, 1995, Tokyo.

Japan Amateur Sports Association.- *Sports for All*. Author, 1991, Tokyo.

Ministry of Education, Science, Sports and Culture.- *Japanese Government Policies in Education, Science, Sports and Culture 1992*. Author, 1993, Tokyo.

Ministry of Education.- *Monbusho*. Author, 1995, Tokyo.

Policy Planning and Research Department of the Ministry of Labour.- *White Paper on Labour 1994*. Japan Institute of Labour, 1994, Tokyo.

National Recreation Association of Japan.- *Annual Report 1994*. Author, 1995, Tokyo.

Sanwa Research Institute.- *Report of Survey on Exercise and Sports 1991*. Commissioned by Ministry of Education, 1992, Tokyo.

Sasakawa Sports Foundation.- *Annual Report 1994*. Author, 1995, Tokyo.

Sport for All Division of Physical Education Bureau of Ministry of Education.- *Report of Investigation on Current States of Sports Facilities in Japan*. Author, 1993, Tokyo.

Sport for All Division of the Ministry of Education.- *Annual Report 1994*. Author, 1995, Tokyo.

Statistics Bureau of Management and Co-ordination Agency.- *Annual Report on Family Income and Expenditure Survey 1994*. Japan Statistics Association, 1994, Tokyo.

Sport management in the Netherlands

Berend Rubingh
European Association for Sport Management,
Groningen, the Netherlands

Introduction

As in all European countries the field of sport management in the Netherlands is a growing one. Because of the increasing complexity of the world of sport, and the diversity of organizations, there is an increasing need for professional managers. This article addresses the questions of how sport in the Netherlands is organized and where "sport managers" can be found. Future developments of sport management and sport management development in the Netherlands are considered in terms of a management concept, in which the most important aspects of management in sports are identified.

Historical developments and their implications for the world of sport

An increasing care by the government for the welfare of citizens after the second World War also resulted in support for sport infrastructure. Since sport was seen as an important means of stimulating social structures in the Netherlands, the sports club was an important organization to help. In the sixties and seventies the sports club became the most important way of practising sport. Sport in school was a rare activity, because teachers in PE (Physical Education) saw sport as a non-educational item within their curriculum. Unlike those in England, for example, schools in the Netherlands had their own way of dealing with physical activity: physical education at schools was something completely different from sport. Physical education had more educational intentions, whereas sport was characterized by more recreational or competitive aspects. This led to a divergence amongst the direct stakeholders which until now has affected the development of sport and its infrastructure in the Netherlands.

Teachers in PE (Physical Education) were educated at institutes for higher professional education known as Academies for Physical Education. These institutes enjoyed higher status, however, because of the degree handed out at the end. Although it was still a Bachelor's degree, it also gave the graduate also the possiblity of teaching PE at all levels of the educational system, a privilege that in all other segments of the educational system was only possible to those who had their Doctorandus degree from a University. The graduates of these institutes were employed in schools and, in the early days, hardly ever in sports organizations, as this was seen as a lower status job: Sport was considered as just competition and recreation and of no educational value.

At the same time, trainers and coaches where educated at completely separate institutes, at a lower level also, the so-called CIOS. These graduates where educated to become sport instructors, trainers, and coaches in sports organizations. Because of the earlier stated assumptions that sport had no educational value and PE had, and the fact that teachers in PE where better paid and had a higher status in society than the graduates from the CIOS, the gap between these two entities increased.

Today, there are still two kinds of institutes, one purely for sport and one purely for Physical Education, although the gap seems to be narrowing as a result of the growing popularity of sport, which has led to an enhanced status for jobs in the world of sport, while the status of the PE teacher has declined. Academies for PE are under pressure nowadays to secure their budgets, especially since they were involved in big mergers in the educational world and therefore they had to justify their special status and their extra costs. They are in search of new markets and the sport market is obviously one.

No competition for the club

In the last few decades, lack of involvement of the schools system in providing sport and competition has strengthened the development of the club system in the Netherlands. At the same time, local authorities have stimulated sport by way of these clubs. In the spirit of building a new nation after the second World War and stimulating a feeling of togetherness, the club was seen as an important organization that could increase the welfare of the nation and strengthen the social structure.

The club ("vereniging" in Dutch)

Sport clubs are private organizations, democratically organized and entirely run by volunteers. At the end of the last century and the beginning of this one, sport clubs started off when, in all branches of society, clubs were formed mainly for recreational or health reasons, but also for reasons of "belonging". As a result of all the efforts of governmental organizations in stimulating the clubs, and the absence of any competitors (for example schools), there are over 35,000 clubs in the Netherlands today. Approximately 1/3 of our population (total = 15 million) is a member of a sports club, and over 600,000 volunteers are somehow involved in these clubs. In the sixties and seventies it was said that if the family could be called the first environment of a child and school the second, the sports club was certainly the third.

The traditional & professional club

Today the traditional club is pressured by many developments. External developments (withdrawal of government support, demographical factors, increasing competition of other suppliers of free-time services) are having their impact on the organization and, at the same time, internal development (changing interests of the members, decreasing support of volunteers) are tending to hinder organizational and management processes. With much talent for improvisation, some clubs have tackled these problems, while others are still under pressure and their existence is in question. If we look at those that have tackled the problems, two extreme strategies can be identified:

- Strengthening traditional values.
In this club, solidarity is still the main value, and the club structure is based on participation by all members. The club has been able to create and strengthen a feeling of "belonging". The members, the board, the instructors, trainers and coaches are the club!

- Strengthening professional services.

In this club, the members are no longer seen as members but as clients: clients with different needs for which the club offers different professional services. The club is seen as a professional organization and is run by professionals, managed as a service company.

These two extreme strategies are oftened combined within one club, which makes it harder to manage. Other clubs do not make a choice on what they want to be, for whom, and which core processes they then want to strengthen. All in all this leads to a growing diversity of organizations offering sports and a growing need for professional (sport management) staff.

The umbrella organizations

In order to organize competitions, sports clubs where organized into federations, for example the Royal Dutch Soccer Federation (6,000 associated clubs and 1 million members in total) or the Royal Dutch Lawn Tennis Federation (1,726 clubs and 700,000 members in total). Some of these federations (the larger ones) are also organized into districts. Decision-making takes place by way of democratic voting processes in General Assemblies of members, these being the sport clubs. These federations are, in turn, members of umbrella organizations. The Netherlands has several umbrella organizations distinguished by their philosphies of life. For example the Netherlands Catholic Sport Federation and the Netherlands Christian Sports Union. The NOC*NSF (Netherlands Olympic Committee and Netherlands Sport Confederation) is the most important one. This organization, with about 90 members, only merged (NOC + NSF) in 1993, and the merger can be explained by an increased interest in top-level sport.

Sport: its characteristics and its financial resources

Whereas in the seventies and eighties great attention was paid to "Sport for All", in the nineties, attention has increasingly been focused on top-level sport; this is due in part to the shift in Dutch society towards a belief that the responsiblity for welfare and wellbeing no longer lies only with governmental organizations. Until the mid-eighties, the main sport structure in the Netherlands consisted of the sports club and its umbrella organization. Therefore, the organizational map of the Netherlands was quite simple (see fig. 1). The club was the central entity and therefore easy to steer from a governmental point of view. Through the federative structure, the national government also had a partner to address for all sport matters (the Netherlands Sport Confederation). Two major resources, government grants and participants' fees, constituted the mainstay of sport. Business as a financial resource for sport has become important only in the last decade. Nowadays, about Ecu 4,300,000,000 are spent on sport by consumers, government and business.

An organizational chart of sport in the Netherlands

Sport in the Netherlands has been influenced by many different developments; one could characterize it as a melting pot of sport activities. There are a great many stakeholders involved in sport and its organizations. This makes the world of sport very complex; in any attempt to paint a map of the Dutch sports world, this essential characteristic is missing. The painting should therefore, rather look like a Picasso than like a Rietveld. However, for reasons one can imagine, the Rietveld method has been chosen to create some clarity in the complex sports world of the Netherlands.

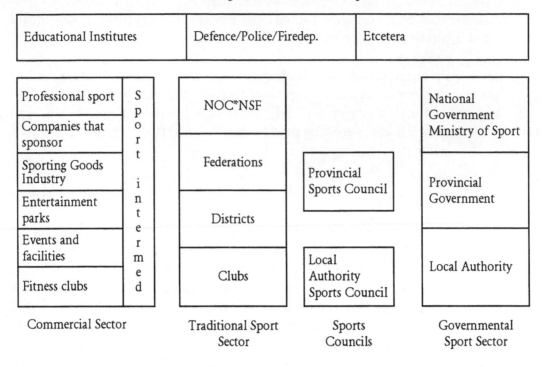

Various Organisations involved in sport

Educational Institutes	Defence/Police/Firedep.	Etcetera

figure 1. *An organizational chart of sport in the Netherlands*

Sport as an open system

Parallel to societal developments (increasing individualism, commercialism, etc.) sport has also developed from a closed and clear system into an open and diverse system. This means that the traditional sport system is partly falling apart. Clubs have been exposed to competition from so-called fitness schools, private, for-profit clubs that provided services for the participants, whereas traditional clubs still relied on solidarity. A solidarity that, in the late eighties and nineties, was hard to find. The discovery of sport as an entertainment instrument, combined with parallel devolopments in the commercial media, has led to an increase in the number of professional and commercial sports organizations. The diversity of the sports market and the diversity of needs within that market have created opportunities for new initiatives. In the world of sport in the Netherlands, sports entrepreneurs are now becoming as common a feature as sports clubs were in the sixties and seventies. The map (see figure 1), would appear to indicate that the growth of the left column (commercial sports organizations) will continue, and that the diversity of sport organizations will also increase. This map reflects a situation that is becoming increasingly diverse and hence harder to steer or to influence, for example for governmental organizations. Whereas politicians used to have a negotiating partner in the Netherlands Sport Confederation, today this umbrella organization no longer represents all activities in the world of sport, although its merge with the Netherlands Olympic Committee increased its status. This also means that the influence of commercial stakeholders will have an increasing impact on sport in the Netherlands, based on market mechanisms.

Consequences for sport management development

In a study of market orientation within the traditional sport organizations (Albronda/Rubingh, 1989) the main sport managers where found within some of the traditional sports organizations. In a later study (Helbig, 1992), the commercial sector, too, was analysed. The conclusion of this study was that this would become an enormous growth sector for management in sport, based also on the assumption that sport would develop parallel to developments in society.

Managers who professionally manage a sport organization and earn their living from it can therefore, be found mainly in three segments:

sport (con)federations, their districts and the provincial sports council
a sport manager in a more organizational/administrative framework
"sport administrator"

public authorities (local authorities)
a sport manager in a more political/policy making framework
"sport policy-maker"

commercial sport organizations
a sport manager in a more entrepreneurial/commercial framework
"sport entrepreneur"

Developments in the sport market and in sport organizations show an increasing need for new management qualities that to suit these developments. Overall, it can be stated that in all three of the above mentioned segments, greater attention has to be paid to the entrepreneurial aspects of management qualities. A three circle model, identifying some of the qualities needed for managing sport, is used to make these changes in management clear.

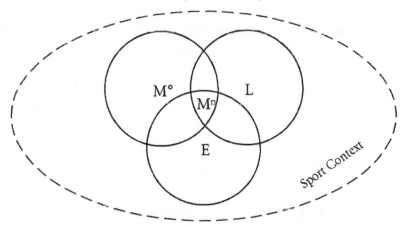

figure 2. Sport management aspects

In this model (see figure 2) the *new management concept* consists of:

L: Leadership
To have the vision and professional knowledge needed to address problems and come up with ideas and solutions as well as the personal social skills implied by the notion of "manager as coach", for example the ability to inspire and to transfer knowledge.

E: Entrepreneurship
To be customer-oriented in offering sport products and services and (dare) to take initiatives.

Mo: Management (old concept)
To have at one's disposal methods and techniques for analysing problems and arriving at views, ideas and solutions (planning, organization and control).

S: Sport context
To have sufficient knowledge of this context to create an optimal fit between the earlier mentioned three skills and the current situation.

The three management styles referred to above (sport administrator, sport policy-maker and sport entrepreneur) and developments in the world of sport, are examined in the light of this three circle model. Assumptions are made in order to identify the main management developments.

The sport administrator

A sport manager in a more organizational/administrative framework; the main activities lie in the area of administrating and managing competitions, their conditions and sports infrastructure. Whereas these organizations relied on government grants in the past, today these managers are confronted with decreasing subsidies, more competitions and a growing complexity of internal and external steering mechanisms. These managers need to move away from the planning, organizing and controlling (Management old style) style of management and acquire more leadership and entrepreneurial qualities to tackle these developments in their organizations.

The sport policy maker

A sport manager in a more political/policy-making framework; the main activities were realizing and creating conditions around sport organizations in which sport was accessible to many. The public sector had a major influence on sport organizations and was one of the providers of sport services. Today, we see the public sector bodies withdrawing from their more executive responsiblities and discussing their key responsibilities in the sport sector. In the discussions, it is becoming apparent that the public authorities feel their main responsibilities to lie in a supportive role towards the private sector and at most an initiating role where the private sector is seen to be failing (for example minority groups, security, standards for safety, etc.). For management, this means that the policy-maker in a public authority has to focus his efforts on the self-supporting skills of the sports private sector. Instead of intervening in sport themselves, sport policy-makers need to increase their support for entrepreneurial activities in sport management. They therefore have to increase their know-how in the areas of entrepreneurial and consultancy (leadership) skills.

The sport entrepreneur

A sport manager in a more entrepreneurial/commercial framework.
Doing business in sport in the Netherlands is, generally speaking, not a way of making big money. The main qualifications for the job are a willingness to work hard and a love of sport. It helps to know the context of the business: sport and its stakeholders. For example, it is important to understand what kinds of grants are available and which governmental influences are positive or negative. Most entrepreneurs in the Netherlands start a business in sport because they are sports lovers, not because they are dyed-in-the-wool entrepreneurs. It could be stated that they have enough, albeit perhaps narrow, know-how of sport, but hardly any skills in entrepreneurship. In this fast-growing sector of sport in the Netherlands, we shall see an increasing institutionalization and professionalization, which will eventually lead towards a new professional field. However, it will be a field that is not traditionally organized, but flexible and changing almost constantly. Change is the constant factor here, i.e. adjusting new supplies to new demands in different organizational settings. Success in entrepreneurship in sport therefore, depends on the adaptability of the entrepreneur and its organization.

Developments & Trends

From the beginning of the nineties sport management became accepted as a new field of expertise both in the professional world and the educational world, although the traditional

Universities still refrain from major involvement. At present, several institutes for Higher Physical Education have the subject in their curriculum, especially in the fourth, bachelor's, year of their programmes. A post-graduate programme is running, both for professionals already working in sport and for initial-phase students with a bachelor's degree in Physical Education or Economics. The Netherlands Olympic Committee*Netherlands Sport Confederation runs short courses in sport management for the staff of the federations. Sport management can also be found in the curricula of several other educational programmes, as for example "Coach Professional Soccer" of the Royal Dutch Soccer Federation, in which sport management is one module. Two trends can therefore be identified:

"Scientification" of sport management

Sport management is slowly being incorporated as a scientific field within the regular educational (academic) framework. There is an increasing demand for sport management know-how from the professional field, and this implies theoretical back-up. The subject is becoming more and more an item studied in the Academic context and it is therefore expected that, in the near future, a chair of sports management will be established at one of the Dutch Universities.

Professionalization of sport managers

The increasing number of educational and training courses over the last five years has created a new professional identity. Through academic involvementen and the foundation of the European Association for Sport Management, sport management and sport managers have gained in status. The number of people who call themselves sport managers is increasing. More and more, it is accepted as a profession, just like other professions, in Dutch society.

Summary

Sport management has only been on the agenda of sport organizations and educational institutes for the last five years. This does not mean, however, that before that no attention was paid to it before that period. Trends in society and the importance of "management" have strengthened the development of sport management as a subject in its own right. Developments in the sport world and a more diverse infrastructure accentuate the need for good management, especially a more market-oriented and entrepreneurial style of management. Both the educational world and the sport world can contribute to the further development of this field. At present, the sport world and the educational world in the Netherlands are loooking for a way to cooperate, in order to bring practice and theory together. The two trends identified above, namely greater interest on the part of from the academic world and further professionalization of the "sport manager", can both benefit from this cooperation. For the time being, however, sport management is still in its infancy.

References

Albronda, B.J., Rubingh, B.- *Marktanalyse na-ervaringsopleiding sportmanagement*, Management Consultancy Center, Groningen, 1989.

Balje, Chr. L., Slik, W.K.H.- *De Sport van een grenzeloos Europa*, Sectie Internationale Organisaties, University Groningen, Groningen, 1992.

Beckers, Th., Serail, S.- *Nieuwe verhoudingen in de sport*, Katholieke Universiteit Brabant, Vrijetijdswetenschappen, Tilburg, 1991.

Chelladurai, P.- Sport management: defining the field, *European Journal for Sport Management*, vol. 1, no. 1, may 1994.

Crum, B.J.- *Over de versporting van de samenleving*, De Vriescheborg, Haarlem, 1992.

Crum, B.J., Kalmthout, J. van.- *Scholingsbehoefte van ambtenaren sport en recreatie*, IVA, Tilburg, 1994.

Heinemann, K., Horch, H.D.- Strukturbesonderheiten des Sportvereins, from: Digel, H., *Sport im Verein und im Verband*, Hofmann Verlag, Schorndorf 1988.

Hattink, B.- *Curriculum design sportmanagement ALO Groningen*, Rijksuniversiteit Groningen, Onderwijskunde, Groningen, 1993.

Helbig, M.- *Sportmanagement in de commerciele sport*, Rijksuniversiteit Groningen, Bedrijfskunde, Groningen, 1990.

Kamphorst, T., Roberts, K.- *Trends in sports*, Giordano Bruno, Culemborg 1989.

Kearney, A.T.- *Sport als bron van inspiratie voor onze samenleving*, NOC*NSF, Amsterdam, 1992.

Rubingh, B.- *Analyse van de sportwereld ten behoeve van een te starten opleiding sportmanagement*, Rijksuniversiteit Groningen, Bewegingswetenschappen, Groningen, 1990.

Rubingh, B., Westerbeek, H.M.- *Besturen van de sportvereniging, kiezen of delen, Spel en sport*, 92/1, Amsterdam, 1992.

Sport Management Committee.- History and organization of sports and sport management in the European Union, *Textbook European Master Seminar on Sport Management*, SMC, Groningen, 1994.

Stokvis, R.- *De sportwereld, een sociologische inleiding*, Samson, Alphen aan den Rijn/Brussel, 1989.

Wegener, G.J.- *Sport in the Netherlands*, Netherlands Olympic Committee*Netherlands Sports Confederation, European Commission, Brussel, 1992.

Sports club management: a comparison

Klaus Heinemann
Institut für Soziologie,
Universität Hamburg,
Germany

Núria Puig
Institut Nacional d'Educació Física de Catalunya,
Universitat de Barcelona,
Spain

Managing a sports club

There are specific aspects to managing a sports club which differ markedly from those involved in running a commercial company or a public organization. This is because the sports club also differs in terms of its characteristics from those of the latter two types of organization. These characteristics are as follows:

1. In a club, *the latter's objectives and members' interests are similar*. Its objective is to satisfy the interests of its members, and as such there is no difference between the club's interests and those of its members. By definition, it is a non-profit-making association which does not aim to generate profit. The position of a commercial company is very different since, although it obviously satisfies the interests of its customers, its ultimate aim is to generate profit. The interests of businessmen, those of their workers and those of their customers are not identical.

2. *Membership of a club is voluntary*. No-one has to belong to a club. People decide to join a club because it offers them something which satisfies them for one or more reasons. A club member is not a worker. Entering or leaving the club is of no consequence for the member but this may be highly significant for the worker who finds himself obliged to leave his employer.

3. *Voluntary work is one of the mainstays of life in a club*. Not only is membership voluntary but there are also people who willingly give up part of their free time to attend to club-related matters. Recent developments in sports clubs illustrate their increasingly professional nature, yet this does not imply the disappearance of voluntary work but the coexistence of the latter with remunerated, professional services. Voluntary work does not exist in the commercial world.

4. *Economic resources*, also, *are different* from those of commercial companies. The main sources of income in most clubs are the members' subscription fees. This enables them to be *independent of third parties*. The type of exchange which is set up is fundamentally different from that of a company: members place their resources in a "pool" (common fund) and, in return, receive the right to take part in decisions as to how this pool of resources will be used and the right to use the services (the products) on offer from the club. A club's economic basis is not a bilateral exchange relationship - as is the case with exchanges in a market economy - but a social agreement.

5. *Decision-making in a club is democratic.* Everyone has the right to make a decision in respect of the use of resources and the type of programmes to be developed (one person, one vote). In a company, on the other hand, only the owner makes decisions.

These elements mean that managing a sports club is fundamentally different from managing other types of organizations. By taking them into account, it is possible to see that sports club management has to deal with the following aspects:

1. *Guaranteeing convergence between its objectives and products and the interests, wishes, capabilities and economic potential of the members.* This requires great sensitivity since, as it does not have a system of market prices geared to the interests of demand, it is difficult to apply itself to all these considerations. The problem becomes more acute when the club has a highly diverse membership or experiences a very dynamic period causing great change in members' interests.

2. *Aspects related to the structure and to the number of members.* A common phenomenon is a drop in the number of members. Clubs which have always had a stable - or increasing - number of members begin to experience an alarming rate of non-renewals, which endangers their very existence. From a management standpoint, it is necessary to look into the reasons for this reorientation of members' interests and to implement the measures required to halt it and reverse it.

In terms of structure, matters relating to the age and sex of members have to be addressed. A club which has traditionally been oriented towards high performance needs to have a high proportion of young people amongst its membership. If, at a given moment, it is noticed that the size of this group in the club has grown smaller, it will be necessary to investigate what type of product should be offered in order to attract more young members. There are also cases of clubs which, amongst their objectives, aim to be a focal point for the entire community but in which the number of female members is very small, with the result that one of the club's priority objectives is not being accomplished. The club should therefore draw up strategies aimed at increasing the number of female members.

3. *Motivating voluntary work.* Managing human resources in a voluntary-type association is perhaps more complex than in companies where work is carried out in exchange for remuneration. "Non-remunerated" means that financial reward does not have to be offered, but this does not mean that the club does not have to offer something in exchange. Another type of reimbursement has to be offered, making voluntary work attractive so that volunteers will feel rewarded by doing it.

Moreover, management of human resources on a voluntary basis has to take the following aspects into account: 1) knowing how to recruit volunteers; 2) checking that motivation is good because this is the only source of support for the project being worked on; 3) guaranteeing that the volunteers are well qualified (even today, there is a widespread belief that if there is good will everything is acceptable, but this can have detrimental consequences for the club's future); 4) finding ways of monitoring the work carried out; and 5) implementing sanctions which are regarded as acceptable within the context of voluntary work.

Finally, the fact that some clubs are currently becoming increasingly professional is creating a new problem in human resources management, namely the relationship between volunteers and professionals. These relationships are not always harmonious and range from power struggles within the organization to a loss of efficiency owing to the ill-feeling which can be generated.

4. *Mobilization of financial resources.* Given the resources which characterize the economic basis of a club, specific ways of generating income have to be sought. Reference has already been made to the need to monitor the number of members given that their subscription fees are an essential budgetary component. The manner of obtaining public assistance implies familiarity

with administrative strategy, both through finding legitimate arguments and by being capable of dealing with a request within the interwoven complexity of official bureaucracy. Finally, finding a sponsor also involves finding convincing arguments and knowing how to develop a sports policy which is adapted to a sponsor's requirements.

However, third-party financing can be a source of conflict in a club. A sponsor may require the club to become more commercial in its activities, thereby distancing it from its initial objectives and therefore failing to satisfy the interests of members or a proportion of members. Similarly, public assistance may lead to the politicization of a club which is also unsatisfactory for members. Management will have to take a decision on the dilemma of commercialization/ politicization in exchange for greater income or a reduction in expenditure to guarantee the club's independence vis-à-vis third parties.

5. *Guaranteeing and facilitating everyone's participation in decision-making.* By taking part in general meetings and other decision-making processes, the members can guide those who manage the club as to their preferences and wishes. This is the means they have at their disposal for making their interests known. Processes whereby a club is ruled by a small group are dangerous since this leads to a feeling of alienation and, in the long term, may give rise to a mass exodus without its having been possible to do anything to prevent this.

A comparison between countries broadens the horizons for sports club management

In 1995, we carried out the first stage of a comparative investigation of sports clubs in Germany and Spain, which reveals major differences between the two countries[1]. These differences also arise in club management. In the second part of this article, in addition to a discussion of the principal results obtained, we illustrate the various problems posed in sports club management in both countries. Owing to the limited space available, the five aspects analysed above have necessarily been summarized.

1. Problems related to club size

The first result requiring our attention is the difference in club size, i.e. the structure and number of members. In Barcelona province, 13.9% of clubs have over 1000 members whereas, in Germany, only 5.5% of all clubs can boast this number. The difference is even more dramatic given the number of people falling into each of these categories since, in Barcelona, 73.3% of people who are members of a club are members in a club with a membership of over 1000, whereas in Germany the figure is only 29.6%.

---

[1] See: Heinemann, K.; Puig, N.; Lopez, C.; Moreno, A., (1995): Clubs deportivos en España y Alemania: una comparación empírica y teórica, Barcelona, Institut Nacional d'Educació Física de Catalunya, unpublished research paper.

The German research results may be consulted in Heinemann, K.; Schubert, M., 1995.

Field work in Spain was carried out by Professor Antonio Moreno from the INEF-Catalunya, in Barcelona. The results are currently being collated.

In this first stage of the research, only data relating to Barcelona province have been dealt with. Therefore, the results must be regarded in hypothetical terms, as suggestions for forthcoming stages. The comparative work consisted of research assistance given to the "Sports clubs in Spain and Germany" project by: 1) the General Directorate for Scientific and Technical Research of the Ministry of Education and Science, within the context of Integrated Hispano-German Actions, 1995, in Spain; and 2) the "Deutscher Akademischer Austauschdienst", within the context of the "Projektbezogener Wissenschaftleraustausch mit Spanien. Programm 1995", in Germany.

Simmel (1968) for groups in general and Heinemann (1990) for sports organizations regard a study of club size as being of utmost importance for at least two reasons:

-Depending on the number of members, its internal structural characteristics vary visibly and affect the type of social relationships which are established within a club. A large club requires a much greater degree of formal relationships than a small club. There have to be rules regarding operation and topics which cannot be resolved within informal, face-to-face discussions. There is also a major difference between the functions of volunteers, and work in the club also has to be tackled much more professionally, thereby requiring a certain level of competence and preparation on the part of all those involved in managing the club. It is of no significance that this is a non-profit-making organization; the size alone requires stricter management.

-The second argument justifying interest in a study of club size relates to their social function and is related to the previous aspect. Generally speaking, a large club has a greater degree of organization and its structure is more bureaucratic, which confers a degree of anonymity on relationships and implies that the product supplied is regarded principally as a service to the members. A small club, on the other hand, makes it possible to get rid of this feeling of anonymity and generates the feeling of "our little world" ("Geselligkeit") or, in other words, "Heimat auf Zeit" (temporary home).

Given the above considerations, the problem facing the management of German sports clubs (which are generally smaller) is that of the clubs' selectivity. It has been observed that the smaller the club the greater the degree of homogeneity it has. If, on the one hand, this implies greater intensity in relationships which are established between the members, they are, on the other hand, more selective and less representative of society as a whole.

In Spain, on the other hand, because clubs are bigger, the problem which arises is that of the loss of the quasi-family atmosphere which is created in a small club. Clubs are less homogeneous and more open to the world at large but, given their more formal structure, their operation has to be regarded as a service. They depend on external income, which makes them less independent, and they have to address the professional level of their staff as well as of their volunteers.

2. Clubs in historical and social context

Differences which depend on the size of clubs caused us to question the origins of such a situation. What historical circumstances can explain this different evolution of sports clubs? Replying to this question makes it possible to understand the socio-political context in which clubs develop.

The difference in the years that clubs were founded, in our opinion, is the answer to this question.
16.4% of German clubs were created before 1918 whereas, in Barcelona province at the same time, only 5.5% of clubs which currently exist had been founded.

Studies carried out in Germany have revealed the importance of the first clubs as focuses of social integration. Many of them have meaningful names in this respect - "Concordance", "Harmony", etc. It has been said that the 19th century in Germany was the century of clubs and friendships. Against a background of great changes profoundly affecting ancient family structures and social links and during which a major trend towards urbanization was witnessed - thereby giving rise to major movements of population -, clubs and the cultivation of friendship (going beyond family ties) were new social references providing individual and group identity. German clubs grew up at the same time as modern physical/sports practices, in a simultaneous process, and this enabled club structure to be shaped in accordance with the requirements of a specific sports philosophy to the point where club and sport come to mean the same thing. Clubs had and continue to have a central role to play on the German sports scene and are, undoubtedly, the cornerstone of German sports development.

The origins and development of sport in Spain are different. Prior to 1918, clubs were set up mostly by members of the emergent middle classes who were confirming their identity as distinct from aristocratic circles, thereby reflecting another concept not only of physical activity but also of society (Lagardera, 1992: 24). The phenomenon was essentially one of creating a distinction mainly vis-à-vis the nobility, the latter refusing to accept the challenges of modernization on account of the obvious loss of power this would represent. However, they did not occupy a central position in sports development because this was only in its infancy. Most clubs in Barcelona are of recent creation, 38.1% of them having been founded between 1981 and 1991, as opposed to 16.4 % in Germany.

As we see it, the youthful nature of Spanish clubs is crucial to an understanding of the differences observed in club size. Most clubs broke onto the Spanish sports scene at the same time as the creation of a sector of the public intent on involvement in the field of personal services which includes, inter alia, sport[2]. This has to be understood on the basis of the collective representation of the State image (Harvey; Beamish; Defrance, 1993) which was created in Spain after the death of Franco. The general feeling was that, in Franco's Spain, scant attention had been given to these services and, after the installation of democracy, the State was required to take them into account. This belief was so firm that Article 43.3 of the Spanish Constitution lays down that "the public authorities shall be responsible for promoting physical activity and sport". That is to say there was unanimous agreement that the public authorities should become involved in sport. From that time onwards, the powers that be followed through their constitutional mandate and embarked on an active sports promotion policy (Puig, 1996). In those places where clubs exist, the trend is one of setting up collaborative, cooperative models. However, the fact that a sizeable proportion of the public is involved in sport beyond the mere construction of facilities obliges clubs to adopt a specific stance regarding sport, namely to safeguard individual space.

The emergence of clubs against a background of different historical processes means that their place in the world of sport varies and that major political consequences ensue. In Germany, the appearance of sport and the setting-up of clubs takes place in parallel. It may be said that clubs hold a monopoly over sport and are able to determine its path as well as establish the conditions under which it is practised. In Spain, on the other hand, clubs are much younger and have developed principally since the 1980s when other types of institutional arrangements (the State and the commercial sector) also took shape (Puig; Heinemann, 1995). The formula legitimizing their existence is their aim to provide a service. They have to find a space within pre-established coordinates and are therefore much more dependent on external circumstances.

3. Economic resources

Finally, an analysis of economic resources also shows up differences between clubs in both countries. On the one hand, Spanish clubs are more "monetarized", i.e. they move a greater volume of money. On the other hand, whereas in Germany membership fees virtually always provide over 50% of income, this is rarely the case in Barcelona, particularly in the big clubs. In this latter case, income originates from the marketing of services or from sponsors, whilst, in

---

[2] In Spain, "personal services" means all fields directly related to people: health, education, culture, social services, youth and sport.

Germany, in addition to subscription fees, donations made by the actual members are also of great importance[3].

From these results, the nature of strategies to be developed with regard to economic resources will clearly be different in the two countries. Bringing in new members to guarantee the club's continued survival principally on the basis of members' contributions and having to mobilize resources originating from the State, sponsors or the services actually offered by the club are two different things. In this sense, Spanish clubs are more greatly affected by the risks inherent in marketing or in politicization given that their funds come from third parties. Sports management must address the consequences of such choices and consider whether, for example, operating with income originating principally from sponsorship does not constitute setting the club on a possible course from which there is no return and which, in the long run, will endanger its very existence.

Conclusions

The comparative research had a sociological aim not centred so much on club management. However, as has been demonstrated, the results obtained do prompt reflection on this subject. In the space available to us, we have given a few outlines. In addition, the comparative view has further enriched the type of assessments made. To view one's own circumstances from another standpoint is an aid in discovering aspects which, since they are regarded as normal, had passed unnoticed.

Finally, it should be pointed out that the differences observed in the comparison carried out between Germany and Spain are a challenge to be addressed within the context of European integration. Taken as a whole, sports clubs are very important to the existence of sport in Europe. We have also been able to offer a number of illustrations to the effect that Europe involves great diversity and that integration cannot mean homogenization but, rather, integration in diversity. For this reason, we believe that the brief outline we have presented is no more than a way of drawing attention to the need to further develop research into sports club management within a specifically European context.

References

Harvey, J., Beamish, R., Defrance, J.- "Physical exercise policy and the Welfare State: a framework for comparative analysis". In *International Review for the Sociology of Sport*, vol. 28, (1), 1993, pp. 53-64.

Heinemann, K.- *Einführung in die Soziologie des Sports*, Hoffmann, Schorndorf, 1990, 3rd edition.

Heinemann, K., Schubert, M.- *Der Sportverein*, Schorndorf, Karl Hoffmann, 1994.

Heinemann, K., Puig, N., Lopez, C., Moreno, A.- *Clubs deportivos en España y Alemania: una comparación empírica y teórica*, Barcelona, Institut Nacional d'Educació Física de Catalunya, unpublished research paper, 1995.

---

[3] The donation formula as a means of supporting sports-based associations and reducing taxes does not exist in Spain unless clubs are able to be recognized as being of service to the public, which is very difficult to achieve.

Lagardera, F.- "De la aristócrata gimnástica al deporte de masas: un siglo de deporte en España". In: *Sistema*, (110-111), 1992, pp. 9-36.

Puig, N., Heinemann, K.- "Poders públics i desenvolupament de l'esport a Catalunya. Proposta de marc teóric interpretatiu", 1995. In *Acàcia*, journal of the Department of Contemporary History, University of Barcelona, pp. 123-143.

Puig, N.- "Sport policy in Spain", 1996. In Johnson, A., Chalip, L., ed. 1996 *International Handbook on National Sport Policies*, Westport, Greenwood Press (in print).

Simmel, G.- *Soziologie - Untersuchungen über die Formen der Vergesellschaftung*, Berlin, 1968, Dunca & Humblot, 5th edition.

II
Sport management: some central concepts

Jean-Claude Killy, Alpine skiing, three times Olympic champion at the X Olympic Winter Games in Grenoble in 1968 (slalom, giant slalom, downhill).

Jean-Claude Killy and Michel Barnier, Co-Presidents of the Organizing Committee of the XVI Olympic Winter Games in Albertville, in a meeting with Juan Antonio Samaranch, Marqués de Samaranch, IOC President.

The purpose of a sports organization: to generate emotion

Jean-Claude Killy
Member of the International Olympic Committee,
France

Great words can give great joys, even where values are in decline:

- Courage
- Internationalism
- The pursuit of perfection
- Respect for others and tolerance
- Solidarity
And even social cohesion, even public health...

These words and, of course, a number of others take on their full meaning in a successful act of sports organization, that is to say the creation of a moment of bliss, be it a dream for the one who looks on or the fulfilment of a dream for the one putting on the show.

The organization of a sports event is first and foremost an expectation: the quality of the response determines the beauty of the instant, the eternal nature of the memory.

A few weeks before the Games in Albertville, the Olympic flame was travelling around France and, sometimes, I followed it: that day, we were in Aubusson, five thousand two hundred inhabitants... and there were ten thousand people that evening, gathered for the celebration.

Just before Aubusson, there is a steep hill. Two farmers were running, holding their berets in their hands so that they would not blow away, the berets they never remove, even to sleep. These men had snowy white foreheads and deeply tanned faces: from working in the fields.

They took off their boots and ran just like that, close to the flame, right in the middle of the Creuse. When you see that, you really ask yourself what is going on.

These unexpected joys are born of the most pragmatic of arrangements: the closer you are to the earth, the fewer clouds there are. Even though it is probably easier for a former athlete or a former champion to become an organizer - he already knows the priorities, the specifications, the mentality - there are a number of necessary steps and there is no question of missing a gate. The first of these concerns the competitors' satisfaction. If you can define the finest sporting act of the day, you have won. The second can be summed up by the word respect: respect of rules, within a schedule established in advance by official authorities; respect for the spectator and the television viewer; respect for the environment and hence for politics in the broadest and finest sense; respect for associates and partners...

Each and every one of us must help sport to live for ever. Making it last is indeed the great idea which should subtend all your action, as sport is rebuilt every day. Even when it is not Olympic, it rests upon Olympic values.

Organizing can mean suffering and tears, but it can also bring the discovery of the fullest sense of the word brotherhood. On the Tour de France, in the descent of the Portet-d'Aspet pass, Fabio Casartelli, former Olympic champion, died. Frightful days and yet the most authentic moment for an organizer to ask himself questions. We buried Fabio in Albesete, a village above Lake Como, in the heat of a crushing sadness. So many people and the church, tiny and charming, overflowing. I shall never forget the Ave Maria that rose from the midst of the choir, sung by a crystalline voice, frail but firm. I shall never forget the moment when a mother, whom we took care of as best we could, placed Marco, her infant son of a few months, on his father's coffin. We all cried, the minister too.

Organizing the Olympic Games, the Tour de France or the Paris-Grenada-Dakar means, first and foremost, giving emotion. Generating it, showing it, controlling it as far as possible. Then and only then can a magic moment of thrilling power come about. My finest story is an anecdote which took place at the Albertville Games and went unnoticed by most people. The medal of an Austrian Nordic combined specialist fell and broke. He was distraught, convinced that the situation was irremediable. The story reached me and I sent for him to come to see me in my COJO office immediately. He mounted the stairs, shoulders hunched, apologizing already. I asked him in English:

"How did you break it?"
"I dropped it."
As he said that, tears welled in his eyes and he lowered his head. I went to the medal cupboard and gave him another one, bronze like his. Then, he stood up straight. With a smile, such a smile as you cannot imagine.

Pál Schmitt, fencing, Olympic team épée champion at the Games of the XIX Olympiad in Mexico City in 1968 and the XX Olympiad in Munich in 1972.

102nd IOC Session in Lillehammer. Pál Schmitt is seated between Marc Hodler, IOC member in Switzerland and President of the International Ski Federation (FIS), and Ashwini Kumar, IOC member in India.

The sports manager's tasks in an Olympic Committee

Pál Schmitt
Member of the International Olympic Committee,
Hungary

The relation and integration of an Olympic Committee (OC) into the national sports movement varies considerably from country to country. Some OCs are responsible for the country's entire sports movement, while some European OCs have merged into the state sports authorities. There are and have been instances where the OC operates as one of the departments of the Ministry of Sport or equivalent authority.

The fundamental duties, the compulsory independence of an OC and the percentage of national sports federation representatives in the membership are clearly stated in the Olympic Charter.

Let us now take a look at the fundamental tasks and the necessary professional background of a manager needed for effective work.

Dissemination of the Olympic Ideals

This task can hardly be connected to a definite profession since the task itself is difficult to determine. In my opinion, teachers, researchers, historians, literary men and philosophers know and sense best what is to be done in this field.

From an organizational point of view, the Olympic academies are the most suitable institutes for this purpose. Their most significant duties are: the promotional work of the media, lectures, commemorative events, solemn occasions, maintenance of traditions, cultural events, organization of quiz games and Olympic days. The Fair Play movement, educating the young in fair play, chivalrousness, honour and respect for each other, forms an integral part of this circle of tasks. The dissemination of the Olympic ideals cannot be closely linked to any expert; by its very nature each member of the OC has to undertake a significant role.

Preparation for and participation in the Olympic Games

This range of tasks is easier to define, so the necessary professional background can also be more easily described.

In the Hungarian Olympic Committee, in order to provide the most appropriate professional guidance to the various sectors, the following permanent working commissions have been established:
- Professional and Scientific

- Medical
- Finance
- Juridical and Ethical
- Press
- Athletes

The commissions are chaired by the most dedicated and educated experts. The commissions have several meetings throughout the year; they report to the executive board on a regular basis and once a year to the general assembly. The professional and scientific activities logically focus upon preparatory plans, establishing aims and cooperating with experts. We should not forget that the sport-specific, professional work is carried out in the clubs and federations, whose competence must always be respected. In decision-making the principle of subsidiarity should be followed: i.e. professional decisions should be taken by the sports experts most closely involved in the living sport. The activity of the OCs in this field is more restricted to co-ordinating and evaluating reports. Naturally, collaboration is also an important characteristic of these activities since the science of sport is an interdisciplinary one, and it is the duty of the professional sports manager to harmonize it effectively. Another type of cooperation is equally important, such as the organization of professional forums for trainers and coaches, and the co-ordination of educational and research programmes with the University of Physical Education, the National Sport Health Institute and other scientific institutes.

The sports-related scientific work requires an overall knowledge and proficiency in living sport. In addition, coaches, researchers and practical experts need to have an original approach to sciences and be capable of adapting the latest results of scientific research. We also expect: considerable innovative ability, receptivity to the new, familiarity with the specialized literature and a knowledge of data processing. Taking the latter into consideration, I have to add that the Hungarian sports movement, including the Hungarian Olympic Committee, is far behind in terms of the opportunities offered by the latest innovations in data processing.

I might not be too popular with my colleagues if I confess that, in the offices of the Hungarian Olympic Committee, the computer is used almost exclusively for word processing, and only two of my fellow workers are able to use it. I might fall into contradiction with myself since, despite this fact, the Hungarian Olympic Committee is one of the most successful in the world. Or perhaps it proves that the real professional work is not carried out in the OC. However, it seems indisputable that as far as employing and using computers is concerned, the sports managers of middle and eastern Europe are left far behind the available opportunities for reasons of economics and differences of attitude.

Sports health and medical care

This activity requires an extremely high degree of expertise and responsibility.

We do not usually call physicians managers, although their activity is also characterized by purposefulness, strategy and team-work. Apart from treating sports injuries, the sports doctor undertakes an important role in prevention, rehabilitation and in the special problems of nutrition and body-weight balancing. The sports doctor assists the coaches in drawing up and scheduling the training stages and cycles, and controls the current work load and level of training. Another significant area of the sports doctor is the special treatment of sportswomen.

In doping control we rely greatly on the help of the sports doctors, since as well as providing prevention and education in this field, the doctor is able to offer scientific alternatives to prohibited substances.

Doctors thus have a very important role in the team, helping the preparation of the athletes. The OCs also need sports doctors or other experts who are able to integrate this scientific layer into the theoretical and practical network of preparation.

Public opinion is not homogeneous on the question as to whether the sports doctor should only cure and treat the ill or injured athlete. In my opinion, we definitely need experts to direct, organize and co-ordinate the sports medical field. If we are fortunate, these experts will also be doctors, who can then be labelled doctor-managers.

Economy and Finance

Due to its complexity, this work also requires special and wide-ranging expertise. Financial accounts have to be prepared; in addition to any state subsidy the possibility of our own resources and income has to be explored, the support system concerning individuals and groups has to be worked out, the operation of the OC has to be ensured and the financial regulations for the operation of social organizations have to be strictly followed. In generating our own revenues, marketing activities are part of the manager's domain, and we rely heavily on his expertise.

This special type of training has only recently been introduced into the curriculum of the University of Physical Education; however, in the absence of well-trained experts and appropriate expertise, we can rely on our own ideas and domestically-adapted international practice. Marketing as a profession has only started developing since the countries in the region converted their economies into free market economies, just a couple of years ago. The level of privatization varies significantly in these countries. The centralized sports authorities and the state financing system did not require such activities. Currently, however, the state has partially or completely withdrawn its support for competitive sport, and the economy is not yet strong enough to offer a proper background for methods of sponsorship and foundations that work well in western Europe.

I often say that the large, prosperous companies we visit to discuss sponsorship opportunities have warm door handles, since numerous sports clubs and federations as well as hundreds of foundations approach them for financial or in-kind support. There are always more pegs than holes to put them in.

In sports marketing well-trained professional experts are necessary both domestically and internationally. Such sports managers need to be fluent negotiators, sensible, persuasive and full of ideas about how to involve sponsors, service them and maintain the partnership in the long run. My perception of this relationship, and what I see as the fundamental principle of leadership in this respect, is that out of every 100 forints at least 20 forints ought to revert to the sponsor himself.

The practice of the Hungarian Olympic Committee is to ensure exclusivity to our sponsors in a sphere or category of services or products. Our sponsorship contracts are signed for four years. We have created categories in accordance with the quantity of the support: an exclusive sponsor club, named after Hungary's first Olympic champion, Alfréd Hajós, gathers together our strongest partners, who provide an annual amount of at least 16 million forints; our golden supporters give us at least 5 million forints per year and with at least 2 million forints yearly we have our official supporters.

While strictly respecting the IOC's marketing activities, the TOP programme, we approach potential sponsors and partners in various categories. The Hungarian Olympic Committee provides them with a specially designed Olympic logo.

As I have pointed out, we make every effort to best service our sponsors since our contracts must rest upon mutual interests. At our own expense, we promote and advertise our partners on TV, in some papers, in the Olympic Bulletin and in the Sports Yearbook. Management representatives are invited to all our occasions, official events, and to the oath taking ceremony prior to the Games. We organize sponsors' evenings. We offer special service for our sponsors in Thermal Hotel Hélia, which is also one of our sponsors. We also provide them with complimentary admission tickets to sports events and competitions. The most popular programme in this field is when the Hungarian Olympic Committee invites the partners to the Olympic Games where they may become more involved in the successes and sense the fantastic atmosphere of the Games, and also have the opportunity to further build their own network of business relations.

Managing and directing foundations for public purposes and interests also requires special expertise and professional knowledge, which has begun to be acquired in the last couple of years.

Managing the financial affairs of an OC consequently requires profound economic and financial education and practical knowledge. The professionals involved ought to be familiar with financial regulations and proficient in tax, VAT, customs clearance, duty and currency matters. They should have a clear view of decision-preparing and -making mechanisms, and be capable of taking rapid action and bearing the responsibility and consequences afterwards.

Legal matters

We may have felt before that we were at the mercy of doctors; however, in our complicated contemporary world we have ended up in the hands of the lawyers. All areas of our lives are regulated and only those who are able to find their way in the vast labyrinth of regulations, orders and directives may expect success and advancement.

Protection of the Olympic symbols, professional structuring, drafting of contracts, and arbitral matters all require special education and expertise, and are impossible to resolve with enthusiastic amateur goodwill any longer. From the less complicated contracts of employment to the more complex foundational contracts, each phase of our activities is regulated by the law, be it an individual or an institutional matter. Obviously, a lawyer or an attorney at law is indispensable in the OCs.

Media

Often one can only with difficulty find one's way in this complicated and peculiar field. My *ars poetica* in my own work is: collect friends with whom you can have a mutually supportive relationship throughout your life and never collect enemies who try to harm you, spread malicious rumours about you or seek revenge throughout your entire life. Well, this more or less describes my relations with the media/press. This does not mean that I am afraid of confrontation, since I myself used to be an athlete. However, I cannot jeopardize the reputation of the OC I lead as a consequence of personal disputes or hostility.

The outstanding role of the media in competitive sport is well-known. In my view the media is the fourth pillar of the Olympic Movement. The other three are often cited: the NOCs, the IFs and the IOC.

In the case of the NOCs, obviously the places of the NOCs and IFs are taken over by the national sports federations and the sports clubs. This is where I think the media have an important and determining role. Well-informed media are able to help our work immensely. Our results may become known nation- and world-wide through them; they can make stars and in some instances heroes out of our successful athletes and coaches.

The activities described previously depend a great deal on the background support provided by the different branches of the media.

Recognizing this fact, the Hungarian Olympic Committee has 9 representatives of the Hungarian sports media among its membership. The HOC regularly holds press conferences, and invites the media to the general assemblies and all major events. Our relationship is maintained by a cooperation agreement with the TV and the most important sports daily and weekly papers.

This field also requires the sports manager, but with specific skills! We expect him/her to have an ability to empathize, a high level of competence in foreign languages, a talent for public speaking and certainly - as I have emphasized on many occasions - an affection for and profound knowledge of sports. Those features, which can hardly be learnt, such as enthusiasm, self-confidence, devotion and charisma, can be a great help in working with the media. Media work and promotional activities, like other fields, ought to have a strategy based on collective, reasoned wisdom.

What kind of managers are necessary in an OC?

Regardless of its being full-time, part-time or volunteer, the OC definitely needs an economist, a lawyer, and in the background physicians, engineers, teachers and educators, organizers, marketing experts, journalists and, in case of special issues, advisers to the executive board or the President in the various specific areas.

Regarding the human features, we may expect devotion, an affection for sport, enthusiasm, optimism, discipline and self-sacrifice. In addition to all these, as for all organizations, the ability to cooperate and the knowledge of and respect for the written and unwritten rules of democracy are fundamental requirements.

If we add to these features technical expertise and other abilities such as knowledge of languages, competence in data and word processing, originality and an affinity for science, we can come to the conclusion that it is not at all easy to find appropriate officials for a well-run OC.

This article was the concluding lecture of the third European Sport Management Congress in Budapest, September 1995.

Distinctive features of sport economics and sport management

Heinz-Dieter Horch
Deutsche Sporthochschule,
Cologne, Germany

Sport goods and sport organizations have many distinctive features which have not received central attention in general economics and business administration. Both traditionally concentrate upon the market-oriented production of goods in large for-profit organizations. The knowledge and especially the recipes of general economics and business administration must therefore be closely examined as to their applicability to sport economics and management. Although most of the following features are neither unique to sport nor relevant to all sport goods and organizations, they are, however, typical of important areas of sport. The point is that these peculiarities of sport economics and sport management form a body of knowledge which traditionally is only of peripheral importance in the education of the average student of business administration but should be central to the education of sport managers.

The following representation is organized in a microeconomic manner concerning distinctive features of goods, demand and markets (see Heinemann, 1984, 1987; Freyer, 1990; Mullin/Hardy/Sutton, 1993; Benner, 1992). Distinctive features of supply form the topic of chapter 2.

Distinctive microeconomic features

1. Goods

Many sport products possess characteristics of public or merit goods or personal services and club goods. In addition to these there are some more specific sport-related features.

1.1. Public and merit goods

Government subsidies, privileges and state-financed infrastructure form an important part of the sport economy in many countries. This is also the case in otherwise strictly market oriented economic systems (including the US) and applies not only to non-profit sport areas but also to a great extent to professional spectator sport. That sport is said to have the characteristics of public and merit goods is given as a justification for these governmental subsidies. The market fails with these two types of goods as a result of a failure either in supply or in demand. Market failure means that goods are either not produced at all or in insufficient quantities in a market-economic type of production.

a) *Public goods* (Samuelson, 1954) can be distinguished from private goods by two criteria: their disadvantage is that the exclusion principle does not operate (first criterion: non-exclusion principle), i.e. once the good has been produced, those that did not pay for it cannot be excluded from its benefits. Free-rider behaviour becomes possible and supply by for-profit organizations is impossible as these are dependent upon voluntary individual purchasing actions. Public goods must therefore be financed primarily through forced contributions like taxes. The advantage of public goods is that they benefit all members of a society (second criterion: non rivalry). External defence and dikes are often mentioned as primary examples of public goods. National representation, youth integration and the economic benefits of the health of society members for the state (not the individual) are given as examples of public goods in sport.

b) *Merit goods* (Musgrave, 1969) can be and are offered on the market. However, the demand from a social political point of view is not great enough owing to distorted consumer preferences. One primarily assumes that consumers overrate short-term benefits to the detriment of long term benefits. Primary examples are school education and vaccinations but also the individual health benefits of sport exercise. As a result of this, government supports the demand (compulsory measures, tax reductions, vouchers) or the production (subsidies, tax reductions) of merit goods.

c) In addition to this it is more or less assumed in all existing market economies that the distribution of income as represented on the factor markets needs some political correction *(distribution failure)*. This can be achieved through the distribution of income (taxes, social transfers) or through specific subsidies for certain goods such as housing or sport exercise. This is the justification in terms of economic policy for subsidizing "sport for all".

1.2. Personal services

Many sport products such as training, therapy and entertainment are personal services (Herder-Dorneich/Kötz, 1972). This presumably represents the product feature with the greatest practical consequences for sport management. Compared to goods such as shoes, personal services are of an immaterial (intangible) nature. Contrary to object services such as installation or reparation, personal services are accomplished upon people. The benefits of *services* are subjectively heterogeneous. Services must be offered irrespective of their use, they are perishable, cannot be stored or transported and show large qualitative differences. In addition to these general features of services, *personal services* can only be produced in spatial, temporal (Uno-actu principle) and especially social contact with the consumer. The consumers are involved in the production and the producers are part of the good. This results in the development of a social relationship alongside the economic one which follows its own logic. These features pose problems for the supplier. Many of the rational mathematical calculations involved with goods cannot be applied. An important consequence of personal services is that the production occurs predominantly in small businesses because this is the only means of establishing the spatial proximity to the consumer. This removes the advantages of large businesses (economies of scale). For instance, small businesses usually do not have the means to employ specialists or conduct research and development.

1.3. Club goods

Club goods (non-pure public goods; Buchanan, 1965) are those to which the exclusion principle applies but to a certain extent have no rivalry in consumption, but only so long as no overcrowding problems occur. The specific economic problem of club goods is that, apart from the price and quantity, the size of membership of the club must also be optimized. Because on the one hand when the size of membership increases, the individual price for each member decreases but on the other hand overcrowding also decreases the individual benefits. This problem is well known in tennis or golf clubs.

1.4. Further distinctive features of sport goods

a) A central theme of sport is the excitement involved due to the *unpredictability* of the developments and the result of any game. Anyone can win. The core product cannot therefore be controlled by the supplier. Therefore he should concentrate on product extensions.

b) The fact that *people*, i.e. the athletes are treated as products in professional sport is unique in modern societies (Büch/Schellhaaß, 1984).

c) Many sport products are *rights*, eg. broadcasting rights or advertising rights.

2. Demand

a) Sport consumers are often attached to certain suppliers due to personal preferences, whether it is a team in spectator sport or a certain fitness trainer in active sport.

b) Sport usually occurs as a form of social consumption together with and dependent on others. Not many people visit a stadium on their own.

c) Sport is often only a part of a wider entertainment programme.

3. Markets

a) As a result of its competitive character spectator sport is distinguished not only by competition but in a similar fashion by cooperation, because sport competitions require the coproduction of at least two partners.

b) This is related to the high degree of regulations. Not only the rules of the sport are set but also fundamental economic parameters such as the amount and time of supply and the number of suppliers.

c) Supplier monopolies such as associations and leagues are typical. Although monopolies are generally to the disadvantage of consumers, this feature may also have a specific rationale in sport, because to have more than one champion in one sport discipline is in contradiction with the competitive logic of sport.

Distinctive features of voluntary associations

The major characteristic of the supplier side is the large number of different institutions which produce sport goods and services. Sport is to a substantial extent produced not in for-profit organizations but by public organizations, private households, and non-profit organizations. This is true not only in Germany but also in the US with substantial offers made by schools, colleges, universities, communities and also by voluntary associations such as the YM(W)CA (Young Men's (Women's) Christian Association). Voluntary associations such as sport clubs and federations typically can be distinguished from for-profit organizations by many socio-economic features. From a business administration point of view these could be divided into: 2.1. goals, 2.2. financing, 2.3. organization and 2.4. effectiveness and efficiency (see Heinemann/Horch, 1981, 1988; Horch, 1983, 1987, 1989, 1992a, 1994).

1. Goals

a) In contrast to a commercial sport studio where the owner wants to make a profit and the customer expects a particular service, the relationship of members to voluntary associations is based not upon satisfying different kinds of interests by means of an interest-exchange contract but rather on an *interest-association*, i.e. a social contract of individuals with common interests.

b) Voluntary associations are *non-profit* organizations. Of course resources must also be economically managed in non-profit organizations. However, the possible profit should not flow into the pockets of a select few - such as the owners in a for-profit firm - but be reinvested in the common goal. This so-called non-distribution constraint (Hansmann, 1980) defines non-profit organizations. The difference between for-profit and non-profit organizations therefore, does not lie in the achieving of profit but in the distribution of the profit.

c) The *sporting goal* of becoming a champion appears always to be of some importance relative to the profit goal even in US professional sport leagues (Heinemann, 1984, 1987).

2. Financing

a) Sport clubs are financed through sales revenues only to some extent. Typically, the members pool resources (Coleman, 1979) instead in order to achieve their common goal. The logic of dues is completely different to that of prices. Through their *contributions* in money and time (volunteering) the members receive a right to take part in the decision-making process and to get a share of the success of the association. The distribution of any goods is, however, decided by internal votes and not by contract. In contrast to exchange contracts, there is no guarantee and also often no desire for the allocation of goods to be equivalent to the contributions made. Each member's part of the goods and services is uncertain and cannot be demanded as in a sales contract because the success of the mutual work is also uncertain. It is also often expected of those who are able to contribute more that they do this out of solidarity. Examples of internal subventioning (Heinemann/Schubert 1994) within sport clubs are elite sportspeople being supported by leisure-time sportspeople, adult members supporting the young and passive members supporting the active, because contributions have to be paid regardless of the concrete use of goods.

b) *Donations*, especially time donations in the form of volunteer work play an important role.

c) The third pillar of sport club financing is composed of *governmental subsidies*: monetary, staff and especially product subventions (sport facilities) and privileges (reduced taxes, tax deductible donations, gambling income).

3. Organization

a) One of the peculiarities of the organizational structure of voluntary associations is that the economic roles are not differentiated as in the market place. The member in *role identity* is simultaneously consumer, producer, financier (owner) and decision maker (manager).

b) The processes of decision making are *democratic*, i.e. power is distributed according to the rule "one man one vote" instead of according to the individual contribution (share).

c) The majority of workers are *volunteers*. They are not a mobile production factor like paid work but work only towards those goals and in a manner they choose.

d) A tense, contradictory *intermediate mixture of structural elements* of formal organizations and informal small groups is the central characteristic of voluntary associations. According to Streeck (1981, 40): "the system problems of voluntary associations can all be traced back to the problem of integrating non-compatible structural forms in the same social unit (H.-D. H.: eg. volunteers and paid workers) or to achieving contradictory functions with one and the same structure (H.-D. H.: eg. instrumental and expressive functions)." The leadership of voluntary associations can therefore be compared to permanently walking a tightrope (Merton, 1976).

4. Effectiveness and efficiency

a) When compared to for-profit organizations voluntary associations possess both economic strengths and weaknesses. Examples of strengths are the *free and intrinsically motivated staff* and the *wide variety of control mechanisms* by which the members can influence the organization, eg. voice, exit and volunteering (Hirschman, 1974).

b) Efficiency weaknesses result for example from the limited rationality of non-profit economies because many benefits and costs are hard to measure and do not have a market price. Insufficient means, particularism of the goals, traditionalism, paternalism and amateurism in the leadership are further aspects of the voluntary failure (Salamon, 1987).

c) Those efficiency problems may be the cause of transformation tendencies such as commercialization, professionalization and bureaucratization which typically occur in voluntary associations when they get bigger and older. However, they may also partially result from adaptation processes in response to socially dominating forms of organization (DiMaggio/Powell, 1983).

d) Voluntary associations function best the younger and smaller they are, when they are locally restricted, the greater the homogeneity of interests and capabilities of the members and the less expertise the tasks require (Weber, 1972, 169).

References

Benner, G.- *Risk Management im professionellen Sport.* (Risk Management in Professional Sport), 1992. Bergisch Gladbach/Köln.

Buchanan, J.M.- An Economic Theory of Clubs, 1965. In: *Economics* 32.

Büch, M.-P., Schellhaaß, H.-M.- Ökonomische Aspekte der Transferentschädigung im bezahlten Mannschaftssport. (Economical Aspects of Transfer Compensation in Paid Team Sport). In: K. Heinemann (Ed.), *Texte zur Ökonomie des Sports.* (Texts on the Economics of Sport). Schorndorf, 1984, pp. 215-236.

Coleman, J.S.- *Macht und Gesellschaftsstruktur.* (Power and Social Structure), 1979. Tübingen.

DiMaggio, P.J., Powell, W.W.- The Iron Cage Revisited. Institutional Isomorphism and Collective Rationality in Organization Fields." In: *American Sociological Review* 48, 1983, pp. 147-160.

Freyer, W.- *Sport-Ökonomie oder Ökonomie des Sports?* (Sport Economics or the Economics of Sport?), 1990. Forschungsinstitut für Tourismus und Sport, Bonn.

Hansmann, H.B.- The Role of Nonprofit Enterprise. *Yale Law Journal,* 1980, 89, 5: pp. 835-901.

Heinemann, K.- Probleme der Ökonomie des Sports. (Problems of the Economics of Sport). In: Heinemann, K. (Ed.), *Texte zur Ökonomie des Sports.* Schorndorf, 1984, pp. 17-51.

Heinemann, K.- Besonderheiten der Betriebswirtschaftslehre des Vereins. (Peculiarities of Business Management Studies of Clubs). In: Heinemann, K. (Ed.), *Betriebswirtschaftliche Grundlagen des Sportvereins.* Schorndorf, 1987, pp. 10-39.

Heinemann, K., Horch, H.-D.- Soziologie der Sportorganisation. (Sociology of Sport Organizations). In: *Sportwissenschaft,* 1981, 11: pp. 123-150.

Heinemann, K., Horch, H.-D.- Strukturbesonderheiten des Sportvereins. (Distinctive Structural Features of Sport Clubs). In: H. Digel (Ed.), *Sport im Verein und im Verband.* (Sport in Clubs and Federations). Schorndorf: 108-122.

Heinemann, K., Schubert, M.- *Der Sportverein.* (The Sport Club), 1994, Schorndorf.

Herderdorneich, Ph., Kötz, W.- *Zur Dienstleistungsökonomie.* (Service Economics), 1972. Berlin.

Hirschman, A.O.- *Abwanderung und Widerspruch.* (Exit, voice and loyality), 1974. Tübingen.

Horch, H.-D.- *Strukturbesonderheiten freiwilliger Vereinigungen.* (Distinctive Structural Features of Voluntary Associations), 1983. Frankfurt/New York.

Horch, H.-D.- Personalwirtschaftliche Aspekte ehrenamtlicher Mitarbeit. (Personal Management Aspects of Volunteer Work). In: K. Heinemann (Ed.), *Betriebswirtschaftliche Grundlagen des Sportvereins.* (Business Management Foundations of Sport Clubs), 1987. Schorndorf: pp. 121-141.

Horch, H.-D.- Sociological Research on Sport Organizations in West Germany. A Review. In: *International Review for the Sociology of Sport,* 1989, 24: pp. 201-216.

Horch, H.-D.- *Geld, Macht und Engagement in freiwilligen Vereinigungen.* (Power and Commitment in Voluntary Associations), 1992a. Berlin.

Horch, H.-D.- On the Socio-Economics of Voluntary Organisations. In: *Voluntas,* 1994, 5/2: pp. 219-230.

Merton, R. K.- Dilemmas of Voluntary Associations. In: Merton, R.K. *Sociological Ambivalence,* 1976, New York: pp. 90-105.

Mullin, B., Hardy, S., Sutton, W.A.- *Sport Marketing,* 1993. Champaign, Ill.

Musgrave, R.- *Finanztheorie.* (Fiscal Theory), 1969. Tübingen.

Salamon, L.M.- Of Market Failure, Voluntary Failure, and Third Party Government: Toward a Theory of Government-Nonprofit Relations in the Modern Welfare State. In: *Journal of Voluntary Action Research,* 1987, pp. 29-49.

Samuelson, P.A.- The Pure Theory of Public Expenditure. In: *Review of Economics and Statistics,* 1954, 36: pp. 387-390.

Streeck, W.- *Gewerkschaftliche Organisationsprobleme in der sozialstaatlichen Demokratie.* (Trade Union Organizational Problems in Social Democracy), 1981. Königstein.

Weber, M.- *Wirtschaft und Gesellschaft.* (Economy and Society), 1972 (5). Tübingen.

Sports values and operational strategies

Pierre Chifflet
Université Joseph Fourier,
Grenoble, France

This paper does not aim to offer a direct analysis of the problems of managing sport. It proposes to identify the cultural or ideological values which serve as references in the organization and administration of various forms of sport. Because sport is not a homogeneous social fact, decision-makers' behaviour is influenced by various complex references at the conscious and unconscious level.

We therefore propose to give an indirect analysis of sports management, given that the sport supply is not a simple response to the demands of those taking part but is a component of the actual process of sport's evolution in practice. In this sociopolitical analysis, the actors have a privileged role to play (Crozier and Friedberg, 1977). We therefore put forward the idea that those involved in sports organizations are the bearers of values which serve as references to define their objectives and strategies. These in turn form the *structure for practical approaches* which sometimes make for complementarity and, fairly often, give rise to competition.

In this way, the values inherent in voluntary help and public service have in many cases created national systems which promote the Olympic model of sport, by virtue of a convergence of interests between those in positions of responsibility in sport and political leaders. However, to offset these reference values which have permitted the development of high-performance sport, other values have become apparent and these are leading to new practical approaches. A number of standard models appear to be emerging and an analysis of these may provide a starting point for understanding the particular interests of sports management and may demonstrate the consequences of this in terms of the sport supply.

Performance and associative strategy

National or international clubs and unions develop the values of *physical effort* and *sports performance*. During the first half of the twentieth century, these values were imposed as the primary points of reference. Athletes took charge of their own affairs, motivated by international bodies such as the International Olympic Committee and the International Sports Federations.

The leaders created an environment for independent action by using an associative framework for organizing sport. In this context, the International Olympic Committee plays a vital, unifying role. As defender of the humanist philosophy of sport and the internationalization of high-performance sport, it represents the associative and volunteer sports management model. This model is based on a symbolic superstructure, namely the Olympic ethic.

The primary objective of leaders is to develop championships around universal conditions of competition: identical rules for everyone, standardization of behaviour in sport, and enhancement of the technical component in sport. These shared objectives encourage leaders and athletes to develop an organizational approach based on privileged relationships *within federations*. The system is one based on representativeness and delegation of power as a response to the development of social values: belief in "scientific" progress (preference given to competition), universality of sporting behaviour (the same sport is offered to everyone), and social interaction (political and religious neutrality). However, association-based sport has progressively moved on from the immediate community, in which individuals group together on the basis of the shared desire to develop the same objectives within a local association, towards the mediate community. In effect, as regulations develop, the community has become more prescriptive in that it requires support for a project which has been created or is being created outside the local group. National and international directives impose on everyone a particular sports model to be developed and local leaders refer primarily to the requirements of a hierarchical organization.

Standardization of the result is becoming the basic operational element (Mintzberg, 1982), with the development of a vertical communication system within the federal system. Management of this type of organization is based on the principle of participation but, as the decision-making becomes more remote, participation is giving way to support for a project sustained by the symbolic profit idea (titles, records, sporting heroes, etc.). This "equal opportunity for self-improvement" project has produced a sports model which, relative to the Olympic ethic, has, in social representations, been transformed into firstly a social ethic and secondly an educational ethic.

High-performance sport may therefore be regarded as having a socializing function and thus as having to be based on a single model. Any major transformation would destroy the creative "philosophy" of the system. It is necessary to preserve the almost mystical "identity" reference for the universal sports fraternity (seen in its more refined version in the Olympic movement), which is promoted in speeches and passes over in silence the political and financial dimensions of high-performance sport.

This first model, which could be called "ideological" since it corresponds to the plan to develop only high-performance sport on a world level, is that of private bodies, i.e. the federations. Their strategy is to become increasingly independent of the public authorities.

Nationalism and public strategy

In most countries, the authorities had little interest in sport prior to 1950, only financial aid being provided for international events, with major towns and cities constructing the facilities. Since then, sports-development policies have been put in place by governments because sport has become of international interest through the spirit of competition which has grown up between different countries.

A form of sports-based nationalism gives rise to the adoption of important measures: national regulation of sports management, construction of sports facilities, development of subsidies to federations and, often, provision of the services of government officials to assist these federations. The aim of all these measures is to enhance national sporting representation. If the prevailing concept of the State is that of the liberal state, its powers being limited to the control of general interests (national defence, security, economic competition, etc.), sport remains in the private sector but often has to conclude agreements on its objectives with governments in order to obtain public funds. If the prevailing concept of the State is that of the welfare state, implying the presence of the authorities in all spheres of economic and social life, sport is generally part of the public sphere. It is certainly possible to distinguish a liberal model, a State model and a joint model on the basis of the presence of the authorities in national sports administration but, in all cases, the principal objective is the setting-up of effective procedures for training champions to represent individual countries in international events. This objective leads to a public-service culture developed by sports executives who have internalized the idea of representation of a State that is at once protective and responsible.

These executives are creating a sports education system in which their role as experts (administrators, trainers, organizers) gives them considerable power, bringing them into competition with traditional leaders in sport. Their points of reference are different because the primary references for the experts are the values of apprenticeship, technical efficiency and sporting knowledge to be passed on.

A convergence of interests can, however, be perceived since, in both cases (administration of sport by the federation system and administration by the authorities), the fundamental ideologies or values all still promote classification in standardized tests and the enhancement of personal performance. In many developing countries, this explains why the sport supply is organized by national sports and political leaders on the basis of the high-performance sports model only.

However, this type of sports management which is both public and private and is driven by the links between international and national bodies such as the National Olympic Committees and the International Olympic Committee, or the International Federations and the National Federations, offers a partial sports service comparable to that of a transport or communications company which offers only partial services, e.g. fixed duration of communications or sole transport destination. This priority given to the results obtained by national champions has, at the close of the 20th century, been undermined by world political developments. For example, the disappearance of the German Democratic Republic demonstrated that the priority given to high-performance sport made it possible to win international titles but was not necessarily proof of social, political and economic development. Reference only to national values is no longer possible, the more so since the development of other points of reference is creating other practical approaches.

Managerial strategy and image

As a system of mass communications, the media play a major role in the way sport is actually perceived. In the case of television, it is no longer only the technical structure of high-performance sport (regulations, technology, movement, etc.) which is involved, but its image (symbol, significance, passion, etc.). The "show" aspect is, to some extent, pushing the technical aspect on to the sidelines and a new reality is coming into existence: the athletes are performers in a show.

Each sporting event therefore takes place against a background of media and financial rivalries and each one has to define its individual strategies to retain media support and sponsorship. This management approach forces leaders to learn to take on management of a market and to work within the economic and administrative constraints of commercial enterprises. In point of fact, commercial activity, which led to a separation between production and the distribution of goods and services, is a very recent phenomenon in many countries in the case of sport.

Producing the show is still primarily the responsibility of the athletes and high-performance sports experts, whereas publicizing it is a task for the organizers and the media. By enhancing the show element, sport ceases to belong solely to the people directly involved; it belongs also to the advertisers and spectators. Consequently, the traditional administrators in sport (sports leaders, public authorities) have to share the sport product with new players who are becoming involved in producing the show, namely television channels, marketing agencies and sponsors.

In the beginning, assistance from the media and sponsors promoted the development of the federation-based sports leaders' power by providing them with financial income; however, sponsors have demanded official contracts specifying the rights and obligations of each party: finance from the sponsor in return for the right to use the champion's name; financial gain for the athletes in return for promoting the product. A "symbol versus profit" exchange system has thus been set up, linking champions, clubs or federations with the impresarios who organize travel, manage tax matters and are becoming progressively more influential than the federation leaders. When the amounts of money provided are considerable, business chiefs incorporate management of sport as a show into their financial considerations or set up private companies to organize sports events directly.

The managerial approach, which makes it possible to meet sport's economic objectives, has therefore become paramount in many sectors. It makes reference to values other than the traditional values of high-performance sport and the interests of the sponsors, the media and managers reinforce the effects of competition between sports, a phenomenon which was virtually non-existent before the development of television sportscasts. Given this situation, federation rules are slowly giving way to labour law, on the one hand, and to economic rules on the other hand, in the increasingly professional world in which sport is a show. The main performers are the commercial organizers, the champions themselves and, sometimes, associations which have been able to acquire business skills, as is the case of the International Olympic Committee.

Individualism and commercial strategy

Given that physical excellence is still a point of reference, other values or ideologies have grown up in connection with the body: pleasure, aesthetic appearance, effectiveness of movement, contact with Nature, etc. Moreover, the satisfaction of individual needs (leisure time, health, family, profession) is, in industrialized countries, tending to replace community needs which favour collective enterprises (political parties, trades unions, the church, national events).

People are turning towards an adapted sport supply which does not involve participation in the associative life of clubs and federations. The requirements are becoming those of the user. Sports facilities and costs are subjected to competition, leading to the development of a commercial system for the sport supply. The market model and local points of reference are partly in conflict with the model of sports organization based on promotion of national interests. Commercial interests favour diversity of sports models. Managers' strategies are becoming differentiated.

An analysis of the specific case of French society reveals at least three types of organization. The first type makes no reference to profit in economic terms and encompasses communal, public authorities and associations offering services which are adapted to the local market. The practical approach is bound by the principles of public management, giving a service below its cost price. The objectives are primarily those of a policy to promote local identity for internal usage (citizen satisfaction) and, secondly, for external usage (fame of the local community). The second type of organization is constituted by local companies offering a commercial service based on symbolic references. The proprietors attempt to make their businesses viable while satisfying their passion for a particular sport. Some of them favour rationalized strategies with reference to economic profitability, while others favour rationalized strategies with reference to symbolic values. The third type of organization is that of commercial enterprises offering multiple, complementary services in return for payment for the right to use them. Ski resorts, marinas, gyms and outdoor activity centres thus take charge of their customer and supply him with all the expected, and paid-for, services. In this case, the economic approach is paramount and the principles of commercial business are applied.

Those involved in the sport supply no longer refer to the values of federation sport. The objective is not to provide a standardized framework to enable athletes to compete against one another with a view to victory. The very notion of competition is giving way to another type of social interaction, namely acceptance of the difference between the various levels and forms of sport. The organizers have to apply a form of management based constant adaptation to demand without relying on rules of competition which are no longer relevant in this case. (See table).

Conclusion

The above analysis reveals the multiple nature of cultural, social, economic or political values which serve as conscious or unconscious points of reference in the choice of sports objectives. Sport is not a homogeneous phenomenon and management of the sport supply requires different strategies leading to conflicting modes of operation.

The ethical references of leaders and the nationalist references of governments have given rise to an international sports model. On the one hand, sport is regarded as independent and governed by particular rules, which explains the existence of private bodies (clubs, federations, the Olympic Committee). On the other hand, high-performance sport is regarded in political terms, which explains the indirect aid or direct intervention on the part of governments. These two points of reference combine to promote a national model of sports management whose perceived objective is to promote high performance.

Now, however, cultural developments, particularly in industrialized countries, have created sufficient diversity to modify the former values of universal community and technical progress. On the one hand, taking into account only the associative model (federations, clubs), sports organizations are no longer adapted to recent developments of sport as a show. A private-management approach has gradually been set up to manage access to the elite (training centres) and professionalism (champions' contracts, media and economic competition). On the other hand, a new sensitivity in sport, based on a restricted form of community identity (informal groups, families) is developing private needs. Importance is attached to active involvement in sport, but such involvement is no longer based on an associative investment. Involvement in sport is no longer regarded as support for codified forms, but refers to individual values.

Therefore, alongside an international model which is controlled jointly by the International Olympic Committee, the International and National Federations, governments, the media, sponsors and other professional organizers, there exist local supplies which respond to the objectives of another sports model.

The objectives of those involved in the sport supply are diverse: high performance, leisure, health, putting on a show, education. The management strategies of the sport supply have to be structured around symbolic and economic interests, with reference to diversified values. However, although apparently in disarray, the initiatives of all those concerned must, nevertheless, take account of competition and role-sharing within the same area of action. It is impossible, therefore, to envisage a single model for sports management, given that sport does not possess a single and exclusive set of cultural, social, political and economic points of reference.

References

Amar, M.- *Nés pour courir. Sport, Pouvoirs et Rebellions 1944-1958*. Grenoble. P.U.G., 1987.

Andreff, W.- *Economie politique du sport*, Paris. Dalloz, 1989.

Bonnes, R.- Le pouvoir sportif: les logiques d'évolution de 1940 à 1986. *Sport et Changement social*. Bordeaux. Société française de sociologie du sport - Maison des Sciences de l'Homme d'Aquitaine, 1987.

Bourg, J.F.- Sport et argent: le football. *Pouvoirs* no 61. Paris. P.U.F., 1992.

Chappelet, J.L.- *Le système olympique*. Grenoble. P.U.G., 1991.

Chifflet, P. & Gouda, S.- Sport et Politique nationale au Bénin de 1975 à 1990. *STAPS*, 1992, no 28, vol. 13, pp. 71-81.

Chifflet, P.- Associations de sportifs ou entreprises du sport, in *Sport et Management* (texts collated by A. Loret). Paris. Dunod, 1993.

Chifflet, P. & Raspaud M.- *Politique sportive intercommunale. Les équipements au sein de l'agglomération grenobloise*. Rapport d'un contrat. E.R.O.S., Université Joseph-Fourier. Grenoble, 1993, 35 pages.

Chifflet, P.- The Sport Supply in France. From Centralization to Segmentation. *Sociology of sport Journal*, 1995. Human Kinetics Publishers, Inc. Champaign.

Clément, J.P.; Defrance, J.; Pociello, C.- *Sport et pouvoirs au XXe siècle*. Grenoble. P.U.G., 1994.

Crozier, M. & Friedberg, E.- *L'acteur et le système*. Paris. Le Seuil, 1977.

Friedberg, E.- *Le Pouvoir et la règle*. Paris. Le Seuil, 1993.

Garrigues, P.- *Evolution de la pratique sportive des Français de 1967 à 1984*. Paris, 1988. Collection INSEE no 595.

Harvey, J. & Cantelon, H. (ed).- *Sport et pouvoir, Les enjeux sociaux au Canada*, 1988. Ottawa University Press.

Jamet, M.- *Le sport dans la société*. Paris, 1991, L'Harmattan (Collection "Logiques sociales").

Loret, A.- *Génération glisse*. Paris, 1995, Editions Autrement (Collection "Mutations").

Loret, A (Ed.).- *Sport et management*. Paris, 1993, Dunod.

Mintzberg, H.- *Structure et dynamique des organisations*. Paris. Ed. d'Organisation, 1982.

Paillou, N.- *Les trois enjeux du sport français*. Paris. Dalloz, 1986.

Ramanantsoa B & Thiery-Baslé C.- *Organisations et Fédérations sportives. Sociologie et Management*. Paris. P.U.F., 1989.

Modelling practical approaches to the sport supply

References (values)	Objectives	Strategies	Practical approach (key elements)	Institutional players (preferred)
Personal effort and performance Cultural symbolism (Olympic-sport)	Standardization Universalization	International competitions Emphasis on technique	Associative approach and volunteerism Vertical communication system and independence	International Olympic Committee Federations - clubs Leaders
National identity Community (National-sport)	Sports promotion Nationalism	Subsidies/nationalization National management	Public-service approach Public/private relationship Apprenticeship and training	Political leaders Public authorities Experts in sports training
Image and fame Economics (Economic-sport)	Profitability Profits	Emphasis on the show element Symbol/profit exchange	Managerial approach Professionalism	Commercial organizers Television channels Businessmen and sponsors
Health, leisure time, relaxation Efficiency of the body Aesthetic appearance of the body (Ego-sport)	Diversification of the supply	Commercial supply Local public supply Marketing	Local-action approach Horizontal communication system	Commercial enterprises Local associations Local public services

Towards Sydney 2000: precipitating sport management planning in Australia

David Shilbury
Deakin University,
Melbourne, Australia

Introduction

Australia will awake to the new millennium with the challenge of organizing the Games of the XXVII Olympiad. Significantly, this will also present an opportunity to reflect on the progress sport has made during the 20th century. For Australia, it will obviously highlight the transition from amateur to professional participation in many sports, as well as the transition from amateur administration to professional management of sporting organizations. This transition has also forced upon many sports a change in culture and a need to adopt traditional principles of management to chart the course of a sport's future. What has occurred in Australia is similar to many other countries. This paper will examine the impact Sydney 2000 will have on Australian sporting organizations. It will focus on the degree to which sporting organizations will have to further professionalize their management systems to cope with the demands of the 21st Century. It is posited in this paper that Australia's hosting of the Games of the XXVII Olympiad will further precipitate the implementation of planning and management systems by sporting organizations. This, in turn, will continue to shape the developing sport management profession.

Planning in Sport

The history of strategic planning and sport in Australia is relatively short. It has only been during the last decade that sporting organizations have begun to plan. The need to plan was precipitated by government through the Australian Sports Commission (ASC). During the mid-1980s, the ASC began to realize that a great deal of money allocated to sporting organizations was wasted. Ultimately, this led to the ASC requiring detailed development plans that mapped out the intended direction of a sport. As most sports relied on government funding to sustain their activities, most were prepared to pay "lip service" to this request.

Sporting organizations differ from traditional businesses in that they are not concerned with measures such as return-on-investment, or net profit levels and similar financial measures. Sporting organizations are interested in factors like participation, membership levels, success at national and international competitions, provision of facilities and, the most basic measure of all, remaining viable. Prior to the need to prepare development plans, even these measures were rarely considered. A great deal has changed in the organization and delivery of sport in Australia since 1972. In 1972, the federal government and a number of state governments began to recognize that sport had become stagnant. The long list of world class athletes was beginning to evaporate, and by 1976 the reality of this stagnation became clear. Australia won only one medal at the Montreal Olympics. This prompted the government of the day to work towards the formation of the Australian Institute of Sport in 1981, and the Australian Sports Commission in 1984.

Federal funding to sporting organizations in 1972/73 was $600,000[1]. By 1975 this had risen to $7.4 million, and more recently (1994/95) a total of $93 million was provided to sport through the National Sporting Organizations. In addition, funding is provided by the Australian government to support the facility infrastructure being developed for the Sydney 2000 Olympic Games. One significant change in terms of human resources has also occurred during this time. Australia's time-honoured system of amateur and honorary administration has slowly been replaced by full-time paid managers. This transition has, at times, been slow and painful as respective power bases have been protected and fought for, right across the country in virtually every sport. In 1995, it is possible to conclude that the trend towards full time paid staff and the professionalization of sport management is irreversible. It is against this background that this paper explores the transition in relation to the traditional business function of strategic planning. The application of strategic planning is considered to provide a guide as to the extent to which sport has truly embarked on professionalization.

Sport Employment in Australia

Sport employment in Australia has risen from near-zero in the late 1960s to an estimated 54,000 positions in 1994. The 1994 Labour Force Survey confirms that 111,628 people are currently employed in the recreation industry. Sport employment constitutes 48 percent of recreation employment. The findings of the 1994 Labour Force study are supported by a 1992 Department of Arts, Sport, Environment and Territories study showing that approximately 66,000 people currently occupy full time positions in sport throughout Australia. The Australian Bureau of Statistics study of Involvement in Sport (1993) showed that 213,000 persons received some payment for their work in sport. This figure includes the multitude of part time jobs required in the organization and delivery of sport. What is not stated is the respective qualifications and backgrounds of the personnel employed in sport. Until recently there were few sport management programmes to educate potential employees in this area. Of more significance, it has only been in the last five years that a recognized need for education via the universities has been seen as essential. Given the evolution of personnel to sport management, it is not surprising to find that many traditional areas of management (such as strategic planning) have not been applied in the sports context. As this paper will show, this is slowly changing.

Funding, Accountability and Planning

By 1984/85, federal sports funding had increased to $38.9 million. It became apparent that the use of this money by sports was not entirely efficient. If it were not, as most suspected, there was no way of determining this as few control systems were in place to ensure the money was well spent. The problem was exacerbated by the general inexperience of sport administrators to effectively plan for their sports future and the subsequent use of the money. During this time, this process was referred to as "Developmental Planning", and in essence, displayed little

---

[1] All amounts in Australian dollars

resemblance to the concept of strategic planning. Sports simply responded to the available funding categories and devised their development plans to suit these criteria. As a consequence, little long-term planning was in reality undertaken.

The irony of this situation was highlighted in 1986/87 when the Australian Sports Commission prepared their first ever strategic plan. The general manager at the time noted:

"This plan is a significant document in the history of sports development in Australia. For the first time, a Federal Government instrumentality specifically responsible for sports development has been obliged, by its enabling legislation, to define a long-term plan as a framework for its activities and decisions. The plan serves a number of purposes. As a process, it provides an opportunity to review long-term directions and priorities in sports development at the national level. As a product, it provides the whole community, and especially the community of sport, with a clear statement of intent about the future ASC policies and programmes." (ASC Strategic Plan, 1986/87 - 1988/89, p. vii)

This phase of developmental planning is closely aligned to the early days of planning in general. For example, strategy formation became a popular topic in the 1950s and 1960s in the USA. This early form of strategy formulation, known as 'long-range' planning, was used to reduce the gap that often existed between anticipated and achieved objectives. This is exactly the level of thinking applied to sport in Australia during the early to mid 1980s. By the 1980s, however, the environment had become far more turbulent and competitive. The events confronted by the Australian Cricket Board in 1977 (the defection of cricketers to a media mogul, in a effort to secure suitable levels of player payments), and the trend towards professionalization exemplify this paradox. It also highlights how the development planning concept came into existence. It was predicated on the notion that any forward thinking would be good for sport.

The issue of funding and accountability was again the centre of public attention in 1989 when the Parliament of Australia's House of Representatives Standing Committee on Public Affairs conducted an inquiry into sports funding and administration. In what was seen as a largely political exercise, sports funding was to increase dramatically as a result of this inquiry. Sport had been able to demonstrate through this process its need for further support. The "Next Step" programme was born out of the two reports ("Going for Gold" and "Can Sport be Bought") to emerge from this inquiry. The government provided $230 million over four years to implement the "Next Step" programme. This was a significant development in sports policy in Australia. In the true meaning of long-term planning, sports were able to plan for up to four years, thus allowing the government to claim it was encouraging sporting bodies to adopt a strategic, forward planning approach.

The success of this programme was evident at the Barcelona Olympic Games where Australia won 27 medals. Although this is clearly not the only means by which success is measured, politically it was enough for the government to commit to a further four-year plan known as 'Maintaining the Momentum', covering the period 1992 to 1996. A total of $293 million was allocated to this four year period. As a consequence of Sydney winning the right to host the 2000 Olympic Games, a further $150 million will be injected into the sports economy between 1995 and 2000. Once again, the importance and significance of strategic planning by sporting organizations is heightened.

The Olympic athlete programme - its impact on planning

"The Olympic Athlete Programme (OAP) is the name given to the ASC's six-year elite development programme aimed at securing 60 medals at the 2000 Olympics and a best-ever result at the Paralympics" (Baker-Finch, 1995, p. 13). As part of the OAP, 900 athletes nominated by all Olympic sports will receive between $2,000 and $10,000 of direct support in each year leading up to Sydney 2000. A total of 14 new national head coaches have been appointed and a series of high performance managers appointed to a range of Olympic sports for the purpose of managing the programmes created by the extra funds. The Australian Institute of Sport and various State-based institutes have also benefited from the extra funding for the OAP.

The Victorian Institute of Sport (VIS), for example, expanded its operations to cater for the injection of funds. The Victorian government recently announced further funding assistance of $2.68 million over five years for the Victorian Institute of Sport. This is in addition to OAP money provided by the federal government. As a consequence of the injection of funds from a number of sources, the VIS, like most sporting organizations, found that their level of business planning significantly increased. The VIS, for example, are currently preparing their business plan cognizant of the impact of the lead-up to Sydney 2000.

An example of a sport having to reassess and re-evaluate its operations is shooting. As a consequence, OAP funding to shooting's four Olympic disciplines (clay target, pistol, rifle and moving target) more than tripled. In 1993/94 shooting received $327,000 from the ASC, and in 1994/95 this increased to $875,000. The infusion of these funds provides a distinct strategic challenge for shooting. Shooting is a relatively low profile sport in Australia with reasonably high registrations (e.g., 25,000 shooters nationally). Strategically, the challenge is to distribute funds to each discipline which is coordinated separately. Forty-five medals are on offer (third highest medal count available at the Games) in 15 different shooting events so, in terms of successfully utilizing this OAP funding, shooting's success at the Games also has strategic significance from a national perspective. Shooting in Australia faces additional challenges to develop its talent base to a level where a steady supply of shooters of international standard are produced. The sport will need to employ specialist full time coaches, improve training and competition facilities, overcome a negative image of the sport and examine ways to reduce the cost of expensive ammunition. In essence, this is a perfect example of a sport that will emerge from the Sydney Olympiad with an infrastructure in place that was previously non-existent. A window of opportunity has presented itself requiring shooting to implement carefully selected strategies through the strategic planning process to move into the 21st Century.

Australian hockey, on the other hand, demonstrates the pressures of maintaining success in a high-profile sport. As opposed to shooting, hockey has a solid infrastructure and a reputation for success that has seen it maintain a top three ranking in both men's and women's competition. Sustaining this level of performance brings with it a different set of pressures. Hockey receives more federal funding than any other team sport. Combined federal funds to men's and women's hockey are in excess of $2 million.

The strategic challenges for hockey are different. Although hockey is considered a successful sport, it is not considered a high-profile sport in Australia outside the Olympic Games. Sport managers have therefore examined ways in which the profile of this sport could be improved. One of the initiatives was the creation of the men's national hockey league which commenced in 1991. The major objectives of the League are to support the Australian team programme and to provide a promotable product which will increase the profile of the game. The League has met with mixed success in its desire to achieve two competing objectives: the ability to attract public attention and the need to provide intense competition in preparing players for international competition. Attracting public attention and interest has meant altering playing conditions to make the game more appealing. This has, in part, been at the expense of players competing under internationally-accepted playing conditions. It is believed that this may have had some effect on the performance of the men's hockey team at the Barcelona Olympics.

OAP funding may now allow for the two conflicting objectives to be achieved via differing mechanisms. OAP funding will allow for intensive training centres to be coordinated with the Australian Institute of Sport programme, thereby increasing competition and training outlets without dismantling the national hockey league. Strategically, this balance is important in managing the resources available to Australian hockey. Success, and maintaining success brings with it a new range of pressures.

Summary

The examples cited, comparing two sports of contrasting profiles and levels of success, and the impact on the institutes of sport of the OAP, clearly illustrate the efficacy of the Olympic Games returning to Australia. Typically, interest is focused on the participating athletes, however, the behind-the-scenes interest in terms of Australian sport will be sport's ability to capitalize on the opportunity to further develop an infrastructure. This includes the adoption of traditional management practices.

Central to this agenda is strategic planning. The process of strategic planning in the first instance is of paramount importance in forcing various groups and splinter groups within sporting associations to consider how to organize their activities in light of a changing environment. This in itself will take some time. Shooting is the perfect example. This sport must integrate and coordinate its activities to a level not seen before. Up until the announcement of Sydney's successful bid, it is unlikely that those responsible for the sport had given this issue much thought. Many other Olympic sports in which Australia has been successful will confront the same challenges (e.g., cycling, volleyball, archery and waterpolo). The second key issue to emerge from increasingly adopting planning systems is to put in place the right strategies. In relation to strategic planning, this remains the greatest unknown - what are the right strategies, and what are the right pattern of actions respective sports need to take to ensure long-term success?

It is clear, 44 years after the Games of the XVI Olympiad in Melbourne, that Australia now has in place an infrastructure for sport that is sufficiently mature to capitalize on the opportunity afforded via the staging of the Olympic Games in Sydney. The implications for sport management in Australia are significant. It will be some time before Australia again has the opportunity to host the Games; infrastructure development must occur now, and as a consequence, the profession of sport management will continue to evolve as will the professionals that currently work in this industry and those that wish to work in it in the future. Strategic planning therefore, is an important business tool in facilitating this process. It is also an important measure of the extent to which sport management is conducted in a business-like manner.

References

Australian Bureau of Statistics.- *Involvement in Australian sport*, ABS (Cat No. 62850)., Commonwealth of Australia, 1993.

Australian Bureau of Statistics.- *The labour force in Australia*, November 1994. (Cat No. 6203.0), Commonwealth of Australia.

Australian Sports Commission.- *Strategic plan 1986/87 - 1988/89*, Australian Government Publishing Service, Canberra, 1986.

Baker-Finch, S.- Towards 2000. The Olympic Athlete Programme in detail, *Sport Report*, 1995, 15 (1), pp. 13-15.

Collins, M.- Shooting aims for Olympic success, *Sport Report*, 1995, 15(3), pp. 18-19.

Commonwealth of Australia.- *Going for gold: The first report on an inquiry into sports funding and administration*, Australian Government Printing Service, Canberra, 1989.

Commonwealth of Australia.- *Can sport be bought: The second report on An inquiry into sports funding and administration*. Australian Government Printing Service, Canberra, 1990.

Prosser, G.- *Economic and employment characteristics of the Australian sport, fitness and recreation industries*, Technical Report No. 6, Prepared for the Commonwealth Department of the Arts, Sport, the Environment and Territories. Australian Government Publishing Service, Canberra, 1992.

Understanding management in sport: concepts, skills, knowledge

Alain Loret
Centre d'Etudes et de Management de l'Innovation Sportive,
Université de Caen,
France

Nowadays, just like the administration and management of a business undertaking, the management of a *sports organization*[1] has to become a logical, consistent process of decisions and actions.

As the twentieth century nears its end, we have in fact come a long way from the extremely simplified forms of management which governed the organization and development of sport in the 1960s. The reason for this trend is easy to understand: sport has become a very important sector of the economy, within which all decisions have consequences that can increasingly be quantified in financial terms. Under these conditions, increasing the efficiency of the ways in which sports structures are administered has become an absolute necessity.

There are two corollaries to this process whereby management of sports organizations has moved towards greater efficiency.

- The first is the obligation imposed upon us to produce a know-how which is specific to a field that, although it falls within the general framework of management sciences, cannot strictly be compared to the business world. Through its history, its organizational forms and its ethical code, sport has a form of management which is all its own. It would be inaccurate to think that the theories that can be applied to a multinational firm, for example, could be transposed to an international sports federation without serious consequences.

- The second corollary derives directly from the first: this specific know-how has to be passed on in order to optimize the action taken by sports management.

Sports management in the coming years will thus be subject to two obligations: first, producing knowledge that is appropriate to the special needs of the sports organizations; and secondly, training effective and efficient management personnel.

In this article, I would like to try to define the theoretical and practical fields within which the training of these future "sports managers" will have to take place. In marking out these areas, I shall divide them into three parts:

---

[1] By "sports organizations" we mean all the structures which operate or work within the institutional and economic field that is sport today: amateur sports associations, professional clubs, committees, national and international federations, municipal and regional sports departments, etc.

1) What are the theoretical *concepts* on which sports management must be based?

2) What are the *skills* which the executives who run sport will need to possess?

3) What types of *knowledge* are we going to have to produce to enable sports managers to bring greater purpose and cohesion to their actions?

The space available will not, unfortunately, enable me to cover the subject in detail. Nevertheless, I shall try to be sufficiently clear and comprehensive to enable the reader to understand the importance which attaches to the production of knowledge today, and the fundamental nature of the issues involved in the training of future sports executives.

The concepts

A. Definition of "sport management"

Managing a sports organization implies implementing four types of decision and action.

- First, it is necessary to *identify the objectives* to be achieved. The search for these objectives will depend, for example, on the history of the organization, its traditional tasks, its identity and how it is financed. It will also depend - increasingly! - on the changes in its environment: new technologies, new legal constraints, new needs among the "consumers" of sports products and services, new techniques, media pressure, sponsors' requirements.

- The next necessity is to be able to distinguish, among all the possible objectives, *those which must be achieved as a priority or necessity.* Once they are identified, these objectives need to be defined as specifically as possible. In particular, they need to be quantified, and periods need to be set for their achievement.

- Once the priority objectives have been determined, it is necessary *to equip oneself with the means* of achieving them, by mobilizing three categories of resources: human, financial and material. One particular factor links these three categories: they are *resources in short supply*. This is why a manager's task is so difficult.

- Finally, the last phase is *monitoring* the results obtained. The question we have to be able to answer is this: was the objective achieved on satisfactory quantitative and qualitative bases and within the periods allowed?

The identification of these various elements enables us to give a precise definition of the notion of "sports management".

The management of a sports organization is a consistent process of decisions and actions based on the ability to determine specific objectives, the capacity to mobilize the necessary means for achieving them, and the aptitude for monitoring the results obtained.

In the more specific context of the Sports Association Movement, this amounts to saying that "managing association sport" comprises *efficiently organizing the human, material and financial resources latent in the "sports environment" to convert them into practical actions beneficial to the development of sports practice.*

B. Why is it necessary to produce specific knowledge?

Every supervisor in sport has, of course, long had a managerial role. After all, he takes action, makes decisions, initiates events and mobilizes resources: in short, he manages in the customary sense of the term.

Hitherto, this sports management has grown up in a particularly stable environment. In the 1960s, it was still possible to say what sport would be like in ten years' time. Technical and technological changes were slow. Amateurism was the order of the day: there was little economic pressure. Legal constraints were not excessively restrictive. The social and demographic profile of sports practitioners and their needs were clearly identified.

Today, all these certainties have been swept away.[2] Sports Organizations exist within a rapidly changing environment. Yesterday's objectives have increasingly little to do with today's, which in turn will probably not be tomorrow's. Under these conditions, sports administrators are confronted by a situation which presents a harsh challenge to the know-how, knowledge and skills they built up during the years of stability.

Now, the prime function of management is to be effective. For a sports administrator, being effective means efficiently channelling the efforts of one's organization to achieve the objectives it has set itself. Since the aims are changing, as is happening today in response to greater and greater economic pressure, the criteria of effectiveness are changing too.

As we can see, we are indeed confronted by the need to redefine many components of sports management procedures. We have no choice, therefore, but to produce new knowledge in order to improve the performance of the executives who will run the sports organizations of the twenty-first century.

C. Understanding management

We are going to define various elements which will enable us to understand both the precise significance of the word "management" and its limitations.

a. The usefulness of management

Management is useful because it makes it possible *to improve the performance* of a sports organization. This improvement is the result of a greater capacity to define the organization's objectives and mobilize its resources.

b. The manager's work

Management is certainly work. It is an activity based on a *logical process of decisions and actions*. The manager is the man who puts this activity into practice: he plans, organizes, initiates and monitors the performance of the tasks undertaken by his colleagues.

c. The role of the manager

Management means carrying out a series of operations in a predetermined and consistent order. The successful manager is thus *a cross between a doer and an organizer*.

---

[2] Alain Loret, *"Génération glisse - dans l'eau, l'air, la neige ... la révolution du sport des années fun"*. [A generation sliding in water, air and snow - the sports revolution of the fun years], Editions Autrement, April 1995. This book analyses changes in contemporary sport and outlines scenarios which are insights into the future of sport. Cf. also *"Sport et management, de l'éthique à la pratique"*, [Sports and management, from ethics to practice], ed. Alain Loret, Paris, Editions EPS, 2nd edition 1995.

d. The difficulty of management

The manager has to achieve his organization's objectives through the efforts of his colleagues. He must therefore be capable of *delegation* and *selecting* competent personnel who will have to carry out the necessary tasks.

e. The reality of management

The act of management is very unusual in that it is, strictly speaking, *invisible*. A manager does not work with tangible realities: he does not process material like a workman, nor does he organize the movement of material like a logistics expert, nor does he produce figures like an accountant. In point of fact, the "substantive" nature of his work only becomes apparent *in the results he produces*.

f. The computerization of management

A computer is not an organizer but an *organizing tool*. This means that the computerization of management is not an end but a means.

g. The personality of the manager

A manager can only work as part of a team. He therefore has to be a *leader*. Listening to and understanding other people (their needs and aspirations) have to be essential concerns for him.

D. The key concepts of management

As we have seen, managing a sports organization means optimizing the use of the available resources to achieve objectives which are perceived as priorities. These simple words conceal difficulties which can sometimes prove insurmountable. To avoid this extremity, the manager has to be capable of distinguishing the various phases and levels of his activities. We will now identify these phases and levels and transform them into key concepts. The objective is to try to understand the various categories of action taken by sports administrators.

1st key concept: identifying, understanding and solving problems

When one sees oneself as an effective manager, it is often the done thing to assert in peremptory tones that "there are no problems, there are only solutions". That may be true, but in order to find the right response to a problem it is still necessary to ask the right questions and formulate them clearly. But things are not always that simple.

For an organization, a problem is always a discrepancy - identified a posteriori - between an objective and a result. However, it should be clearly understood that these discrepancies - the problems, in other words - fuel the activities of managers. *A manager with no problems to solve would be of no use at all.*

To solve a problem it is first necessary to pose it - in other words, to identify its causes. The next step is to analyse the problem data in order to understand them. And the final step is to take the decisions necessary to bring into play new resources designed to reduce the discrepancy identified between the actual position and the objective which one has selected and failed to achieve.

2nd key concept - taking decisions

Taking a decision means reaching a conclusion at the outcome of a process of problem analysis in order *to take action*.

A manager is rarely confronted by a situation in which there are not several possible courses of action. The necessity, then, is to identify the various options accurately in order to choose that which best suits the situation in question. However, a decision is *never of the either-or type* (digital, in other words black and white). It is always of the *more or less* type (analog, in other words grey). In fact, a right decision is a rarity, and a manager will often look no further than finding the *least bad* decision.

3rd key concept: steering an accurate course

There is a famous adage attributable to Seneca: "The sailor who knows not where he is going never has a favourable wind." It seems an elementary matter to know the objective for which an organization's resources have been mobilized. However, this requires a clear and precise definition of the objective to be achieved. In the absence of this clarity and precision, the manager will have no chance of optimizing the use of the scarce resources (human, material and financial) he will mobilize to achieve the objective the organization has set itself.

4th key concept: planning

Planning means putting into practice a consistent plan of action within which one can mobilize the resources available to the organization. This planning is based on the ability to determine the tasks to be undertaken, the aptitude to arrange them in order of priority, the faculty of determining a maximum period within which to achieve them, and the opportunity to allocate to them people who have the necessary skills to undertake them.

Planning is a form of "future intelligence", in the sense that it has to make it possible to foresee difficulties by anticipation, in other words by asking such questions as "what would happen if such and such decisions or choices were made in the course of events?"

5th key concept: structuring the organization

Objectives are achieved by way of what is habitually called "optimization" of the use of the available resources. This in turn is achieved *by linking up* one's resources. For example, effective links will have to be created between individuals, enabling them to gain access to the information or knowledge produced by teams other than that to which they belong. From this standpoint, computerized communication (networking) of data is essential.

Whatever the chosen structure (hierarchy, matrix, network, etc.), it will have to foster collaboration between the players in the organization so as to improve that collaboration.

6th key concept: managing the human resources

Motivation, inspiration, galvanization ... all these words imply the same fundamental factor which determines the success or failure of a manager: *his ability to mobilize everyone's energy* in order to achieve objectives within the periods allowed.

Management of human resources goes through four levels of action:
- recruitment which is appropriate to needs;
- the delegation of tasks as a function of skills;
- recognition by the manager of each individual's aspirations (expectations or ambitions);
- the handling of conflicts.

7th key concept: monitoring results

In an organization, monitoring comprises assessing the differential which exists between the objective which was aimed at and the result achieved.

Two broad categories of monitoring activity can be distinguished: quantitative monitoring and qualitative monitoring. Monitoring procedures are given names like, for example, "management control", "audits" (financial, strategic, human resources, etc.) and use the concepts of "ratios" (of liquidity, activity, profitability, etc.).

As the final activity of the management process, monitoring makes it possible to verify that all the organization's functions and resources have in fact been mobilized in an optimum manner.

A. How to define the "competent sports manager"

We have seen previously that "management in sport" means efficiently organizing the resources of the club or federation to *transform* them into practical benefits which favour the development of the sports activity.

In this sentence, the important word in the context of the subject with which we are dealing is the verb "transform". From this aspect, management will be a sort of enhanced capacity to transform scarce resources with a view to obtaining the best possible results for the development of the sport in the town or country. The fact remains that the success of a manager is something very "relative", since it can only be measured in terms of the resources available to him. Consequently, the most efficient manager will be the one who proves capable of getting the maximum benefit out of those resources. Hence the concept of optimizing the use of the human, material and financial resources of the organization.

It can be said, then, that management is a permanent process of improving the utilization of the available resources with a view to a hoped-for result. Under these conditions, *the competent manager will be the one who proves capable of obtaining the best result possible in terms of development of his club or federation on the basis of the best possible exploitation of the necessarily limited resources available to him.*

B. The assessment of competence

As we have also seen, the competence of the manager is always measured in terms of the results of his actions. In very broad terms, it can be said that the results achieved must never be less than the objectives set. This does not alter the fact that the results of a management process in the field of sport must be evaluated on the basis of specific criteria.

We shall adopt three criteria.

- ***First criterion***: the competence of the manager results in the production of a profitable service.

Whether sport is regarded as a televized spectacle, an educational undertaking, an activity related to health or leisure, or a competitive event, it is always to be considered as a service. Sport clearly forms one of the activities of the "tertiary sector". The sports manager, then, is running an organization which produces a particular service intended for a television viewer, a school pupil, a health-conscious person or a competitor.

The first criterion for evaluating the activity of the sports organization, then, will be the number of persons who have aquired, consumed or participated in the service offered (audience rating, number of participants or licensees, etc.).

Under these conditions, the concept of *productivity* - measured in terms of indices of participation in the service produced by the organization - must be constantly in the manager's mind, since it will very often determine his success or failure. From this point of view, the result of the sports management process must be of a "value" (social or economic value) which exceeds the cost of its production. *"Getting value"* out of the equipment, grants and personnel made available by a local authority, for example, will thus be the primary concern of the chairman of a municipal club.

- ***Second criterion***: the competence of the manager provides *control over the production costs* of the service.

The providers of grants and sponsorship are paying increasing attention to the way in which the sums they grant to sports organizations are used. This attitude is the result of the economic crisis: the days when institutional and business sources allocated substantial sums to sport without any real control are long gone. The concept of the *"agreement on objectives"* is now regularly associated with the granting of the funds necessary for sports organizations to function.

Bearing in mind the current budgetary constraints, the production costs of sports services are increasingly becoming the *direct measure* of managers' competence. Hence, within the framework of a specific objective, compliance with the budgets allocated to the achievement of that objective can no longer be regarded as a secondary factor (as was long the case) by sports administrators. Control over costs has to become their creed.

- **Third criterion**: the competence of the manager results in the production of a *diversified and quality sports service*.

The *quality* of sports services is a very recent factor. Consequently, it is a factor that has not been fully mastered by the Sports Movement. The fact remains that it is an essential factor, in so far as the sports associations are increasingly in competition with economic bodies which, rightly, are extremely attentive to the quality of the service they offer.

In the future, we are probably going to be forced to define a standardization of sports services, which will take the form of a label. It might be termed the "quality sport label", for example, and, might define the level of quality which the services offered are supposed to achieve.

Moreover, there is no escaping the fact today that there has been a definite change in the way in which sports associations have to regard their members. Over the last twenty-five years, those members have moved from the status of *"users"* to that of *"customers"*.

A user has very little choice, because he is confronted by a single service offer (a monopoly, like the postal services or public transport, for example). This monopoly situation still applied to the supply of sports services in the 1970s.

The customer, by contrast, is in the position to choose the service he wants to buy. That, in fact, is what is happening today: a great many economically oriented organizations are in competition with the associations, especially in the field of "leisure sport".

It has to be accepted, therefore, that sport regarded as a *public service* - without distinguishing the "public", which could only be competition enthusiasts - has to change into a *service for the public* (men and women, young and old, competition enthusiasts or enthusiasts of "fun sports"). Sports managers therefore have *to diversify* the sports services they offer. In addition, they have to understand that the level of quality directly affects the *"performance"* of the service offered by the organizations they manage. Consequently, the quality of the service offered will largely determine the number of members, spectators or customers.

The modelling of the sports management process

Figure 1 reproduces in diagram form the logic which has to govern the decisions and actions of sports managers. It goes without saying that this model is a substantial simplification of reality. It will therefore have to be used with reference to all the factors dealt with in parts I and II of this article.

Figure 1

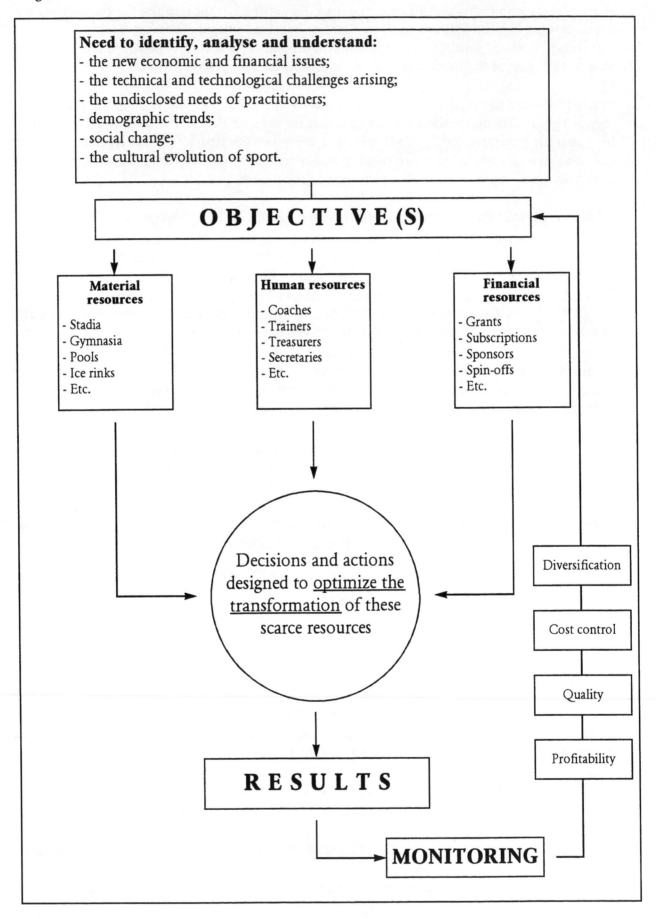

1. Sports management: a fundamental issue

As we have seen, the obligation to produce the necessary knowledge for managing sports organizations, immersed in a rapidly changing environment, goes hand in hand with the need to pass on that knowledge. The training of future sports managers will probably be one of the major challenges that the Sports Movement will have to face in future years.

It is also necessary to appreciate the fact that the *management of sports organizations* is a very recent university discipline. Consequently, it has not yet fully defined the framework of research and training which will enable it to find the right response to the legitimate demands of the Sports Movement. Over and above the management of association sport, it will also be necessary to consider the needs of economically oriented organizations (firms which manufacture and distribute sports equipment, producers of events, thematic televison and media, sponsors, advertising agencies, etc.). In fact, a very wide field of research and training is opening up. The capacity to mobilize the skills, resources and, perhaps most of all, goodwill which the Sports Movement will demonstrate in this enterprise will determine the degree of control over sports development which the international sports institutions achieve during the next thirty years.

Within the limits of this article, I want to try to outline the body of knowledge which the executives of sport - in the broadest sense of the term, i.e. amateur and professional sport - will have to master in future years.

I should stress the fact that the concept of *anticipation of training needs* must today be the prime concern of all those involved in the sports system: delegates of the sports movement, those with political responsibility, heads of businesses, practitioners, trainee managers and, of course, university lecturers and researchers. The contact between these various categories of individual, each with their special though different vision of the future of sport, is what will give birth to the conceptual framework within which future training courses will be incorporated. As this framework has yet to be devised, may I suggest that it has, at present, no internationally established intake structure[3] which would make it possible to construct it ...

2. What knowledge?

The strategy of producing knowledge in the field with which we are concerned must take account of one very special factor: management is a matter of disciplinary fragmentation. Far from being uniform, the knowledge needed for the administration of sports organizations lies within separate fields. For reasons of clarity, I have decided to consider six of those fields, my objective being not to lay any claim to being comprehensive but to open some avenues of approach as regards research and training. We are going to move through each of these six areas, endeavouring to illustrate in each case the specific nature of sports management. Although it will be too brief - and I apologize in advance for the simplifying nature of what I now have to say - this presentation of the fields of knowledge needed for mastery of the expansion of sports organizations will nevertheless be sufficient to show the width of the subject and clarify its content to some extent.

---

[3] The international character of such a "think-tank" structure would be essential because of the globalization of the sports phenomenon.

1a. Knowledge relating to the management of human resources

If we were to measure the assets of the Sports Movement, the only yardstick we could use would be the voluntary commitment of the men and women who have set it up over the course of the twentieth century. Human resources are the dominant force behind sports associations.

Managing these assets presupposes accurate knowledge of the motivations, aspirations and values which, to a large extent, determine the voluntary commitment to tasks relating to the development of sport. Accurate knowledge, because the objectives of each individual administrator are not necessarily identical with the objectives of the association or federation to which it belongs. This amounts to saying that the effectiveness of the president of a federation, for example, will be directly linked to his capacity to make individuals with different motivations and objectives *work together*.

It will thus be essential to have a knowledge of the various North American theories of teamwork motivation. The Z theory of William Ouchi, for example, forms part of a participative management model. According to this theory, participative management satisfies the sociological motivations relating to the voluntary membership and involvement of the individual in achieving the objectives which the organization has adopted.

The Z theory can be combined with the concept of Participative Management By Objectives (PMBO). This is a process of decisions and actions which makes it possible to determine for each official (a committee chairman, for example) sub-objectives which determine an appropriate number of specific functions together with deadlines for undertaking them and strict requirements in terms of performance level.

Human resources management is conditional upon the choice of a method of administration. It will therefore be necessary to know the various possibilities in this area. The choice of a *centralized functional structure*, a *decentralized divisional structure*, a *matric structure* or any other form of organizational structure will thus produce significant results.

1.b. Knowledge relating to the financial aspects

Optimizing the use of financial resources - which can be considered as being in particularly short supply! - of sports organizations is necessarily one of the priority concerns of executive personnel. It is commonly said that a manager cannot be happy in his work if his decisions constantly fall foul of funding problems. Yet this seems to be exactly what happens with many managers in sport ...

Under these conditions, full familarity with the balance sheet (assets and liabilities) in the context of the continuity of the action to be taken in order to achieve the organization's objectives is essential. Furthermore, achieving a reliable accounting result is a necessary condition for obtaining full value from sources of finance, especially grants, as we have seen. This result will, therefore, have to fit within the framework of constraints imposed by the general budget. It may also, in the case of management by PMBO, for example, be present in the form of an account showing the results for each function.

A knowledge of all the procedures allowing full familiarization with the financial constraints inherent in the management of sports organizations seems necessary in order to follow and, above all, predict their development.

1.c. Knowledge relating to the production of sports services

We have seen that sport forms part of the tertiary sector - the services sector. "Manufacturing" a sports service, such as for example a keep-fit gymnastics course for adults or football training for the young, is the highly specific "trade" of the sports associations. All the activities devised by the managers of these associations are designed to produce a quality service which is ideally adapted to the needs of those who take advantage of it.

Various criteria have to be taken into account in order to produce a quality sports service. Intrinsically, each of these criteria has to be at the highest level possible in terms of the resources available to the organization: the coach of the junior football team needs to be well trained, the pitch in good condition, and the players well equipped, for example.

But the intrinsic quality of each criterion is not enough. Quality service actually derives from the positive interaction - or synergy - between all the criteria. Now, in order to create this synergy, it is necessary to know the precise nature of the objective which it is desired to achieve. In the present case, considering a team of young footballers, that question can be asked. Is the objective sports success (case no. 1)? Is it physical education (case no. 2)? Is it the social integration of disadvantaged young people (case no. 3)? Is it just a matter of filling spare time (case no. 4)?

As we can see, there are at least four separate objectives: so there are at least four types of service whose "manufacture" will call for different skills. If we consider only the skills of the training personnel, each case will be different:

case no. 1 will need a coach;
case no. 2 will need a physical education teacher;
case no. 3 will need an educationalist;
case no. 4 will need an organizer.

Producing a quality sports service, then, requires a specific knowledge of the purpose of the organization in order to design a coherent and "transparent" product. Only the coherence and "transparency" of the service produced will make it possible to obtain, from the local authority for example, resources adequate to meet the objectives.

1.d. Knowledge relating to the computerizaton of sports organizations
The introduction of computer hardware into the machinery and functions of the organization must help the manager to work more efficiently. If we go no further than that, the service provided by applying computer technology to the specific needs of sports associations will be cost-effective. In all other cases, there is a danger of underestimating or overestimating the need for computerization.

The increasing pace of obsolescence of computer technology (hardware, software and networks) makes training in this field particularly difficult. From this standpoint, the necessary knowledge will have to be not so much technical or technological as capable of redefining the working procedures and "production" processes of a quality service (computerized management of tennis court reservations, for example). Over and above this, it will be necessary to provide information capable of improving decisions regarding the purchase of hardware which is strictly in line with what is needed.

1.e. Knowledge relating to the "strategic management" of sports organizations
If we consider the rapid pace of change in the environment of sports organizations, this (along with the next section-marketing and futurology) is probably the most important part of this chapter dealing with knowledge. Indeed, I would almost go so far as to say that the survival of many association or federation structures in the next twenty years will depend on the strategic ability demonstrated by managers in sport.

This opinion is based, in particular, on the following observation: the development of sports services is increasingly taking place within a competitive arena. The competition is played out between various players and at several levels.

First, competition is growing up between the associative sports movement and firms providing sports services (in the field of leisure, keep-fit or the production of televized events, for example). The emergence of these new players, often highly dynamic, makes it absolutely necessary for administrators to develop their strategic capabilities.

Next, it must be recognized that sports associations and federations are in competition among themselves. In addition, they are in a position of rivalry with the numerous new organizations which come into existence as soon as unfamiliar activities appear: snowboarding, roller-blading, mountain bikes, windsurfing and before long cybersports.

Under these circumstances, managers in sport will have to have the ability to intervene strategically in the following sectors:

- the capacity for developing a *"competitive advantage"* based on an acknowledged strong point of their organization or a positioning which corresponds to a key success factor in their field of activity;
- the capacity for analysis of the *"value chain"* which structures the activity of their organization to optimize the quality of the services offered;
- the capacity for developing *processes for taking decisions* of a strategic nature;
- the capacity for *designing* flexible *organizational structures* with a view to adapting the sports organization to changes in the environment;
- the capacity for *understanding* the real *issues*: practitioners' needs and expectations, competitors' strengths, substitutional sports techniques and technologies;
- the capacity for *analysing the strengths and weaknesses* of their organization on the basis of exploitation of traditional matrices (BCG, ADL, Mc Kinsey) or new methodologies which are better adapted to the specific nature of sports organizations (P.I.S.T.E.S. methods, for example[4]);
- the capacity for *formalizing* the functioning of the organization within the context of strategic planning.

1.f. Knowledge relating to marketing and futurology

Contrary to what happens in the United States, research and knowledge relating to sports marketing are relatively underdeveloped in Europe. As regards futurology applied to sport, apart from the work undertaken by Professor Pociello's French team at Paris-Sud-Orsay University [5], research is still in its infancy in every country. Furthermore, as far as I know, the concept of "sports innovation management" which we are trying to develop in France, at Caen University, has not yet attracted any researchers or lecturers outside that university.

Although underdeveloped, knowledge about marketing and futurology as applied to the production of sports services will be necessary to sports managers. It seems to me, indeed, that this is a field where the production of know-how is essential, in so far as it will make it possible to understand and integrate three phenomena, all different and yet complementary, into the development strategies of sports organizations.

---

[4] P.I.S.T.E.S. stands for the French "Programme d'Investigations Stratégiques des Tendances d'Evolution du Sport."[Programme of Strategic Investigations into Sports Trends]. This is a method of investigation developed by the Sports Innovation Management and Study Centre of Caen University.

[5] See the latest work by Christian Pociello: *"Les cultures sportives"*, [Sports cultures], Paris, PUF, 1995.

First phenomenon: sports techniques and technologies are developing considerably and very rapidly. This development means that the know-how of the technical personnel becomes out of date almost instantaneously. This is reflected by the abrupt changes in the areas of teaching skills, for example. From this strict standpoint, in terms of human resources management, the capacity for integration of technical and technological innovation will be one of the main features of sports management tomorrow.

Second phenomenon: the needs and expectations of practitioners are changing just as rapidly as techniques and technologies. The profile of today's sports enthusiast - older, more likely to be female, more interested in companionship than in competition - has little in common with that of the 1970s. This is reflected by the emergence of new "market segments". These little-known sectors of action correspond to an unfamiliar public of "consumers" whom the organizations will have to satisfy unless they want to risk losing "market shares".

Third phenomenon: technical and technological developments combined with changing needs will find expression in new expectations regarding sports services. Under these circumstances, it would be inconsistent to try to satisfy a new public, using a new technique based on the exploitation of an original technology, by offering it an antiquated service - meaning a service which is obsolete in terms of the many and multifarious innovations on which the sportsman's commitment to his activity will be based.

The combination of these three phenomena, all different and yet complementary, opens up many lines of development for sports organizations. Some of these lines are opportunities, while others are dead ends. Figure 2 can be used to identify the promising lines and mark off the dead ends.

This model (figure 2), analysing strategic opportunities and dead ends, can be read as follows:

Let us consider the case of the French Ski Federation (FFS), confronted with the emergence of a new technique - snowboarding. We write FFS in the "Organization" box.

The next step is to identify snowboarding in technical and/or technological terms. We can agree that it is certainly a new technique. So the line begins like this:

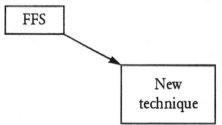

More and more people are taking up snowboarding, and the FFS will legitimately want to take advantage of this new activity for its own development. The next step, then, is to determine whether or not snowboarders are a new market. They are younger, they use different locations, they report new needs - so the reply is clearly in the affirmative; which gives us this line:

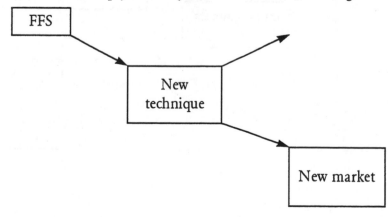

Figure 2

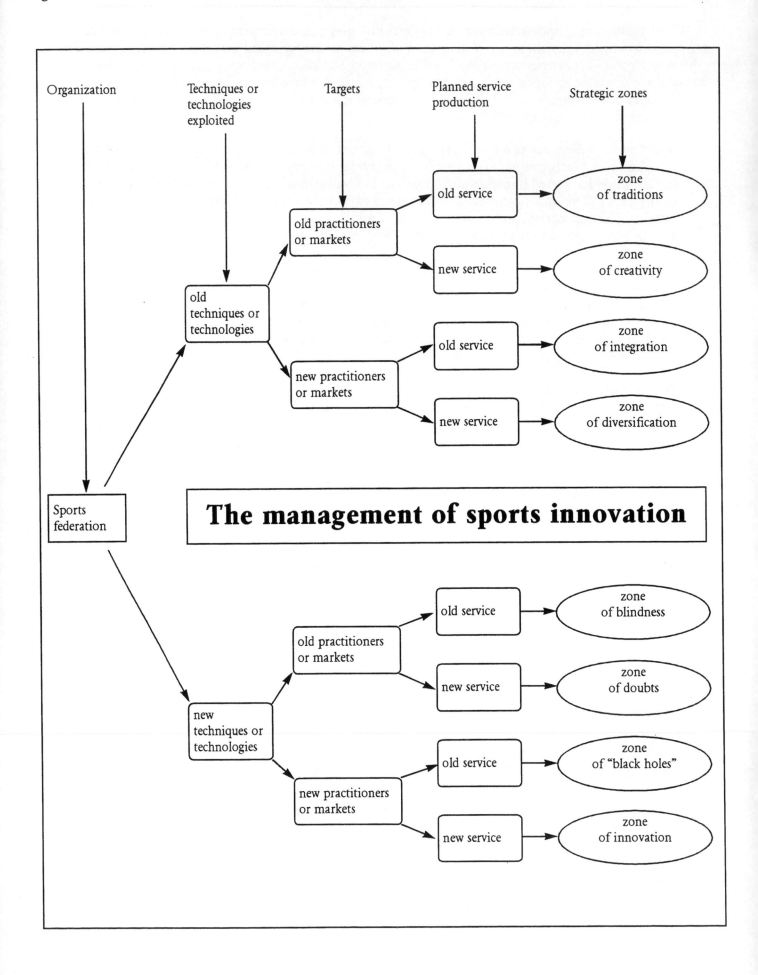

This is the point where things become difficult, because two totally contrasting strategic options arise.

One is that the FFS will refuse to redefine the service it has traditionally offered to skiers, in which case it will embark upon a strategic option which is a genuine dead end: the zone of "black holes", in which all its efforts will lead to nothing. Alternatively, by contrast, it can accept the challenge to its traditional "trade" and design a new service which meets the unfamiliar needs of snowboarders. In this case, the line which it follows will lead to the zone of innovation. This immediately indicates that, in order to incorporate these new practitioners, the administrators of the FFS will become genuine managers, diversifying the service they offer.

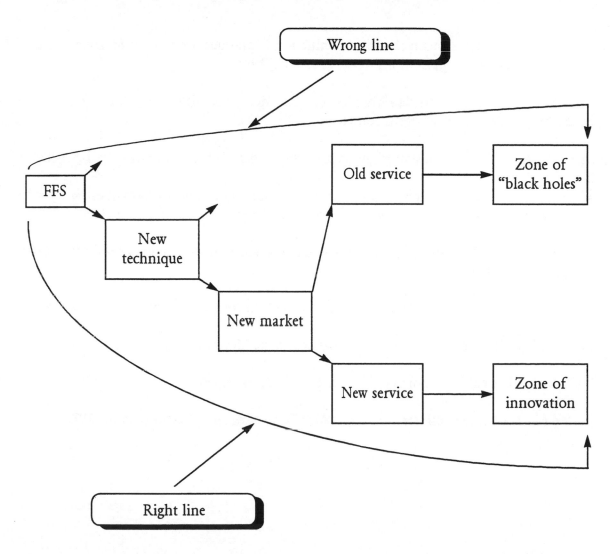

The concept of "Management of sports innovation" formalized in Figure 2, can thus be broken down on the basis of different strategic lines leading to very different zones of decision and action. The capacity for identifying the right road and refusing to turn down dead ends is the whole point of the concept of management as applied to sports organizations.

References

Burlot, A. and Simon, C.J.- Analyse des coûts et contrôle de gestion *Cost analysis and management monitoring,* Vuibert Gestion, Paris, 1987.

Dumoulin, C.- Management des systèmes d'information *Information systems management*, Editions d'Organization, Paris, 1986.

Eiglier, P. and Langeard, E.- Servuction, le marketing des services *"Servuction", the marketing of services*, McGraw-Hill, Paris, 1988.

Gelinier, O.- La direction participative par objectif *Participative management by objective*, Editions Hommes et Techniques, Paris, 1979.

Igalens, J. and Peretti, J.M.- Le bilan social de l'entreprise, *The company balance sheet*, PUF, Paris, 1982.

Loret, A. (ed.).- Sport et management, de l'éthique à la pratique *Sport and management - from ethics to practice*, second edition, Editions Révue EPS, Paris, 1995.

Loret, A.- Génération Glisse, la révolution du sport des années fun *A generation sliding - the sports revolution of the fun years*, Editions Autrement, Paris, 1995.

Martinet, A.C.- Diagnostic stratégique *Strategic diagnostics*, Vuibert Entreprise, Paris, 1988.

Mathis, L. et al.- Gestion prévisionnelle et valorisation des ressources humaines *Forward-looking management and valorization of human resources*, Editions d'Organization, Paris, 1983.

Mintzberg, H.- Le pouvoir dans les organizations *Power in organizations*, Editions d'Organization, Paris, 1986.

Mullin, B.J. et al.- *Sport Marketing*, Human Kinetics Publishers, Champaign (USA), 1993.

Thietart, R.A.- La stratégie d'entreprise *Business strategy*, McGraw-Hill, Paris, 1984.

Pociello, C.- Les cultures sportives *Sports cultures*, PUF, Paris, 1995.

Porter, M.- L'avantage concurrentiel *Competitive advantage*, Inter Editions, Paris, 1986.

Ethics in sport management

Marc Maes
Comité Olympique et Interfédéral Belge,
Bruxelles, Belgium

Newspapers and magazines churn out articles and exposés of all types dealing with the ethical problems encountered in business. No organization - political, cultural or economic - seems to be spared. The same applies to sports organizations. This situation is all the more worrying in that it runs precisely counter to the fundamental, universal sports values on which the Olympic Movement is based.

Management and ethics

Given that management is based on human actions, in accordance with which techniques and strategies conceived by man are employed, these actions fall within a legal and ethical framework. Any management action must take this framework into consideration, the ethical aspect being broader here than the legal aspect. This is because the legal aspect is exclusively based on rules and laws which are laid down with the greatest precision and are subject to continuous evolution. This evolution is due partly to the influence of empirical development within this legal framework, and partly to modifications or new arrangements which anticipate socio-economic developments.

The ethical aspect goes beyond the legal aspect in so far as it is based not only on established laws and duly notified provisions but also on unwritten agreements and on empathic perceptions in the social context, on guiding principles and on commonly accepted values and standards.

Unlike the lower animals, man's actions are not based on instinct; we must therefore presuppose the existence of guiding principles or criteria. In his actions, man often refers to the lack of or need for orientation. Plato, long ago, called attention to the existence of a natural need for orientation, for the compilation of a scale of values or standards. Since man is not bound by any strict, inevitable predetermination, he can distinguish himself from other living creatures through such concepts as liberty, thought, intelligence, discernment, wisdom and perspicacity.

In the context of any cultural activity, including management, man has acapacity for seeking and finding guidance for his own actions within the world which surrounds him, and so for positively stimulating his self-realization. Ethics are understood as a process of thinking about the orientation of human actions, since man has to find the action criterion which will serve as an exchange standard between himself and his environment. The fact of finding such a criterion or having such a criterion come to him is thus of vital importance, in view of the fact that man has alternative courses of action available. The orientation of these actions is entirely a matter for him.

The basic meaning of "ethic" is ambit, enclosure, habitation or accustomed place; it refers to the complete set of habits and customs amid which man is born and which surround him, and which thus set the limits beyond which he may not go. The orientation which administrators select for themselves is subject to various pressures and is increasingly threatened by the negative consequences of the rapid changes in our supposedly highly civilized society. Money and power often devalue administrators' scope of action. Personal dignity and self-respect are very often discarded.

Management has something in common with war, and can thus be subject to the same negative degradation. Sport, too, is becoming more and more of a battle in which the objective is no longer the sport but the prize. This presupposes a totally different concept, and different strategies. When the prize - money - becomes the main objective, there is a great temptation to achieve that objective by less high-minded means. Managers promise financial rewards for victory; that is within the bounds of acceptability. But things go too far when some managers promise money in the event of defeat. This sounds an ethical alarm, even if the participant no longer makes the distinction, because the financial gains have become the primary objective. It is clear that, in this latter case, the most fundamental values of sport are being trampled underfoot.

Sport is increasingly at risk from factors such as the stardom cult, drug-taking, violence within and around sport, exaggerated nationalism and chauvinism, overcommercialization, financial greed, corruption and fraud, facile media presentation, discrimination and the auctioning of services within sport itself, so that it is obvious that the manager whose duty it is to keep a sports enterprise running must have the benefit of an extremely sound ethical profile if he is to be able to stand up to these various threats.

The factors which threaten sport

We know full well that we live amid the cultural flowering that we deserve, or perhaps we should speak of cultural decadence. Sport, as a cultural asset, is no exception to this rule. As the mirror of the society in which it evolves, culture clearly reflects what takes place within that society, through a wide variety of forms of expression. Above all, though, it reflects the way in which it satisfies the concept of a standard which is specific both to the society and to the individual. If we accept sport as one of the forms of expression of the cultural process, as the mirror of society, we will find that sport - because of its elemental universality, irrespective of the linguistic aspect - operates more like a convex mirror which primarily exaggerates the disastrous excesses of society.

This is why sources of information on sport always seem to pay greater attention to its negative aspects than to the positive elements. Frank Taylor, President of the International Sports Press Association (AIPS) rightly says that "too often the bad news of sport gets bigger headlines than the good news".

If we take this into consideration, we can say that the factors which threaten sport are not specific to it but are instead social phenomena which sport reflects, so to speak, in a magnifying mirror. Let us briefly consider some of them.

The cult of stardom

The cult of stardom has always existed in the most varied forms of human activity, in politics, academia, the arts (cinema, theatre, variety, pop or classical music, etc.), in business, or even in the ecclesiastical world or the media. Nothing could be more normal than to admire the skills of others, the sublime and virtuosic manifestation of talent. This is the excellence so dear to Coubertin.

We can see this excellence in a person capable of interpreting a concerto in an almost miraculous manner, with a musical and technical perfection worthy of the greatest virtuosi, or in the climber who conquers the world's highest peaks. But we can also find it in the farmer who shows the greatest skill in cultivating his land, the bus driver who delivers thousands of passengers safely to their destinations every day, or the housewife who keeps smiling as she prepares her offspring to face a future which is not always easy.

It is, of course, a mistake to admire someone for what he is - for his title or social position. What matters is to be able to respect the way in which a person occupies his position in life and gives meaning to it. Society wants chief executives and stars with "integrity", concerned with combating corruption and fraud, and endowed with charisma to motivate their colleagues and followers, offering them an honest, ethical role model.

The flowering of talent in the absence of any ethical dimension is worthless. In antiquity, a "talent" represented a fortune, equivalent to about 14 kg of silver coins or some 6,000 drachmas. Today, "talent" is undoubtedly man's most precious asset. The sports administrator, therefore, has a duty to safeguard this talent. Experience has shown us that a child star can rapidly prove a flash in the pan, a phenomenon which sometimes gives rise to unexpected human suffering. The football star who has just scored a miraculous goal and excites his admirers by climbing the fence and making vulgar gestures is unworthy of any consideration. Here again, the role of the sports administrator is of considerable importance - after all, his responsibilities include the behaviour of his players.

The problem of drug taking

This extremely serious threat to sport is far from being peculiar to it. After all, studies have shown that millions of young people throughout the world take drugs simply to portray themselves in a better light, to come closer to this ideal of attractiveness which is imposed upon them: a pseudo-aesthetic image redolent of superficiality and false happiness.

Hundreds of thousands of sports fanatics use caffeine to improve their performances, or resort to stimulants. But there are also hundreds of thousands who use stimulants as a way of enhancing non-sports performance at activities such as dancing or evenings out. In sport, it is the athletes involved in power sports - body-building enthusiasts, long-distance cyclists, etc. - who are most inclined to take drugs, not the sports elites. Sport is the first sector - and the only one to date - in which drug tests are carried out, and those tests are not confined to competitions but even extend to training sessions and a variety of disciplines, even including golf and shooting. The drugs taken there are for the most part tranquillizers, such as beta-blockers.

These are also used by executives and heads of companies, politicians, musicians, students and other groups which have never been subjected to any checks. This is another area in which the role of the sports administrator is a very important one, as any lapse implies the bankruptcy of the whole system of sports management and an inevitable devaluing of the image of sport.

Overcommercialization

At many competitions and other sports events, it has become almost impossible to find the sportsmen amidst the innumerable advertising messages displayed on and around the pitches, on

T-shirts, shorts, shoes and socks, in the boxes and on the hoardings and other advertising media. Only the Olympic stadia and Wimbledon have so far succeeded in resisting all forms of advertising, though advertising was permitted on an Olympic stadium - for the first and, fortunately, last occasion - at the Olympic Games of 1924 in Paris.

Sponsorship is a phenomenon which has always existed. In the days of the original Olympics, athletes were already being supported and protected by wealthy sponsors or by the towns or villages in which they lived. When the first modern Olympics were organized, private donations accounted for more than two-thirds of the income. Without the contributions made by George Averof, who was responsible in particular for the cost of building the Olympic stadium, it would quite simply have been impossible for those early Games to be organized. These private donations were a form of patronage. Today, the scene is dominated almost exclusively by the rule of the "quid pro quo" and "you win, I win" - which leads to sponsorship.

Firms are willing to invest, but they expect a return: increased public awareness of their product or strengthening of their brand image. What they want is to be associated with sport and with the values which normally go hand in hand with that concept: victory, coolness, speed, power, perseverance, etc.

Unfortunately, there are many factors with which firms do not want to be assoicated, such as violence, hooliganism, drug taking and so on, which are a direct threat to sport. Hence the extremely important part played by the sports administrator, whose particular task is to ensure that his sphere of influence retains complete integrity and is undisturbed by any undesirable element. He is also called upon to protect his sport against unreasonable requests and expectations on the part of the sponsor. He has to avoid the situation where the sponsor can harm his sport and the integrity of the sportsmen. The overloading of the sports calendar is one example of this. In a good many sports disciplines, athletes complain that their programme is too busy, the pressure too great. It is the sports managers who have to steel themselves to make choices in favour of the physical and moral well-being of their athletes, and so in favour of sport. It is up to them to have the courage to turn down what are sometimes very alluring proposals. Above all, the sports administrator has to protect young sportsmen against the tentacles of economic interests. As was pointed out earlier, it is not unusual for the careers of young sports stars to come to a sad and premature end, not just because they have proved unable to cope with their precocious fame and the excessive interest shown in them by the public and the media, but also because they have simply been unable to cope with the physical and moral demands made upon them. In order to provide effective control of sponsors' influence, it is necessary to limit their numbers. A brief analysis of the sponsors of the various summer Olympic Games will illustrate this. The number of sponsors increased considerably after the Los Angeles Games (1932), reaching a peak at Montreal (1976) where the total number of sponsors was 628. Today, Montreal is still trying to recover from the financial débâcle of the Games. Los Angeles (1984) marked a turning point in the financing of the Olympics. The number of sponsors, suppliers and licence holders was considerably reduced and contracts were worded more carefully. TOP - The Olympic Program - came into existence with the Games at Seoul (1988) and Calgary. For the 1985 - 1988 Olympiad, the I.S.L. agency received the support of 9 multinationals, with a total sum of 95 million dollars. For Lillehammer and Atlanta, TOP III should bring in about 300 million dollars. Coca-Cola, whose 1995 turnover is estimated at 15,000 million dollars (producing profits of 2,500 million), has contributed no less than 44 million dollars to Atlanta.

Since no advertising activity is permitted within the stadia, the oldest sponsor of the Games - its support dates back to 1928 - has allocated an additional sum of 67 million dollars to advertising spots and about 100 million dollars to worldwide campaigns designed to publicize its sponsorship of the Olympics. Obviously, these astronomical sums oblige the marketing executives to devise all sorts of systems and strategies to ensure that the return is as substantial as possible, sometimes at the expense of sport and the athletes. But a contract which is properly drawn up by the sports manager, covering every detail and containing no ambiguities, will make it possible to avoid any disappointment. Apart from purely commercial agreements, it is also necessary for the contract to refer to a code of conduct imposed on the sponsor. Some products, too, are so incompatible with the healthy pursuit of sport that they have to be rejected. Some sports disciplines are still too closely associated with alcoholic drinks or brands of cigarettes. The cover of the programme at the Antwerp Games (1920) was half-filled by advertisement for a brand of cigarette. "Olympias" was the official cigarette of the Tokyo Games (1964) and brought in more than one million dollars. Fortunately, tobacco manufacturers were subsequently banned from the sponsorship programmes.

But all this is nothing new. Nor is the introduction of boxes and other "business seats" in the modern stadia - a practice which can hardly fail to accentuate class differences and segregation. Centuries ago, family and patrons' pews were already to be found in churches, so as to enable dignitaries to attend religious services. These comfortable padded seats bore a plaque showing the owner's name, and were bought by the better-off dignitaries of the parish or village.

Merchandising is no novelty, either. After all, if the sale of medallions, candles, scapulars, relics, holy pictures and indulgences was not marketing, then what was it? Today these have been replaced by badges, T-shirts, stickers and key-rings which sell very successfuly.

Media coverage

The substantial impact of television on the commercial scene which centres on the Olympic Games is clearly apparent from the astronomical sums spent on acquiring TV rights. For the Nagano and Sydney Games (2000), a sum of more than 1,200 million dollars is being counted on. Clearly, for sums of this kind, the intention is to reach the widest possible audience and, at the same time, to obtain the greatest possible effect in terms of spectacle. The fact that sport and television will, in future, be increasingly closely associated is positive in itself, provided of course that sport is able to retain its identity, and that the integrity and health of the sportsman is not tainted or jeopardized by any tendency to adapt to the media.

The way in which some sports organizations have changed the rules of their games to make them more telegenic may be acceptable, but - at the very least - this process of modification should be a decision taken by the sports organization itself and have no adverse consequences either for the game or for those that play it.

What is more worrying, however, is that the time at which a competition takes place is being decided not in the interests of the athlete's comfort but to suit the audience. For example, during the football World Cup, matches were played in Orlando at midday, with a temperature that varied between 35 and 45°C and extremely high humidity levels. To organize an Olympic marathon under such conditions would be irresponsible.

Violence in sport

This is a particularly deplorable phenomenon, but one which is certainly not specific to sport. Nor is it anything new. What about the combats and boxing matches to the death seen in the days of the ancient Greeks? What about the frequent deaths resulting from injuries during football matches played in England in the late Middle Ages - at a time when teams numbered several hundred people and the pitch measured several square kilometres in area? Today, the most innocuous tackle in the heat of the moment is replayed on all our television screens, from every conceivable and inconceivable angle, and preferably in slow motion! To the best of my knowledge, acts of violence - and, more particularly, of moral violence - which take place elsewhere in society are not always so closely scrutinized by journalists, and are certainly far from being broadcast from all possible angles, still less in slow motion. However, the aggression to be found in competitive sport can certainly not meet with our approval. Some journalists play down bad behaviour and violence, citing the prevailing atmosphere of stress and the insane sums at stake. Bernard Destreman, President of Racing-Club de France, for his part believes that "it is precisely because these are professional athletes, highly paid and well off, that they should behave better than if they were just anybody". This duty of exemplary behaviour applies not only to the losers but also to the winners. The excessively provocative behaviour of players and coaches when a goal is scored is often the cause of uncontrolled behaviour by the supporters.

Excessive profits

Some high-level sportsmen earn fortunes. This point, again, attracts the attention of the media more often than the millions handled by other cultural sectors. It is rare for a "top thirty" of the world's greatest earners in cinema, music, theatre, etc. to be published. Some high-level sportsmen are opposed to this excessive kind of financial profit: others, whose efforts earn thousands of millions for the media and the organizers, demand their slice of the cake. There is nothing new about this. As long ago as 590 B.C., a law of Solon laid down that a substantial sum (500 drachmas) was to be granted to winners at the Olympic Games (about half the annual earnings of a worker). The excessive financial profit was one of the reasons that led to the loss of the ancient Games. This should provide food for thought for today's sports managers.

The foregoing facts show that sport, as presented by the media, seems to be held responsible for a number of defects in society which, though not specific to sport, are certainly a threat to it.

This failure on the part of society, illustrated in this article through the example of sport, relates in every case to a potential incompatibility between man's freedom and his sense of responsibility. It is apparent from all this that the direct involvement of the business world in the sports world should be avoided. However, this seems extremely difficult to achieve, bearing in mind the fact that many sports clubs are managed by people whose origins lie in the business world.

The potential results of this are illustrated by news bulletins referring to bankruptcies and collapses among sports clubs and cycling teams because the financial backing has ceased to exist.

The sports administrator - an ethical benchmark

There is no need for him to be more catholic than the Pope. Nevertheless, the sports administrator, in his capacity as a representative or even a "symbol" of sport, and of all the values associated with that concept, should strictly observe a number of principles and constraints which ethics impose on his activities. His policy has to be distinguished by an internal direction which appeals to the individual's conscience. We referred earlier to various social factors which represent a threat to sport, factors which he must be able to overcome. But he also needs to play a benchmark role not just for all those who work with him but also for all sportsmen, coaches, club managers and other volunteers concerned. He must be able to develop a long-term vision and to pursue a multidisciplinary approach within the various teams which are to achieve the final objective. Additionally, he must act as a "super facilitator", and as initiator of change, a person capable of taking calculated risks. Thus, he must have a genuine notion of quality, and be endowed with flexibility, open-mindedness, creativity, motivation, the ability to synthesize and analyse, social graces, the capacity to stimulate his co-workers and to dynamize (not dynamite) them.... He must demonstrate real power of persuasion, genuine charisma and the ability to solve problems. The administrator also has to be a guide, know how to create favourable conditions and generate a feeling of involvement. He needs to be aware of the fact that peak performances are first and foremost the result of an outstanding capability for managing others. When managers are selected, mention is often made of the 5-factor model established by MCrae & Costa. A more in-depth analysis shows that virtually all these factors relate to motivation and emotional response rather than to technicality or knowledge, i.e. vulnerability (emotional stability) and openness of mind/intellect. The world is changing, and the future will obviously require the administrator to demonstrate other basic skills. Global efficiency is more important today than traditional productivity. Over the last century, sport has changed from being a social practice to being an economic activity. And this is reflected by transition from practical sports management to the practice of sports management.

Seeking corporate sponsorship: some factors limiting the success of national sport organization initiatives

Trevor Slack & Tim Berrett
The Faculty of Physical Education and Recreation,
University of Alberta,
Edmonton, Alberta, Canada

Since the early 1970s Canada's national sport organizations (NSOs) have been the recipients of funding from the federal government. For the vast majority of these organizations this is their primary source of income. As recently as 1992 the Federal Government's most recent task force report Sport: The Way Ahead indicated that government support of NSOs ranged from 5% to 95% of their total income, with the average being around 75%.

However, since 1987 the real and nominal contributions of the federal government to funding Canada's NSOs have been considerably reduced. So severe is this reduction that on March 31st 1995 it was announced that some NSOs would have their entire government contribution eliminated in the 1996-97 federal budget. Those that do not have their budget totally eliminated will see cuts of up to 50% of 1994-95 funding levels.

Implicit in this move to reduce federal government funding for NSOs is the assumption that these organizations can generate other sources of revenue for their operations. This thinking was evidenced in the *Sport: The Way Ahead* document when it was suggested that:
"part of each sport's agenda should be to reduce dependence on government funding and broaden the resource base. To accomplish this, sport must diversify its sources of funding, supplementing the traditional government sources with new and creative sources" (Canada 1992, p. 243).

Although not specifically stated as such, the main source to which it is expected NSOs will turn to enhance their funding is the corporate sector. Despite the implicit appeal of having these organizations approach private sector organizations for support, Berrett (1993, p. 324) contends that there has "been little done within the current sport system in Canada to assist NSOs in developing a strategy for accessing funds from [this] sector." Consequently the purpose of this paper is to examine the initiatives that are being taken by Canada's NSOs in seeking sponsorship from the corporate sector and to outline some of the factors that are working to limit their success in this area.

Method

The data for the study come from a series of interviews conducted with those individuals responsible for marketing and sponsorship in a sample of 32 Canadian NSOs. The NSOs used in the study reflect variation in such factors as size, media profile, structural form, and type of sport (team/individual, summer/winter). Some of the NSOs we surveyed had full- or part-time marketing directors, others placed the responsibility for seeking sponsorship support in the hands of their Executive Director. The interviews which lasted approximately 60 to 90 minutes were recorded and then transcribed verbatim. Data were solicited on a wide range of topics related to the involvement of these organizations in corporate sponsorship.

Results and Discussion

The approaches taken by the different NSOs in our study, in their attempts to secure sponsorship, can be grouped into three broad categories. First, a small number of organizations (4 NSOs or 12.5% of our sample) used what has been termed the shotgun approach. Here the NSO staff member responsible for sponsorship sends out a large number of requests in the hopes that a few will "hit the target". That is to say a corporation's interest will be sufficiently aroused that they will at least agree to meet with a representative from the NSO to discuss sponsorship possibilities. For the most part the success rate using this approach is low. As one individual responsible for sponsorship told us "I might get a meeting out of ten percent of four to five hundred [requests] ... and ten of them might result in deals".

The vast majority of NSOs had at one time another used the shotgun approach but many had now moved to using the second method of seeking support, a more focused approach. Here a smaller number of corporations were targeted as potential sponsors. The level of sophistication in these targeting efforts varied considerably. Most NSOs made their first approach to organizations directly linked to their sport, e.g. equipment manufacturers, then sought out unrelated companies. A number of the more sophisticated NSOs sought out information about the corporate strategy and previous giving patterns of companies they were planning to approach. As one Executive Director told us "a little secret I rarely tell people is the *Financial Post*". This individual indicated that he used the newspaper as a source of information about companies that he could possibly approach for sponsorship support and claimed he could "correlate his biggest successes" with what he had learned from the paper.

By taking the time to find out about the companies they were seeking sponsorship from marketing personnel can work to develop what McDonald (1991) calls the "subtle effects" of sponsorship. That is to say those unique linkages that provide a synergy between the sport and the company supporting it. The sport of freestyle skiing was able to do this by forging links with Owens Corning, an insulation company which was trying to expand its market and present an image of an innovative and exciting company, qualities it saw in freestyle. So too was Figure skating who secured an agreement with the Royal Bank because they felt figure skating's image of a "clean, classy, Canadian, and family-oriented sport" fit with the values it was trying to promote. Such linkages if properly established can be presented to potential sponsors as a resource which is capable of generating for their company a sustainable competitive advantage (Peteraf, 1993). However, establishing such linkages requires careful researching of companies before approaching them as potential sponsors. Unfortunately few NSOs had the foresight or resources to undertake this type of initiative.

Some NSOs focused their efforts on those corporations that had already shown an interest in sponsoring a particular sporting festival, such as the Commonwealth Games, a World Championships, or the Olympics, in which their sport was on the programme. The approach taken in these instances was to attempt to illustrate to the corporation in question that, for little extra outlay, they could leverage the major deal with a "side-deal". Such regional or local tie-ins to more global campaigns can provide the sponsoring company with a multi-layered marketing campaign (Gronroos, 1990). In some cases this approach proved to be successful and sponsoring companies were keen to reap the benefits of a global campaign while still positioning and promoting their product in a regional market. However, many NSOs received a standard response that the sponsorship budget had been committed to the primary event.

The final group of NSOs are those who were in the enviable position of having sponsors approach them to ask if they could sponsor their sport. Of the 32 organizations in our sample only four (12.5%) were in this category. Of the sports that these organizations represent one was played at the professional league level in North America and the other three were activities in which top competitors received large sums of money for performing. It is important to note about this group of NSOs that they did not just sit back and wait for sponsors to provide them with money. Even though they were approached by potential supporters each proposal was carefully evaluated by the NSO staff and considerable care was taken to try to ensure complementary sponsorship.

In some of those NSOs that had seen little success in their attempts to attract non-related corporations, i.e., those directly linked to the sport, there was a certain sense of acquiescence. As one Executive Director told us "I don't see our sport getting major sponsors. I don't see the [name of a large corporation] being interested." While this may well be the case, for the most part NSOs had not developed the necessary infrastructure in the form of policies and procedures to help guide this aspect of their operation nor had they undertaken the type of planning required to secure the ongoing commitment of top level corporations. Even in many of those NSOs that used a more focused method of seeking sponsorship, policy formulation and planning was still relatively ad hoc.

Of the NSOs we surveyed only ten (29%) had any type of policy to guide their operations with regard to sponsorship. For those who did have this type of documentation this varied from "one-off" agreements with committees hosting national championship and special events to formal statements detailing the rights and responsibilities of all actors involved in a sponsorship arrangement. The reasons given by those who did not have policies mainly related to a lack of time to formulate this type of material and the constant state of turmoil these organizations found themselves in. As one Executive Director put it "given that this whole area is in a constant state of change, any policy that we did draw up would be out of date by the time the board passed it."

While the development of policies can be a time-consuming task, those who had made the effort to formulate some type of procedural guidelines suggested that they were helpful in implementing their sponsorship programmes. Three specific areas, where policies were useful, emanated from our interview data. The first of these related to the servicing of existing sponsors. Here policies guided the manner in which NSO personnel dealt with current sponsors thus helping ensure the continuation of existing contracts. Second policies were used to help with the evaluation of sponsorship agreements. While this is a difficult area to objectively assess (Abratt & Grobler, 1989) policies helped identify "a priori" the objectives of sponsorship agreements thus making evaluations somewhat more definitive. Finally, policies were used to help limit any possible conflicts that could arise between the NSO securing the sponsorship and its constituent groups. These included athletes who may have sponsorship agreements with companies which were in competition with the NSO's sponsor; with provincial (regional) sport organizations who often operated independently from the NSO in terms of seeking sponsorships; and with the hosting committees of the NSO's events and championship who would also seek their own local-level sponsorships.

Given that less than one in three of the NSOs we surveyed had no policies in place to guide their operations in terms of sponsorship it is not surprising that only 14 (44%) had any type of marketing plan. Eight (25%) indicated that they were in the process of developing a plan. Of those NSOs that already had a plan, there was wide variation in the level of sophistication they exhibited. One organization had a multi-year plan which contained membership targets, details of media exposure, and the type of corporations they planned to approach. The executive director in this organization had clearly recognized the ramifications of government cutbacks. He described the plan as "a natural evolution from a state run sport to trying to meet the demands of corporate sponsors in order to get their business". Unfortunately this type of foresight was sadly lacking in most NSOs. Ten (31%) had no plan at all and even in a number of those who had developed plans we were told it was not being followed. A lack of time and expertise were the most frequently cited reasons for the plan not being implemented. As one Executive Director told us:

"the plan was written in 1991 and marketing was identified as priority number one, but I'm not sure its been priority number one. It's a difficult area for volunteers to manage. ... They all recognize that something's got to be done, but they are not sure how to do it."

The reference to volunteer involvement in marketing highlights another limitation NSOs face in obtaining corporate sponsorship.

Only nine NSOs (28%) acknowledged having an active marketing committee, three (9%) used an external agency in lieu of a committee. The remaining 20 organizations (63%) had no committee or an inactive committee. In most NSOs (20 or 63%) the responsibility for seeking corporate sponsorship was delegated to the Executive Director, an individual who already had a significant workload administering the day to day operations of the NSO. Only nine (28%) organizations had a person with the title Marketing Director and in some cases this also included the communications or public relations portfolio.

A number of respondents indicated that their NSO had previously hired someone to fill the role of Marketing Director then subsequently eliminated the position. This is somewhat of the short term view of building sponsorship opportunities which seemed to prevail in these organizations. Given the relatively weak competitive position of many of these organizations within the sponsorship marketplace it should have been anticipated that it would take a number of years to build a strong relationship with a company that was willing to commit significant amounts of money to an event, programme, or team. To expect a Marketing Director to secure such deals in a relatively short space of time, which seems to have been the belief in many NSOs, would seem to be a rather tall order. Rather than being viewed as a long term investment, the position of Marketing Director, appeared to have been seen as a "quick fix" solution to the longer term problem of lack of funds.

Another problem which was highlighted by those who had hired and subsequently released Marketing Directors was the qualifications of the person they employed. Only nine (28%) organizations had hired someone who possessed what could be described as a significant background in marketing. Almost half of the people hired were graduates from a physical education degree (or equivalent). While not wishing to understate the abilities of some of these people, most would have little more than two or three courses in marketing. It seems rather optimistic to expect someone with such limited expertise to generate significant revenues over a short time horizon.

Also a limiting factor is the amount of money paid to these people; most received a salary of less than $30,000 (Cdn) per year. Although monetary compensation is not the only way to attract qualified people to a position it is realistic to expect that those with more experience in the marketing field will be able to command a higher compensatory package in the private sector. This is not to imply that the solution to a NSO's marketing problem is merely to employ a full-time Marketing Director at a salary competitive with the private sector. Of the 9 NSOs (28%) that had a person in a position who spent most or all of his/her time on marketing, perhaps only three were in the position of earning a level of income that could be compared to that which could be garnered in the private sector. However, the nine that had made this commitment appeared to be among the most successful organizations in terms of securing sponsorship.

In part this success may be tied to the fact that in those NSOs which had made the commitment to hiring a full time Marketing Director there was an indication that more time was spent on sponsorship activities. Fifteen (47%) of the NSOs in our sample indicated that the person designated to this area spent less than 20% of the time his/her time in this area. A factor that is no doubt related to the relative lack of success NSOs have had in securing ongoing sponsorships. As noted some NSOs used an external marketing agency and among those that did the rationale for this approach stemmed from a belief that the people in the organization did not have the necessary expertise to do the marketing. As the Executive Directors from one of these sport remarked, when the agency was signed, he and his staff "can get on with running the sport". Another noted "I can get back to what I do best, which is administering the sport".

Conclusion

What this brief overview of the results of our study shows is that despite the pressures being placed on NSOs in Canada to seek corporate sponsorship most are limited in their ability to access these type of funds. These limitations stem from the relatively unsophisticated approaches being used in seeking sponsorship, the lack of policies and plans to guide sponsorship initiatives, and the lack of time and in some cases expertise exhibited by those individuals charged with the responsibility for seeking sponsorship. Consequently we would offer the following recommendations to these and similar organizations as they seek to obtain support from the corporate sectors.

1. National sport organizations should seek to formulate formal strategic plans for their marketing and sponsorship activities in order to maximize their efforts in these areas.

2. The employment of a Marketing Director should be seen as a long term investment.

3. The boards of NSOs which rely on their Executive Director for sponsorship and marketing activities should not have unreasonably high expectations of revenue generation from these sources unless an adequate number of support staff is also provided.

4. For those NSOs lacking expertise in marketing and sponsorship, it should be recognized that external agencies might be able to provide some or all of the personnel and effort required for success.

5. It is important that corporate sponsors be adequately serviced if it is hoped they will continue their association with the NSO.

6. An active marketing committee is likely to assist an NSO in its sponsorship activities. However, there should be clear guidelines outlining the precise role of such a committee.

7. The overall corporate strategies of potential sponsors should be tracked by NSOs prior to their making a sponsorship proposal. It is evident that the "shotgun" approach is inappropriate.

References

Abratt, R., & Grobler, P. S.- The evaluation of sport sponsorships. *International Journal of Advertising*, 1989, 8, 351-362.

Berrett, T.- The sponsorship of amateur sport: Government, national sport organization, and corporate perspectives. *Loisir et Société / Society and Leisure,* 1993, 16, 323-346.

Canada.- *Sport: The Way Ahead. Minister's Task Force on Federal Sport Policy.* Ottawa Minister of Supply and Service, 1992.

Gronroos, C.- *Service Management and Marketing: Managing the Moments of Truth in Service Competition,* Lexington, M.A.: DC. Heath and Co./Lexington Books, 1990.

McDonald, C.- Sponsorship and the image of the sponsor. *European Journal of Marketing,* 1991, 25, 31-38.

Peteraf, M.A.- The cornerstones of competitive advantage: A resource-based view. *Strategic Management Journal,* 1993, 14, 179-191.

Negotiating sponsorship and endorsements

John Cheffers
School of Education,
Boston University,
Boston, Massachusetts, United States of America

As sport grows in importance, more professional expertise in management is called for. Managers are attracted from the business community and universities and colleges are introducing Sports Management programmes into their curricula. The day of the full-time chief executive officer (CEO) in the management of sport is at hand. This article will concentrate on the important aspect of negotiating sponsorships and endorsements for sporting enterprises. It centres, specifically, on the Australian Institute of Sport (AIS), which has emerged, since its inception in 1981, as a critical mass in the sport development and service world.

Very little important development in the world of service occurs without support of some kind. This support tends to come either from government sources or the private sector. Occasionally individual philanthropists will sponsor their own schemes with bequests that are used to promote or develop service plans. Mostly, however, government, assisted by big business, provides the support, even the impetus, for community development. Very little sponsorship occurs without strings attached. This brings the question of ethics and preference into consideration along with choices that are not infrequently difficult to make. The sporting world in Australia is currently reeling from the effects of the withdrawal of cigarette industry sponsorship. Although replacement in the form of cigarette tax monies has been made, large organizations have been unable to continue their promotions. The two competing benefactors in most developmental schemes - the government and private industry - are sometimes in conflict over goals and objectives. Government sponsorship is always tied to political feasibility and bureaucratic control, whilst private sponsorship is subject to a range of objectives, some whimsical, some solid. And in all but perhaps two countries - the United States and Germany - the private sector is limited with contributions restricted in number and size. So sponsorship and endorsements are subject to controls, whimsy, sudden change and a wide range of ethical considerations. These problems notwithstanding, few sporting bodies or service organizations can survive without the aid of major communal enclaves.

Personal and institutional causes

Where an individual is sufficiently advanced in need identification, personal sponsorship can be pursued. Individuals seeking support for material, overseas expense support and competition service support are motivated to seek the kind of endorsement that will keep their career active and efforts improving. More often, institutions seek endorsement and sponsorship. These range from small community groups to large visible organizations. In the case of individuals, resolution and justification is fairly easily reached. With institutions, however, years might pass before the true value of a sponsorship is learned. Such agreements tend to be subject to interim evaluations and sudden changes in support direction. There is also the question of essential versus nonessential support service. It might be argued that all sporting bodies fall into the nonessential category. Music, literature, art, craft and entertainment are similarly placed. Groups supplying primary and secondary needs might therefore be in a better position to secure the necessary sponsorship. But there is not a single reader who would support this contention. The emotion-satisfying communal activities are so appealing, even alluring, that sponsorship is provided readily for supposedly nonessential activities. Indeed, it is easier to get sponsorship for sport and the arts than it is for the schools and other educational institutions. People with leisure time, and this is increasing in quantity, and people whose interests range beyond work and duty, are attracted to sport and the arts in huge numbers. Where people gather together and where competitive interest is aroused, great energy, enthusiasm and effort are expended, and visibility is vast. It is therefore in the interests of business enclaves and government personnel to be associated authentically and beneficially.

Contact

Sporting groups wishing to attract sponsorship have first to make contact with potential donors. The mechanics of such effort are worth considering. Very rarely will serious sponsorship efforts succeed through casual or amateur contact. This fact has given rise to a host of consulting enterprises, all seeking to promote and raise money for the various sporting groups. Brochures and memorabilia are used to set bait. Films, audio systems, symbols and trivial items comprise this bait. The huge profit of $250 million recorded by Los Angeles during the 1984 Olympic Games is attributed mostly to this source. They produced T-shirts, flags, caps, cups, coasters, posters and other symbolism, all designed to help people remember their experiences and give away to friends and neighbours who could not attend. Where the local population is vast and can afford such trivia, memorabilia is an excellent way to raise money and interest sponsors. International events possess the credibility of attracting important involvement. This explains why even the most outlandish of sports can attract support services provided they have the credibility of staging "the World Championships". The local sponsor will always find that much of the sponsorship money will automatically accrue to international sources. Other means of contact are diverse and often very difficult. Mail order and telephone contacts frequently result in overflowing trashbins and abortive conversations. Door-to-door salespeople frequently experience the same problems. Most marketing people, therefore, fall back on a few tested and tried methods. Add-on sales are used where people already contacted and under contract are introduced to a new line or new sponsorship opportunities. A sponsor happily ensconced with a viable product is more vulnerable to new opportunities than one who has not yet to experience the credibility of the association. TV and press advertising are also true and tried techniques for attracting attention, although there are also much more expensive.

One fact in this process of contact that cannot be overlooked is the phenomenon of "layers of impression". Unless the marketing agent has the luxury of inside contact or equal opportunity contact, the agent has to be prepared to reach the decision-making desk only after encountering many protective layers beforehand: the secretary who takes the call or opens the mail, the third assistant who feels out the nature and promise of the endorsement, the assistant to the public relations chief, who records all the details of the proposed co-adventure, and, finally, the public relations chief, whose task it to formulate the proposal that goes to the chief executive officer. Many times this CEO then has to consult a board of management. Almost by definition, public boards consist of various positions on the philosophic spectrum. Some directors are generous, others give nothing at any time to anybody. So a "number-crunching" operation has to be mounted if the enterprise is to succeed. During this process the sponsorship seekers have to continue to provide information, (accessibility) answers and renewed enthusiasm as each layer of the onion is peeled away. This process takes time and is nerve-wracking, but it is probably the only way in which new organizations will attract sponsorship of any substance.

Quid pro quo

Whether it be government or private sponsorship, few organizations will provide support without, in return, receiving something substantial from the agreement. Many examples exist of politicians providing generous assistance when their needs so decree.

Australian treasurer (in the 80's), Paul Keating, suddenly became a rabid Collingwood supporter (Australian Football League) when he realized that it would be a good way to defuse communication of an unpopular budget. That same astute politician also recognized that 1990 could well be the year in which the most heavily supported Australian football club would reverse 32 years of failure and win the coveted Premiership. Collingwood obliged and Mr. Keatings's smile has yet to be removed from his lean features. Prime Minister of the day, Robert J. Hawke, and former Prime Minister, Malcolm Fraser, have been guilty of similar manoeuvres in support of unpopular policies. Perhaps the best example of politicians leaning heavily on sport in recent times was the visit of Richard M. Nixon to China in the mid-seventies. Aware that U.S. sports was vastly superior to all but one of the Chinese sports, he chose that single exception, table tennis, to promote a sporting exchange, symbolizing the new relationships between the U.S. and the People's Republic of China. The U.S. team was worsted, a happening rare to the United States sporting public, but accepted graciously on all sides because it represented a bending over the giant to facilitate the new friendship. Much press was devoted to this lopsided competition. The fact that the second sport to visit China, the U.S. Track and Field team, lost only one event on three weeks of competition, receiving little publicity, substantiates sport's usefulness in the world of politics.

So a quid pro quo position usually permeates all sponsorship arrangement in sports. Occasionally a gift of unfettered money is received and always welcomed. Mostly, however, such arrangements as "one for one" and "kind for cash" or "cash for kind", are the standing orders of each sponsorship day. Ingenious arrangements where both sides receive strong promotion, are preferred. John Purnell, resourceful public relations director at the Australian Institute of Sport, was particularly lucid in such developments. His "Come and Play Sport" weekends with the Lend-Lease Organization meant that developmental teaching units and institute promotional activities would be taken into the large shopping centres run by the Lend-Lease Organization. Young children benefited, parents were interested and informed, and businesses saw swollen attendances, all bearing fruit. Other Australian Institute of Sport (AIS) initiatives to succeed are also worth recording :

1) naming of seats in the auditorium - over 300 seats in the beautiful weight-lifting auditorium were "sold" to individual names for a modest sum. The names were affixed to the backs of the chairs, thus preserving aesthetic appeal. Monies collected provided an annual scholarship in the name of a deceased AIS coach to deserving track and field aspirants;

2) naming of residence rooms - naming rights to these rooms were "sold" to large business concerns at a considerable one-time sum. $250,000 was raised for the Institute in the first 12 months of this scheme. A plaque on the wall next to the door recorded the sponsor's name, and a yearly history of its inmates was recorded. Tradition and sponsorship monies were enhanced by this scheme;

3) naming of individual teams at the Institute - large business concerns were offered primary sponsorship of each of the 10 teams at AIS. To qualify, they had to promise a tidy sum of money for a three-year period. This scheme left very few of the teams unsponsored after the first year of its existence. The sponsor's name was displayed prominently on the uniforms and

equipment of the specific team. Naturally, the more prominent the television coverage was the better the attraction, and further sponsors were found for this team;

4) naming of programmes - programmes of great interest and attraction were also sold to individual sponsors. One of Australia's four largest banks took over the sponsorship of the National Training Scheme, which was set up to attract sports that were not permanent at the AIS. In one year over 105 training camps were organized for more than 50 individual sports. It is not difficult to imagine how successful this programme was in attracting press coverage and grass roots activities around Australia;

5) support for scientific investigations - the exciting activities in the sports medicine and sports science areas provided sponsorship opportunities, and, in particular, endorsement openings for enterprises wishing to link up with the AIS. Protein supplement companies, vitamin groups, medication businesses and a myriad of supply organizations, hooked into this benefit happily and generously;

6) proportional or sliding scale sponsorship - this activity implies that start-up monies are given by the sponsoring body and are replaced by the normal budgeting arrangements in the later years. In this case, the initial two years' financial burden was placed upon the sponsor but the onus shifted to the organization as the enterprise developed. Such an arrangement helps with the initial, perhaps risky, activities, but implies essential partnership upon completion of the initiative. Trust is a very important feature of the sliding scale sponsorship concept.

Visibility

Little substantial service assistance will be provided without visibility. Occasionally anonymous gifts are received, but these are rare and unheralded, often unsolicited. Most enterprises seeking sponsorship do so in answer to problems posed within their own organization. The chairman of the board will say : "We need greater exposure on this..." or "In order to launch this new product we need..." or "We have some bad odours with the public - let us support popular causes..." or "In order to promote our managing director into national presidency, we need some good feelings from this area..." Since 1956, the leading visibility form in Australia has been television. Sponsorship efforts are likely to succeed if television visibility is present and continuous. To a lesser extent, but also important, is the capacity to attract the print media and the periodical press. At the local level, billboards, working equipment, motor vehicles, even trams sporting the sponsor's name will attract donor support.

Probably an essential ingredient is the appearance of harmony within the organization, although agents have found that the larger and more diverse a sporting organization the less affected it will by internal struggling or systematic bias. Some organizations attract support for parochial reasons. This is always dangerous, as the organizations become associated and praised or condemned with their causes to a point where general sponsorship opportunities recede.

Government regulations

Where an organization can claim tax exempt status, the likelihood of support increases exponentially. If the donor can contribute to the sporting group in lieu of paying taxes, then he or she will probably respond favourably. Direct sponsorship ensures that the normally-taxed monies of a group will be directionally given rather than unilaterally surrendered. Therefore tax exempt status is an important condition for most sporting organizations. There are, however, many variations and interpretations within the Tax Act itself. It is in the interests of the organizations to maintain close contact with the taxation department on this issue. An illustration is worth recording. In 1985 goods for use by the AIS (the national body) were specifically declared not exempt from taxation under Item 63A. In the same year the Homebush Bay State Sport Centre in Sydney (the regional body) was declared tax exempt under Article 74, because it was an authority completely controlled by, and its expenditure exclusively born by, the government of the Commonwealth of Australia. Both institutions, one at the federal and one at the state level, were given opposite rulings by the tax authorities of the day. Groups and institutes should test the taxation waters continuously to preserve the precious "taxations exempt" status. It must also be pointed out that the taxation officials interpret the laws as best they can under often conflicting circumstances. They do not object to inquiries or challenges. It is in the best interests of the groups seeking sponsorship to test every aspect of their official status.

Controls

As soon as an organization seeks sponsorship, it surrenders exclusive control over its products, its activities and its governorship. Very few sponsors will accept conditions otherwise. The controls over goods, buildings, training methods, team activities, even performance, are now shared with the major sponsors. The team's success is allied as much with sponsorship pride as it is with the efforts and status of the immediate performers and administrators. Sometimes such shared control is unspoken, rather implied, but most times the need for success is a shared experience. Few business concerns or governments, for the matter, will continue association with disreputable teams or individuals. Controversies are not always unpopular, but often are disreputable. Indeed, a controversy can draw public attention to an individual, resulting in increased sales or prestige. The public tends to side with the individuals affected, especially where the dispute involves government and an individual, thus a loyal sponsor is seen in the best possible light. But disreputation implies dishonesty, shallowness, fractured goals and a spoiling of the sporting enterprise. This odour is far less acceptable to the public.

Such important mundane activities as stock control, publications, mailing lists and sundry merchandises are also shared with major sponsors. Where contribution can be made in kind, fewer opportunities exist for misplacement or corruption. Where the contributions are made in cash, very tight regulatory control must exist, and strict accountability be maintained.

As we move to the 21st century, sport will rely more heavily on sponsorships and endorsements. More professional agencies will arise and develop, less crude techniques for soliciting support and, hopefully, the jarring effect of crude advertising will be lessened also. But it must be remembered that research has clearly indicated certain techniques for attracting attention are more successful than others. The public, therefore, will have to get used to such activities as repeated announcements, controversial events, hero worship and more subliminal techniques. As sponsorship enters increasing sophistication, so the ethicists will be called upon for increased vigilance and courageous pronouncement.

References

Cheffers, John.- *Raw and Resilient*, 1992. Wm.C. Brown & Benchmark, Dubuque, Iowa.

Hardy, Stephen., Mullin, Bernard J., and Sutton, William A.- *Sport Managing*, 1993. Human Kinetics Publishers, Champaigne, Illinois.

Service quality as a success factor in sports management

Klaus Zieschang & Thomas Bezold
Universität Bayreuth,
Germany

Sports management and the services society

By international custom, a country's economic processes are divided into three sectors (cf. CLARK 1957). The primary sector covers the recovery of raw materials and agricultural production; in the secondary sector the raw products are upgraded and processed; and the tertiary sector includes services in tourism, commerce and public administration. In global terms, the more sophisticated and differentiated a nation's economy becomes, the more the weight shifts towards the services society. As a consequence, employment in the tertiary sector increases steadily, with a corresponding rise in its share of the gross domestic product.

This trend is also, and especially, to be found in sport. Apart from the manufacture of sports equipment and the sporting goods industry, virtually all fields of activity in sport are connected with services. This is true internationally in sport, and applies equally to profit-making and non-profit-making organizations.

Sports organizations and organizers are well advised to make the quality of their services the central focus of their endeavours. They will be in good company: the subject of "service quality" is one which is discussed with special intensity in business practice and business management theory (cf. Zeithaml/Parasuraman/Berry 1991; Bezold 1996). Two sets of circumstances were primarily responsible for initiating this trend. First, the empirical results of strategic research into success factors disclosed that the "quality" feature was the single most important variable in determining the success of a services enterprise (Buzzle/Gale 1989, 41 and 240). Secondly, following the worldwide recession, the early 1980s saw the beginning of a more pronounced quality orientation, the main expression of which is to be found in the intensive preoccupation with the popular "Total Quality Management" (cf. Stauss 1994).

In uncontested and saturated buyer's market situations, deliberate quality orientation on the part of an enterprise represents a promising strategic option (cf. Porter 1990, 65-69). High service quality creates a positive image, generates customer satisfaction, promotes positive word-of-mouth propaganda, makes it easier to obtain sponsors and so allows a high-price strategy to be successfully implemented. Service quality, then, creates comparative competitive advantages! This is particularly important for suppliers in the sports sector when they find themselves confronted by a notably competitive situation. More and more service undertakings organized on private enterprise lines are entering the market to offer sports services for a wide variety of target groups (examples being fitness studios, sports schools, sports marketing agencies, etc.). As one example of the wide range of sporting services (cf. the summary in Chelladurai 1994), we shall consider the promotion sector. Service quality plays an exceptionally important part in the management of national and inter-national sporting events. Examples which may be mentioned include the Olympic Games, World Championships and the championships of the various continents as well as major national events in specific disciplines such as athletics or swimming, and league activities in football or basketball. Sporting events such as these call for the planning, organization and implementation of a number of complex services such as transport, board and lodging, training facilities for the athletes, accreditation of media representatives, security and ticketing for widely varied target groups.

In the past, the success of sporting events was measured primarily in terms of organizer-oriented indicators such as total number of spectators, percentage of capacity taken up, media reporting and advertising figures, number of countries participating or the setting of international records. In addition to these, and taking into account the worldwide professionalization of event management, service quality should also be included here as a modern evaluation parameter. This criterion makes it possible to pay attention to the satisfaction of all groups of persons actively or passively involved in the sporting event. Specifically, this means athletes, referees, spectators, media recipients, media representatives, agencies, sponsors and officials. In this context, due note should be taken of the scientifically established finding that each individual assesses his satisfaction with the service subjectively (Stauss 1993, 43). Logically, then, the organizer should record the evaluations of the service quality formed by the various groups of individuals.

This turns our attention to those processes of market research which are suitable for systematically recording and analysing the quality of sports services. In the past - with a few exceptions - no systematic information has been gathered regarding the evaluation by the various groups of individuals of the quality of service offered at major sporting events.

Many services are becoming, or already are, largely circumscribed by structural conditions. This, however, is no bar whatever to improving the operational procedures before, during and after the event. In order to do this, of course, one central prerequisite has to exist: the identification of problems perceived in the service process by those involved. Successful quality management is possible only if the supplier is aware of the variety and significance of service-specific customer problems. There are various reasons for this (cf. Berry 1987; Brandt 1989):

Customers usually experience the problems that arise with the service package as an annoyance. The objective, then, is to restrict customer problems to a minimum so as to minimize negative customer reactions such as boycotts or a change of supplier and negative word-of-mouth propaganda. Secondly, problems in the process of providing a service cannot be completely avoided, so that the organizational and human resources for finding rapid and non-bureaucratic solutions should be set in place. In addition, information on customer problems provides differentiated indications of the appropriateness of the existing quality level and can serve as a basis for ideas on service variations and innovations. Finally, the customer problems recorded are important for maintaining and monitoring the quality of the service because they highlight the relevant quality features and indicate whether and to what extent existing quality standards are being maintained.

The above remarks indicate that service providers should be comprehensively and thoroughly informed about the problems which customers experience with a service package. This raises the question of which procedures are particularly suited to identifying and analysing the problems associated with sports services. In this article, we are able to recommend an empirically tried and tested procedure based on a number of analytical studies of the quality of service offered by profit-making and non-profit-making organizations in the sporting economy. In detail, these studies were carried out at the Olympia Park in Munich (Olympia Tower, football matches in the Olympic Stadium, the 1993 World Ice Hockey Championships and the tennis Grand Slam Cup in the Olympia Hall), and in multi-purpose sports facilities, fitness studios and swimming pools.

Sports services have two special features which are important for evaluation of the service quality from the customer standpoint: need for contact and intangibility. Sport services can be provided only if supplier and customer come into direct contact. This brings the customer into contact with the various elements of the service package. In the case of a spectator attending an event, these elements include the parking situation, the approach to the ground, the purchase of tickets, access to the ground, kind of seating, etc., and aspects of more general importance such as safety and cleanliness within the ground. The intangibility referred to is to be understood as a promise of service, because the purchase of the ticket provides the purchaser not with a material asset but merely with a certificate of entitlement to be present at an event. Because of this intangibility, the proportion of features which the customer can check before purchasing or using the ticket is relatively low, while the proportion which cannot be evaluated until after the purchase is comparatively high. Accordingly, perception of quality takes place to a large extent while the service is being provided (cf. Bezold 1996, 77-80). In the process of providing the service, the service provider is reliant on the participation of the customer, with mental and physical involvement taking place to differing extents. The result of the service is initially open and can be standardized only within limits. Whether the visit is judged positively or negatively is something the customer can only decide retrospectively. The customer's perception of quality takes place at the contact points where he encounters personal and substantive elements of the service offered. These contact points are the moments of truth. This is what decides how the service quality is judged. If service providers fail to identify these moments of truth, then they lack the starting points for controlling the service quality.

How to single out the contact points

The first stage is to run through the entire service procedure in the context of a participatory study from the customer's standpoint. The aim here is to record, in chronological sequence, those points at which visitors come into contact with substantive and/or personal elements of the service package. The customer contact points identified are displayed graphically in a flow diagram (blueprint). Fig. 1 shows, by way of example, the flow diagram for a visit to Munich's Olympia Tower.

```
┌─────────────────────────────────────┐
│ I. Arrival at the Olympia Park       │
└─────────────────────────────────────┘

┌─────────────────────────────────────┐
│ II. Transit to the Olympia Tower     │
└─────────────────────────────────────┘

┌─────────────────────────────────────┐
│ III. Queuing to buy ticket           │
└─────────────────────────────────────┘

┌─────────────────────────────────────┐
│ IV. Buying ticket                    │
└─────────────────────────────────────┘

┌─────────────────────────────────────┐
│ V. Queuing to ascend tower           │
└─────────────────────────────────────┘

┌─────────────────────────────────────┐
│ VI. Ascending tower                  │
└─────────────────────────────────────┘

┌─────────────────────────────────────┐
│ VII. Circling the viewing platforms  │
└─────────────────────────────────────┘

┌─────────────────────────────────────┐
│ VIII. Visiting the revolving restaurant │
└─────────────────────────────────────┘

┌─────────────────────────────────────┐
│ IX. Descending the tower             │
└─────────────────────────────────────┘

┌─────────────────────────────────────┐
│ X. Leaving the Olympic Park          │
└─────────────────────────────────────┘
```

Fig. 1: Service-specific flow-chart for the Olympia Tower in Munich with the various customer contact points

Since the various customer contact points are not of equal importance, they should be weighted in accordance with their significance. The flow-chart serves as a basis for the customer survey. The users experience the complete service as a sequence of incidents from contact point to contact point.

Incidents which the customers experience at the contact points are memorized as stories or episodes. This finding is utilized in order to ascertain quality, the customers reporting on incidents which they experience at each individual customer contact.

Result-oriented survey on the customer contact points
Via an oral survey, the incidents experienced by the customers at the contact points are determined. They are shown the flow-chart as an aide-mémoire. Then the interviewer guides the customer through the various customer contact points with the aid of the flow-chart and asks him to recapitulate the thoughts/emotions produced in him by his experience of the service. Then the customer is asked, by means of open, structured questions, to describe in detail his positive and negative experiences of each contact point and to say which aspects of the quality of the service he perceived as good or bad or as pleasant or unpleasant. The answers are noted by the interviewer, the only ones being recorded being those which can be clearly allocated to a time (discrete episodes), can be influenced by the service provider and report a specific incident (no general impressions or preferences).

The procedure roughly outlined here corresponds, in principle, to the sequential incident technique, which our empirical results suggest is currently the best suited to a detailed analysis of the service quality (cf. Bezold 1996, 265 et seq. and 283-288). The reasons for this are as follows. First, it identifies both the positive and the negative incidents relating to quality, so that the strengths and weaknesses of the service package can all be isolated. Secondly, the survey based on the flow-chart has the advantage that the subject recalls and reports significantly more incidents than with the spontaneous procedure using the critical incident technique. Whereas the critical incident technique covers only the serious, critical incidents, relating to drastic service failures, the sequential incident technique also includes those incidents which, though less significance is attached to them, nevertheless substantially influence the overall quality assessment (cf. Stauss 1993, 46-49).

In addition, the reported incidents are so specific (e.g. "No women's car parks indicated"; "No signposts to the underground") that direct measures to improve quality can be inferred from them. The sequential incident method is also superior to complaint analysis because it reveals those shortcomings of quality which are below the threshold of a personal complaint - and there are a significant number of these!

What can be done with the results?
When a survey is conducted by the sequential incident method, the questioner obtains a copious supply of quality information.
The analysis should be so designed as to differentiate on the basis of the following criteria:
- positive personal,
- positive non-personal,
- negative personal and
- negative non-personal.

This provides the possibility of analysing the service quality on a differentiated basis. The first step is usually to count the incidents under each of these four categories. This provides an overview of the breakdown of positive and negative incidents, which represents a global assessment of the service quality. The "personal versus non-personal" breakdown provides information as to the extent to which customers anchor their assessment of service quality to the personnel or to substantive elements of the service.

It is also advisable to carry out the analysis at contact point level. This is done for all four categories of incident for each contact point. Arranging the contact points in order of absolute frequencies provides information as to the importance of the various contact points in the customer's quality assessment (cf. Fig. 2).

Customer contact points	Incidents	Positive incidents		Negative incidents	
	Total (as %)	Personal	Non-personal	Personal	Non-personal
1. CCP VI: Changing	141 (29.3%)	0	5	0	136
2. CCP VII: Catering	54 (11.2%)	16	29	5	4
3. CCP III: Parking	44 (9.2%)	0	20	0	24
4. CCP I: Tel. enquiry	42 (8.8%)	23	7	12	0
5. CCP II: Signposting	42 (8.8%)	0	3	0	39
6. CCP IV: Reception	39 (8.2%)	19	3	9	8
7. CCP Va: Tennis	36 (7.2%)	0	14	0	22
8. CCP Vc: Badminton	32 (6.6%)	0	11	0	21
9. CCP Vb: Squash	20 (4.2%)	0	12	0	8
10. CCP VIII: Cash desk	16 (3.3%)	11	0	5	0
11. CCP IX: Departure	14 (2.9%)	0	3	0	11
		176 (36.7%)		304 (63.3%)	
Total	480 (100%)	69	107	31	273

Fig. 2: Customer contact points at a multipurpose sports facility, arranged in order of frequency of incidents

The individual analysis of the customer contact points constitutes the step from numerical analysis to the specific incident. A list of the specific incidents gives a very clear impression of the relative proportions of the four categories and offers optimum starting points for working out specific improvements. This is made clear by Fig. 3, which refers to the customer contact point "Reception" of a multi-purpose sports facility.

AT RECEPTION (39)			
22 positive incidents (55.3%)		17 negative incidents (44.7%)	
Personal (19)	Non-personal (3)	Personal (9)	Non-personal (8)
- Friendly, courteous welcome (14) - Smooth processing (3) - Quick, informal procedure (1)	- Clear, because reception right by entrance (2) - No rackets available for hire (1)	- Badly organized (4) - Rarely manned (4) - Little customer service (1)	- Untidy office (4) - Doors stick (2) - No plants (2)

Fig. 3: Individual analysis of the customer contact point "At Reception" of a multipurpose sports facility

Conclusions

The use of the sequential incident technique for analysing profit-making and non-profit-making organizations in sport is always appropriate if the service quality has not yet been systematically analysed. The initial quality survey made necessary by this indicates the most important quality features from the customer's viewpoint, enables them to be weighted and so provides the prerequisites for monitoring service quality in regular future surveys. In the medium term, the incident-oriented quality information can serve as a basis for continuous quality assurance. Sports organizations which commission or hold events thus obtain an instrument which helps them to develop guidelines for contracts and monitor compliance with them.

The service quality as a success factor is becoming increasingly important as sports management becomes more professional. This trend is intensified by the changing expectations of the groups involved, such as sportsmen, spectators, media representatives, officials and sponsors, who want the standards they have developed in other service sectors to be met in sport as well.

References

Berry, L.- Big Ideas in Service Marketing. In: *Journal of Services Marketing*, 1 (Summer), 1987, pp. 5-10.

Bezold, T.- *Zur Messung der Dienstleistungsqualität in sportökonomischen Einsatzfeldern*. Diss. Universität Bayreuth, 1996 [On the measurement of service quality in sports economic applications] Dissertation, Bayreuth University 1996 (at press).

Brandt, R.D.- Focusing on Customer Problems to Improve Service Quality. In: *Journal of Services Marketing*, (3) (Fall), 1989, pp. 5-14.

Buzzle, R.D.; Gale B.T.- *Das PIMS-Programm. Strategien und Unternehmenserfolg* (The PIMS programme. Strategies and corporate success) Wiesbaden, 1989.

Chelladurai, P.- Sports Management: Defining the Field: In: *European Journal of Sports Management*, 1, 1994, 1, pp. 7-21.

Clark, C.- *The Conditions of Economic Progress*. London, 1957.

Porter, M.E.- *Competitive strategy*. New York, 1990.

Stauss, B.- Service Problem Deployment. In: *International Journal of Service Industry*, 4, 1993, 2, pp. 41-62.

Stauss, B.- Total Quality Management and Marketing. In: *Marketing - Zeitschrift für Forschung und Praxis* (Marketing Journal for Research and Practice), Volume 3, 1994, pp. 149-159.

Zeithaml, V.; Parasuraman, A.; Berry, L.- *Delivering Service Quality*. New York, 1991.

Sport management and multiculturalism

Joy T. DeSensi
University of Tennessee,
Knoxville, Tennessee, United States of America

The world of competitive sport calls us to risk our performance abilities against worthy opponents, challenges us to give the best of ourselves, and to meet others on an equal ground. It is a setting in which we give our best to each other as individual competitors and see ourselves striving together no matter how different we may be.

Within the educational setting in the United States, the issues associated with multiculturalism have been addressed at length, yet in the study of sport and sport management or administration, little has been done to address this topic until recently. Sport on the surface appears to be a bastion free from discrimination, yet such issues are posing dilemmas in abounding numbers and affect multitudes of individuals. This has been the case not only at a local or national level, but even at the international levels of organized sport. We need only look at those racial, cultural, gender, religion, and political ideology differences which have historically had fatal consequences. It is precisely these reasons which make it imperative that those preparing to assume sport management or administration positions develop their background on the issues of multiculturalism.

Since this article is one which brings to attention very sensitive issues, it may not meet with favour by all those who read it. The article calls to our attention local, national, and international concerns and carries an important message which is vital to everyone. The message it carries is concerned with the topic of social justice which is inclusive of gender, race, ethnicity, and class discrimination, in addition to oppression, power/authority, and the manner in which these concepts are dealt with by those who govern and manage sport. There is a never-ending need for those individuals who prepare sport managers in educational institutions and those who already hold such positions to make a commitment to reflect and directly address the issues of multiculturalism. It is my hope that this brief article will raise or reaffirm the social consciousness of each of us, serve as a base for further questioning and potentially initiate social action regarding the issues presented. (DeSensi, 1994)

In order to develop a true multicultural setting, developing an appreciation of peoples' differences associated with the heritage, characteristics, and values of different groups is vital. Multiculturalism also involves respecting the uniqueness of each individual. (Morrison, 1992) It is thought that in organizations which aspire to using a multicultural approach that conflict is low because there appreciation and respect for difference is evident and that there is an absence of bias and discrimination. (Powell, 1993) Since highly organized sport settings appear to be steeped in patriarchy and exclusivity, achieving a true multicultural organization may appear to be more an ideal than an actuality especially when those who are team owners, managers, coaches, players, sponsors, athletic directors, and spectators are examined in a context which compares their positions and more negative behaviours.

The term 'cultural diversity' refers to those differences of people in any workplace who are associated with characteristics which makes them dissimilar. Kessler (1990) points out that the term 'cultural diversity' at first glance appears to be restricted to equal employment opportunity laws as refer to sex, race, national origin, religion, age, disability, and veteran status, but it also includes differences regarding personality, sexual orientation, physical appearance, marital status and parental status. Thomas (1991) points out that cultural diversity should be expanded to include civil rights, women's rights, humanitarianism, moral responsibility and social responsibility since we in the United States have traditionally thought of diversity in relation to moral or legal imperatives. If valuing differences were promoted and interpersonal relationships enhanced among individuals, it would seem that blatant expressions of all types of discrimination would be eliminated if we seek to live according to our moral beliefs and do "what is right" and to accept our social responsibility by being "good corporate citizens".

Returning to the educational setting once again, Thomas, (1991) indicates that managing diversity is needed by all organizations in order to empower diverse groups of people to reach their full potential. This can be achieved if the proper foundation and opportunity for exploring the issues are included in the sport manager's preparation. The objectives of the educational program would need to include the following:

1) fostering awareness and acceptance of individual differences
2) fostering greater understanding of the nature and dynamics of individual differences
3) helping individuals understand their own feelings and attitudes about people who are different from themselves
4) exploring how differences might be tapped as assets in the workplace
5) enhancing work relations between people who are different from each other

Exploring our own thoughts and feelings regarding authentic acceptance of a multicultural setting in sport, we must consider those factors which may influence our beliefs regarding this issue. Within everyday life, we have been in the past and will continue to be in the future influenced by our own backgrounds; that is, our own race, gender ethnicity, religion, age, abilities, sexual orientation, geographical location, education, socialization, social group affiliation and political ideologies. Considering these factors, it is easier to understand the premises upon which our beliefs are predicated. What we need to understand is that multicultural education is about knowing about others, but more about knowing about ourselves. Since the factors noted above hold much significance and influence, the previous statement becomes even more significant. All forms of discrimination, including stereotyping are deterrents to developing a social responsibility for multiculturalism. Since decisions are influenced by the overall culture of the setting, significant problems arise when the decisions of the sport organizations are based on these discriminatory behaviours. (DeSensi, 1994)

Multicultural Issues Related to Sport

It is critical that sport managers be conscious of the various forms of discrimination which manifest themselves in different ways within the various levels of sport, but it is not possible to address all of the issues in this brief article. The following points address only a few of the issues within multiculturalism, but relay pertinent information regarding race and gender discrimination:

Race Discrimination
Race discrimination is well documented in college and professional levels of sport. 'Stacking,' which is a function of 'centrality' or spatial location in a team sport according to Loy and

McElvogue (1970). In stacking, blacks are overrepresented in the peripheral or noncentral positions, while whites occupy the central positions. Situations in which minority group members are disproportionately found in specific team positions and underrepresented in others has been supported by research. With the increase in proportion of blacks in racially mixed teams, stacking in basketball has been somewhat broken down.

Stacking is substantiated in the literature by the following quote:

In women's intercollegiate volleyball, blacks are overrepresented at the hitter position and whites at the setter (which is a central position) and bumper (Eitzen & Furst, 1989). In Canadian hockey, French Canadians are overrepresented at the central position of goalie and English Canadians are disproportionately represented in defensive positions (Lavoie, 1989). In British soccer, Black West Indians and Black Africans are overrepresented in the wide forward position and whites at the central positions of midfielder and goal (Maguire, 1988; Melnick, 1988). In Australian rugby, whites are overrepresented in the central team positions and Aborigines are found disproportionately in the wide positions (Halliman, 1991). (DeSensi, 1994, p. 66)

Gender Discrimination

Monitoring issues of gender equality is not an easy task for the sport manager or administrator. The primary question raised within this topic is; Are all levels of competition offering equal opportunity for participation? Once again, we rely on our moral obligations and social responsibility. Title IX (which was to ensure gender equity in institutions receiving federal funding) was passed in the United States in 1972, yet athletic departments in high schools and colleges and universities are just now responding to this law. It would be wonderful to think that sport managers and administrators would address this issue even if the law did not exist.

Multiculturalism and the Future of Sport Management

The education of future sport leaders regarding the concept of multiculturalism is critical. Bennett (1992) offers the following points to consider for developing an approach to how diversity can be implemented in various settings of which sport is no exception:

1) Intercultural sensitivity cannot be developed through confrontation with difference and cannot be adequately developed by simply pointing out examples of ethnocentricism and racism. Understanding cultural differences is a developmental goal, and diversity initiatives need to be designed along these lines.

2) Living in a multicultural society demands more than tolerance for difference, it requires respect and appreciation for those differences. One time 'fix it' solutions to intolerance are insufficient to deal with such issues.

3) Everyone in the educational setting, administrators, students, faculty, and staff are all responsible for developing intercultural competence.

4) While we might include individuals of diversity in our administrative and management ranks of sport, this does not ensure that diversity will be valued. The resource that individuals of diversity represent for a community, state, or nation must be emphasized.

5) Knowledge without understanding is dangerous. The study of cultures and mastery of intercultural interaction has to be a part of the educational process in order to develop a transformation of perspective, intercultural relations and social action.

6) Successful diversity initiatives must be supported within educational institutions from the upper administration, faculty, staff, and student groups, especially groups formed to study this issue in sport management. Unrelenting dialogue in a supportive climate is most important to help with this initiative.

While these points will assist those students studying sport management and administration as well as those professionals currently holding such positions, my concern is for the future of multiculturalism. Unless sport managers and administrators take their social, moral, and personal responsibility seriously the oppression of all people through racism, sexism, classism, ageism, able-ism, homophobia, and other forms of discrimination, they will be contributing to the perpetuation of barriers for sport competitors at all levels of sport competition.

Education is only a beginning step toward the goal of multiculturalism, my hope is for a true multicultural understanding within sport and especially on the part of our sport managers and those educators preparing these professionals. A commitment toward this end is a necessity.

References

Bennett, M. J.- An intercultural approach to diversity in education, some tentative principles. Unpublished manuscript, 1992. The Intercultural Communication Institute, Portland, OR.

DeSensi, J. T.- Multiculturalism as an issue in sport management. *Quest*, 1994, 8, pp. 63-74.

Eitzen, D. S. & Furst, D.- Racial bias in women's intercollegiate sports. *Journal of Sport and Social Issues*, 1989, *13*, pp. 46-51.

Hallinan, C.- Aborigines and positional segregation in the Australian rugby league. *International Review for the Sociology of Sport*, 1991, *26*, pp. 69-81.

Kessler, L. L.- *Managing diversity in an equal opportunity workplace: A primer for today's manager*, 1990. Washington, DC: National Foundation for the Study of Employment Policy.

Lavoie, M.- Stacking, performance differentials, and salary discrimination in professional ice hockey. *Sociology of Sport Journal*, 1989, 6, pp. 17-35.

Loy, J. W. & McElvogue, J.F.- Racial segregation in American sport. *International Review of Sport Sociology*, 1970, 5, pp. 5-24.

Maguire, J. A.- Assignment in English soccer. *Sociology of Sport Journal*, 1988, 5, pp. 257-269.

Melnick, M.- Racial segregation by playing position in the English football league. *Journal of Sport and Social Issues*, 1988, *12*, pp. 122-130.

Morrison, A. M.- *The new leaders: Guidelines on leadership diversity in America*. San Francisco: Jossey-Bass, 1992.

Powell, G. N.- *Women and men in management*, (2nd ed.). London: Sage, 1993.

Thomas, R. R., Jr.- *Beyond race and gender*. New York: American Management Association, 1991.

Sport as a management model

Jean-Loup Chappelet
Institut de Hautes Etudes en Administration Publique,
Lausanne, Switzerland

Sports management is traditionally considered as the application of managerial knowledge to the sports sphere and the organizations which belong to it. These organizations may be: public like a sports ministry; private like a tennis-shoe manufacturer; or, more commonly still, associative like a national or international federation. For some fifteen years now, the discipline "sports management" has been structuring and defining itself at various congresses and through numerous publications. In reality, the issue is not simply to stick management on to sport, but to try to adapt it to the specific features of sports bodies, for example widespread use of volunteers, the non-profit nature of the body in question and its assumed public interest mission.

There are those who deny sports management the status of a fully-fledged discipline. They see it as nothing more or less than management (of a general nature). They are doubtless not wrong when it comes to running and managing a sports goods firm such as Nike or Mizuno, or an agency that organizes sport as entertainment, which is what the professional football, basketball, baseball and ice-hockey clubs in the United States have become. However, when a sports body belongs to the non-commercial sector, as is very often the case, its management takes on a quite specific character. And, just as public management can be distinguished from general (private) management, it is quite possible to conceive a form of management specific to associative sport and classify it in more general terms as part of the management of the tertiary sector, somewhere between public and private, in which non-profit organizations, in particular, are to be found.

Another, more ambitious way of affirming the existence of sport management as a discipline would be to demonstrate that a study of it can lead to new insights for management itself. This is what this article attempts to do. In the event, I shall seek to explore the idea that sport can serve as a model for modern management, not only for sports bodies but also for non-sports bodies such as private companies and public administrations.

In the first section, the omnipresence of the sporting metaphor in the managerial sphere will be highlighted through numerous examples which, taken as a whole, become significant. In the second section, three main sports-based supports for a new management will be developed with a view to identifying a "sports model" for the way an entity is run and managed. In conclusion, a link will be established with the four generic roles of management, in contrast with the predominant "military" model.

The sports metaphor in the managerial sphere

Following Alain Ehrenberg (1991) and others, it has become relatively commonplace to point out the constant use of sports metaphor in the corporate sector. The most obvious evidence of this is doubtless commercial advertising which uses and abuses athletes and sports scenes to sell products and services that have little to do with sport. This is particularly the case in the computer industry, most of whose companies have on one occasion or another displayed themselves with sportsmen or -women, for instance an American football team (Oki), women sprinters (Dell), rowers (IBM) or triathletes (ICL). The frenzied competition to develop ever more powerful hardware and software is in perfect symbiosis with the Olympic motto "citius, altius, fortius" (faster, higher, stronger).

This partnership between sport and the corporation becomes even more apparent when advertising is associated with sports sponsorship. Such actions are directed towards clients, but also and doubtless primarily towards members of staff. Perhaps the most significant example, still in the data-processing sector, is the Bull company and its boat "team spirit", which took part in a round-the-world race in 1986, or its mountaineering employees who climbed Annapurna in 1988 with their employer's support. Recruitment advertisements, which are a form of indirect advertising, also make frequent reference to sport through such words as "challenge, endurance, victory, records to be beaten", etc.

A second application of the sports metaphor is the employment of high-level athletes inside corporations. This practice began with sports goods manufacturers and, in particular, Adidas, which recruited numerous champions in the '70s and '80s. It has gradually spread to all sectors of the economy. Today, although elite athletes sometimes have problems switching careers, they are generally given a better reception than other young people with the same qualifications. Top athletes even sometimes end up running companies. The most famous examples are doubtless the French skier Jean-Claude Killy and the American golfer Mark McCormack. The identification of the top athlete with a winning company is sometimes so strong that it seems quite natural for a champion to rescue a struggling company (Cf. LNQ, 1995). Conversely, the most flamboyant rescuer of companies of the early '90s, Frenchman Bernard Tapie, felt the need to invent himself a youthful sporting career (Cf. Maitrot, 1995).

The aura of champions is often transferred to successful coaches. In football, for example, Roy Hodgson (coach of the Swiss 1994 World Cup squad) and Michel Hidalgo (who led the French team in the 1986 World Cup) gave numerous seminars on the best way to manage on the basis of their professional experience as leaders.

The practice of sport within the company provides another approach. It was formerly reserved for workers who played in clubs run by their employers to occupy their Sunday leisure. The football teams Sochaux (financed by Peugeot) and Leverkusen (Bayer), or the many and varied sports associations of the European postal authorities are the prototypes of this corporate use of sport. But today, it is managers too who, alongside the rank and file, practise sport in fitness facilities provided by companies. Intra- and inter- company competitions aslo provide new forms of stimulus.

An intra-company competition is open to all employees willing to practise a variety of more or less competitive sports. It has a similar function to the office party. Its principal aim is to strengthen good relations among employees. An inter-company competition is a more serious proposition. It is open to teams each representing a company within a region or a country.

These teams compete in various generally highly competitive sports and are often run by senior company executives. The aim is to galvanize the team members (more effectively that by proxy as with sports sponsorship). Inter-company competitions culminate in the "World Corporate Games" which have been held in a different city every year since 1989 under the aegis of a private organization.[1] As Gary Tribou writes (1993), "The discreet entrepreneur, whose puritan ethos is epitomized by May Weber, is transformed into a high-profile champion leading his team towards a collective triumph."

"Outward bound" sports seminars or adventure and survival courses constitute another, more concentrated type of training, generally reserved for top executives and imported, it appears, from Japan. They generally seek to inculcate the "thirst for victory" and to forge through often extreme physical activity a corporate culture and solidarity in the face of adversity. (Ehrenberg, 1988).

Through these seminars and other sports activities in the corporate context, competition sport has become a sort of informal school of management, rather as rugby and football served to build the characters of future gentlemen in English public schools in the 19th century.

Management literature has contributed not a little in recent years to the arrival of sport in the corporate world. In terms of form, first of all, one may observe titles or covers which use the sporting metaphor without any link with the sports experience, for example "Japan as number one", by Ezra Vogel (1980) or "Le décathlon du manager" (The Manager's Decathlon) by Gilbert Labat (1995), or "Le management" by Alice Hubel (1991), the cover of which shows a manager in suit and tie running on a switchback statistical curve, or "The Brass Tacks manager" by Pat Kaufman and Cindy Wetmore (1994), which shows a manager fencing against a background of mountain peaks.

In terms of substance, several works seek to draw parallels between a sports experience and a managerial one. For example, in their book "The Way to Win: Strategies for Success in Business and Sport" (1995), Will Carling, the English rugby international, and Robert Heller, author of management books, try to extract the vital substance from the experience of a dozen or so great English athletes (Sebastian Coe, Adrian Moorhouse, Daley Thompson, etc.). "Passes croisées entre rugby et entreprise" (Cross passing between rugby and the firm) (Delabare, 1995) is another example. One can also include in this category Kenneth Blanchard's work "The One Minute Manager Gets Fit" (1987) which recommends regular physical exercise as indispensable to an effective manager. This idea is reflected, in terms of the company as a whole, in the concept of a "lean organization", recently brought up to date in the terms "agile" or "fit" as applied to an organization, or even the terms slim and muscular (Cf. Goldman, 1995). According to the Director General of Swissair (Loepfe, 1995), "agility calls for an active management that anticipates the changes necessary to success...".

Bernard Guétin is one of those who have taken the comparison between the business and sports worlds farthest (Guétin, 1989). He sees the learning of sports rules as a good preparation for the assimilation of the game rules that govern each industrial sector or each society. He states, in English, ten tips for success in an American company: "know the environment, be mobile, be a doer, report, be a pro, seek excellence, don't be modest, be open, be a team player, be a nice guy." We may recognize in these tips several sports values which will be examined in the second part of this article.

I shall conclude this brief overview of sports-inspired management literature with a reference to a book by Miyomoto Musashi (1645), considered by experts to be the bedside reading of Japanese managers. It is primarily a treatise on fencing. This work, written in the mid seventeenth century, is entitled "Gorin-no-Sho" or "A Book of Five Rings", anticipating by

---

[1] These "games" have been held succesively in San Francisco, Hawai, Lille, London, Kuala Lumpur, Johannesburg and Geneva.

several centuries Coubertin's design of the interlinked rings which have become the Olympic symbol!

The accumulation of all these signs is not so surprising at all if one considers that competition sport has become a metaphor for our postindustrial society, a society characterized by an increasingly tough competition between individuals (the struggle for performance), between companies (the trade war) and even between nations (see the "World Competitiveness Report" published every year by IMD in Lausanne, which classifies countries like tennis players). "The sports model is the key to success for companies engaged in the struggle", says the top executive of a major French company who is also President of a Paris football club (Largardère quoted by Ragot, 1992). One is therefore prompted to wonder whether certain features of the dominant sports culture cannot serve to rejuvenate the management of companies immersed in this society in which competition, effort, surpassing of oneself, the will to win and success have become potentially important values.

Sports-based supports for a new management

A perusal of management literature enables one to identify three main supports for a "sports model" of management. These are the concepts of excellence, the team and coaching. We shall examine them in this order.

Excellence

Excellence became a key term in management in the early 'eighties following the publication of a best-seller by Tom Peters and Robert Waterman entitled "In search of Excellence" (1983). The work sought to identify, on the basis of a study of large and well-managed American companies, the generic conditions for success, which it summed up in eight principal points. This book has been widely criticized since in view of the fact that some of the companies it identified as exemplary have suffered enormous financial losses in recent years.[2] It nevertheless served to highlight this need to excel oneself that is a natural property of many employees and which a company must know how to harness in order to beat its competitors. Excellence marries perfectly the obligation to compete and the need for self-actualization. It certainly constitutes an alternative to the Taylorian disciplinary model in which the human being is forgotten or rather considered as a machine.

Peters and Waterman put forward the figure of the "champion" who believes in an innovative product or service and who pushes its development in the teeth of difficulties and the incredulousness of his colleagues. Around him, they construct a framework of ongoing innovation (championing system). Companies which excel encourage autonomy. They support the entrepreneurial spirit and allow internal competition among ideas to function as a means of selecting the best. We find here a reflection of the relatively unorganized system of training of the American sports elite in contrast to the early detection and systematic maturation systems practised in other countries. Similar ideas are developed by David Hemery in his work entitled "Sporting Excellence: What Makes a Champion" (1991) in which he stresses the importance of mindset in sport as in the company.

Together with other psychologists, Guy Missoum of the INSEP (Institut national des sports et de l'éducation physique, in Paris) has explored the deep-lying impulses that push men and

---

[2] Cf. for example the cover of *Business Week* of 5th November 1984.

companies to excel, to win like an athlete. In a first work (1990), he identifies four dimensions of the winner's psychological potential (cognitive, emotional, relational and behavioural) and seven strategies for entrepreneurial success directly inspired by those applied by champions. In a second work (1994), he explores in depth the concept of excellence as "the capacity to mobilize, in oneself and others, the specific resources which make it possible to obtain satisfactory results in relation to the objectives pursued." For him, excellence is not an elitist concept which separates the "sheep" from the "goats", but a concept of collective progress which can be imported into and developed within companies with the aid of a suitable style of management: modelling of excellence.

This collective modelling necessitates a symbolic model that the sports phenomenon can provide. Sport makes it possible, in an initial phase, to transfer excellence into the organization, then to train for excellence and, finally, to manage excellence. The transfer of excellence can take place in part through the use of sport's positive image, for example on the occasion of sponsoring actions, or, more generally, by encouragement of the practice of sport and its specific values within the company (see first part of this article). Training for excellence may draw direct inspiration from the techniques of mental preparation used by champions. Management of excellence requires a manager who, like the coach of a sports team, knows how to mobilize his players/employees to make them win as a team but also as individuals, by setting them ambitious objectives.

This last remark leads on quite naturally to the concepts of team and coaching.

The Team
The number of books devoted, since the 1930's, to the team or the small group as a tool of effective management is a sure sign of the importance of this idea which is commonplace not only in so-called... "team" sports, but also in individual sports, where it is reflected in the idea of the sports club and interclub competition.

The team is a form of organization based on the fairly obvious idea that it is difficult to find all skills in a single individual, especially if contradictory qualities are needed for a particular job. It is, however, possible to gather together various talents within a group and to transform it into a team, i.e. a coordinated set of personalities acting towards a goal which is inaccessible to them individually. One may refer, for example, to the work by Darrel Ray and Howard Bronstein entitled "Teaming Up: Making the Transition to a Self-Directed Team-Based Organization" (1995), whose cover is illustrated with a coxed eights rowing boat, symbol par excellence of individual effectiveness bent to a collective task.

But there are various types of team operations. Here too, the sporting analogy is helpful. Cresencio Torres and Jerry Spiegel (1994) identify five types, comparing them with different sports. The great management guru, Peter Drucker, pinpoints three (1993). The first is that of the baseball or cricket team (or the surgical team) in which each person occupies fixed post and where the players do not help each other much. This type of organization is suitable for companies which have repetitive tasks and well-established operating rules. The second type is represented by the soccer team (or the symphony orchestra) which, when well trained, forms a whole that favours cooperation. The third type, which is compared to a doubles pair in tennis (or a jazz group) are the most efficacious, as each player constantly adjusts to the strengths and weakness of his or her partner(s); however, they call for great self-discipline. It is possible to organize any form of human work on the basis of one of these types of team.

In a number of publications, Robert Keidel (1985, 1987, 1989) also identifies three sports, namely baseball, American football and basketball, as the archetypes of the three main types of organizational structure: decentralized, centralized or based on small groups. These he synthesizes around three concepts which must be constantly maintained in equilibrium for the sake of good management, namely: autonomy, control and cooperation (Keidel, 1995). It will be noted in passing that the system of sports federations, leagues and clubs constitutes an example of a highly decentralized organization with a strong centre nevertheless.

Keidel sums up the task that awaits the players in symbolic terms: "Fill out the lineup card" in baseball; "Prepare the game plan" in football; "Influence the flow" in basketball. Along the same lines, according to the results of a survey published by the Washington Post, basketball appears to have ousted the languorous baseball as Americans' national pastime because it constitutes a better metaphor of the world in which we live, "unpredictable, divided and in constant evolution", while the "infernal rhythms" of American football are increasingly rejected (LES, 1995).

Several authors point out that teams do not always work very well and that particular conditions have to be managed to make them successful (Cf., for example, Robbins, 1995). This is an obvious truth in sport, where it is not enough just to put together a team in order to win a match. In a collective work devoted to the conditions necessary for effective team-work (Hackman, 1990), Jack Wood takes the example of the Nighthawks, the AHL[3] professional ice-hockey team of New Haven (Conneticut). At the end of the season under consideration, the team was eliminated in the first round of the play-offs despite having players and a coach of a good standard. The explanation therefore had to be sought in the particular context of the Nighthawks team, which served as a breeding ground for talent for the Los Angeles NHL team. Indeed, its best players joined this team, while New Haven received those who no longer made the grade in California. Thus, from week to week, the Nighthawks' lineup varied and the players never really constituted a team, but rather a number of individuals in strong competition (seeking promotion) or highly demotivated (after a relegation). Thus, the necessary cooperation on the ice never really happened, in contrast to other AHL teams which maintained a stable nucleus of players. Moreover, no collective reward system operated in case of a team success. The Nighthawks coaches were typically in the highly uncomfortable position of the intermediate manager (caught between the players and the managers of the Los Angeles team), and they were regularly sacked.

This state of affairs is a far cry from those companies in which the employees are referred to as "team-member", as in Johnsonville (Cf. Stayer, 1992) or, so they say, at McDonald's. And a further one still from so-called "democratic" corporations in which participative management prevails and a circular form of management replaces the autocratic and pyramidal type of organization (Cf. Ackoff, 1994). As pointed out by Raymond Chappuis and Raymond Thomas (1988), the bases of teamwork are not to be found in a mechanistic conception of performance with victory for the coach and obedience on the part of the players as the sole aims. Operational efficacy, in sport as in business, calls for a degree of emotional cohesion on the part of the team-members.

Coaching

In origin, coaching is the way in which a coach gives a sports team or an individual athlete and passes on to it/him/her a certain know-how. It concerns much more the form than the substance of the teaching process. This word entered the fashionable vocabulary of management in the late 1970's. It is a concept whose origins are truly to be found in sport. One of the first

---

[3] The AHL (American Hockey League) is the second American professional league after the NHL (National Hockey League).

people to realize that the relationship between the sports instructor and his pupil was more important than the technical instruction was the Harvard educational theorist Timothy Gallwey. He applied his ideas initially to tennis, then to skiing and to golf in a series of three books whose titles referred to the personal or "inner" experience of the learner (Gallwey, 1975, 1977, 1979). The idea was to break down gradually the pupil's internal psychological barriers in order to release his natural potential, and to give him confidence.

From the learner sportsman to the corporate employee, the step was but a short one, and the Gallwey School of Coaching was founded. In its wake, many managers took to "coaching" as a method of leading and motivating their teams. It would really be more accurate to speak of self-motivation, as the idea of coaching is to encourage the staff member to take full responsibility for his own work. Given its recreational aspects, this is relatively easy to achieve in sport, which Bernard Jeu (1994) defined as "working at play" (in the case of amateurs) or "playing at work" (in the case of professionals). In the company, the recreational side of things is rarer.[4] The secret is knowing how to give each employee real responsibilities which enable him to affirm his personal identity while contributing to a collective project.

The manager-coach must monitor his charge with varying degrees of closeness, but should never leave him to his own devices. This brings us back to the meaning given to the word manager in the 18th century, namely the adviser (of an athlete). According to Bill Walsh, legendary American football coach, it is essential to create the conditions which will enable the individual to develop, to participate in decision-making and to subscribe to the objectives that have been laid down (HBR, 1993). "The main thing is to participate", as Coubertin himself said in another context.

According to the English rugby coach and consultant Eric Parsloe, a good coach needs three key skills: a good command of body language, the ability to listen and observe and mastery of the art questioning based on Socrates' maieutics. The coach's remarks and questions must not be general but precise and incisive. According to John Whitmore (1992), the whole coaching process depends on periodic consideration of the following four fundamental questions: "What do you want? (goal) What is happening? (reality) What can you do about it? (options) What will you do? (action)". He sums up these questions by the English initials GROW (Goal, Reality, Options, Will)". Coaching thus becomes an ongoing and structured form of management.

Conclusions

The three concepts of excellence, team and coaching set out above can be associated with three of the main functions of management as identified by Henri Fayol, namely: planning, organizing and directing (Cf. for example Thiétart, 1980). Indeed, planning can today no longer satisfy itself with quantitative productivity targets; it must also aim for the pursuit of excellence in relation to the competition (in a process known as "benchmarking") and to the qualitative expectations of the consuming public (Cf. "Total quality management). By the same token, traditional hierarchical organization symbolized by the army or the state bureaucracy is not longer in tune with our times; it can be replaced to good effect by an organization based on autonomous and evolving teams in which everyone can achieve self-actualization. Finally, the classic and disciplinary leadership applied in companies and administrations, based on a

---

[4] Although Crozer and Friedberg see in play the instrument devised by men to regulate their cooperation, for instance in the company conceived as a set of interlocking games. Cf. Michel Crozer & Erhard Friedberg, *L'acteur et le système*, Seuil, Paris, 1977.

minimum of delegation and uniquely financial motivation, must give way to a form of leadership that encourages cooperation between members of a team, of the type advocated by coaching which is, as it were, a way of "cloning excellence" (Missoum, 1994). We have seen how these three fundamental functions of management can draw inspiration from sporting concepts.

The fourth and, traditionally, last function of management, is that of controlling. Is not it too inspired by competition sport where the result falls ineluctably at the end of each event and where every hierarchy is purely provisional? Alvin Toffler (1981) describes as "adhocratic" a society in which acquired statuses are constantly and legitimately questioned, in contract to our essentially meritocratic society. Henry Mintzberg (1989) sees in adhocracy one of the corporate organizational forms best adapted to continual change. One cannot but observe that the sporting society in general and the team in the field in particular offer one of the rare real models of this type of modus operandi: highly effective individuals pursuing a common cause in an egalitarian framework of "fair competition", to use Alain Ehrenberg's expression (1991).

One might therefore suggest that sport and, more particularly the sports club, could provide a management model alternative to the perennial army model, whereby positive sporting values would replace forms of military mobilization, to no one's regret. Sport having often been presented as a civilized way of waging war, we are currently witnessing the progressive transition from one model to another, as shown in the diagram below.

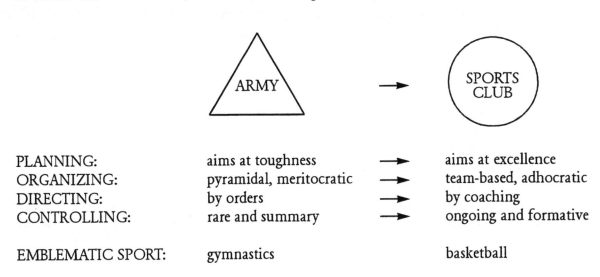

PLANNING:	aims at toughness	→	aims at excellence
ORGANIZING:	pyramidal, meritocratic	→	team-based, adhocratic
DIRECTING:	by orders	→	by coaching
CONTROLLING:	rare and summary	→	ongoing and formative
EMBLEMATIC SPORT:	gymnastics		basketball

In a parallel development, the associative sports community, made up of clubs leagues and federations, is gradually assimilating techniques of management. Thus, sport and managment, two phenomena which came into being independently at the end of the 19th century and have developed throughout the 20th, may perhaps find ways of enriching one another for the years to come.

References

Ackoff, Rusell L.- *The Democratic Corporation*, Oxford University Press, New York, 1994.

Blanchard, K. Kenneth & Edington, D.W.- *The One Minute Manager Gets Fit*, Morrow, New York, 1987.

Carling, Will & Heller, Robert.- *The Way to Win: Strategies for Success in Business and Sport*, Little, Brown & Co, London, 1995.

Chappuis, Raymond & Thomas, Raymond.- *L'équipe sportive*, PUF, Paris, 1988.

Delabare, Pierre-Jean et al.- *Passes croisées entre rugby et entreprise*, Presses du management, Paris, 1995.

Drucker, Peter F.- *Post-capitalist Society*, Butterworth, Oxford, 1993.

Ehrenberg, Alain.- «L'âge de l'héroïsme», *Cahiers internationaux de sociologie*, vol. 85, juillet-décembre, 1988.

Ehrenberg, Alain.- *Le culte de la performance*, Calmann-Lévy, Paris, 1991.

Gallwey, Timothy (1975, 1977, 1979).- *The Inner Game of Tennis*, Random House, New York, 1975; avec B. Kriegel, *Inner Skiing*, Random House, New York, 1977; *The Inner Game of Golf*, Random House, New York, 1979.

Goldman, Steven L. et al.- *Agile Competitors and Virtual Organizations: Strategies for Enriching the Customer*, Random House, New York, 1995.

Guétin, Bernard.- *10 conseils si vous travaillez pour une société américaine*, Publi-Union, Paris, 1989.

HBR.- «*To Build a Winning Team*», interview with Bill Walsh by Richard Rapaport, *Harvard Business Review*, January-February, 1993.

Hemery, David.- *Sporting Excellence: What Makes a Champion*, Collins Willow, London, 1991.

Hubel, Alice.- *Le management*, Marabout, Alleur (Belgique), 1991.

Jeu, Bernard.- «La définition du sport et les enjeux de cette définition» in Collectif, *Pour un humanisme du sport*, CNOSF - Revue EPS, Paris, 1994.

Kaufman, Pat & Wetmore, Cindy.- *The Brass Tacks Manager*. Doubleday, New York, 1994.

Keidel, Robert W. (1985, 1987, 1989).- *Game Plans: Sports Strategies for Business*, Dutton, New York, 1985. «Team Sports Models as a Generic Organizational Framework», Human Relations, 40(9), 1987, pp. 591-612. *Corporate Players: Designs for Working and Winning Together*, Dutton, New York, 1989.

Keidel, Robert W.- *Seeing Organizational Patterns: A New Theory and Language of Organizational Design*, Berrett-Koehler, San Francisco, 1995.

Labat, Gilbert.- *Le management global ou le décathlon du manager*, Presses du management, Paris, 1995.

LES.- *La Lettre de l'économie du sport*, n° 308, 28 juin 1995, p. 5.

LNQ.- *Le Nouveau Quotidien*, «Une championne de natation se lance dans le sauvetage du transport fluvial suisse», 9 juin 1995.

Loepfe, Otto, (1995).- «Agility as a Leadership Quality» in *Swissair Gazette*, 9/95, p. 5.

Maitrot, Eric.- *Sport et télé, les liaisons secrètes*, Flammarion, Paris, 1995, p. 159.

Mintzberg, Henry.- *Mintzberg on Management: Inside our Strange World of Organizations*, Free Press, New York, 1989.

Missoum, Guy & Minard, Jean-Luc.- *L'art de réussir, l'esprit du sport appliqué à l'entreprise*, Editions d'organisation, Paris, 1990.

Missoum, Guy & Selva, Chantal.- *Le modelage de l'excellence*, ESF Editeur, Paris, 1994.

Musashi, Miyamoto (1645).- Traduit en français par M. et M. Shibata sous le titre *Ecrits sur les cinq roues*, Maisonneuve & Larose, Paris, 1977. (Translated into English by V. Harris, under the title *A Book of Five Rings*, Allen, London, 1987.)

Parsloe, Eric.- *The Manager as Coach and Mentor*, IPD, London, 1995, p. 11.

Peters, Thomas J. & Waterman, Robert H.- *In Search of Excellence: Lessons from America's Best-Run Companies*, Harper Collins, New York, 1982.

Ragot, Nathalie.- «Sport: logique sportive, logique d'entreprise», *Revue française de marketing*, n° 138, 1992/3, p. 104.

Ray, Darrel & Bronstein, Howard.- *Teaming Up: Making the Transition to a Self-Directed Team-Based Organization*, McGraw-Hill, New York, 1995.

Robbins, Harvey & Finley, Michael.- *Why Teams Don't Work*, Peterson's/Pacesetter Books, Princeton, 1995.

Stayer, Ralph.- «How I learned to let my workers lead», *Harvard Business Review*, November/December 1992, cité par John Whitmore, *Coaching for Performance*, op. cit.

Thiétart, Raymond.- *Le Management*, QSJ-PUF, Paris, 1980.

Toffler, Alvin.- *The Third Wave*, Bantam, New York, 1981.

Torres, Cresencio & Spiegel, Jerry.- *Self-Directed Work Teams: a Primer*, Pfeiffer, London, 1994.

Tribou, Gary.- «Ethique sportive et culture d'entreprise», in *Sport et Management*, Alain Loret (Ed.), Dunod, Paris, 1993.

Ezra Vogel.- *Japan as number one*, Harvard University Press, Cambridge, 1980.

Whitmore, John.- *Coaching for Performance: A Practical Guide to Growing Your Own Skills*, Brealey Publishing, London, 1992.

Wood, Jack D.- «New Haven Nighthawks» (Chapter 16) in J. Richard Hackman (Ed.), *Groups That Work (and Those That Don't): Creating Conditions for Effective Teamwork*, Jossey-Bass Publishers, San Francisco, 1990.